Text-Based Learning and Reasoning
Studies in History

Text-Based Learning and Reasoning
Studies in History

Charles A. Perfetti
M. Anne Britt
Mara C. Georgi
University of Pittsburgh

1995

LAWRENCE ERLBAUM ASSOCIATES, PUBLISHERS
Hillsdale, New Jersey   Hove, UK

Lawrence Erlbaum Associates, Inc., Publishers
365 Broadway
Hillsdale, New Jersey 07642

Cover design by Jan Melchior

Library of Congress Cataloging-in-Publication Data

Perfetti, Charles A.
    Text-based learning and reasoning : studies in history / Charles A.
Perfetti, M. Anne Britt, and Mara C. Georgi.
        p.   cm.
    Includes bibliographical references and index.
    ISBN 0-8058-1643-7 (acid-free paper).—ISBN 0-8058-1977-0
    1. History—Study and teaching—United States.   I. Britt, M. Anne.
II. Georgi, Mara C.   III. Title.
D16.3.P36   1995
907'.2073—dc20   95-18002
                                                                CIP

Books published by Lawrence Erlbaum Associates are printed on
acid-free paper, and their bindings are chosen for strength and durability.

Printed in the United States of America
10 9 8 7 6 5 4 3 2 1

Contents

Preface

Our effort in this book is to examine the learning of a small piece of history as a problem of cognition. History is both an academic discipline and a school subject matter. As a discipline, it fosters a systematic way of discovering and evaluating the events of the past. As a school subject matter, American history is a staple of middle grades and high school curricula in the United States. And, in higher education, it is part of the liberal arts education tradition. Its role in school learning provides a context for our approach to history as a topic of learning. In reading history, students engage in cognitive processes of learning, text processing, and reasoning. Our examination touches on each of these cognitive problems, centered on an in-depth study of college students' text learning and extended to broader issues of text understanding, the cognitive structures that enable learning of history, and reasoning about historical problems.

To some extent, we use history merely as an interesting subject-matter window on these cognitive problems. Ours is not a contribution to how students acquire knowledge in the discipline of history, although we do discuss some comparisons of history "experts" and novices. However, history is not an arbitrary choice of subject matter. From a learner's point of view, it has properties that make it typical of narrative learning; less visible to the beginning student are its distinctive discipline properties that allow the evaluation of evidence in support of competing interpretations. We examine these and other issues of learning and reasoning in history, drawing primarily from a study of a handful of students learning about the history of the Panama Canal, and linking this study to others we have since carried out.

ACKNOWLEDGMENTS

We wish to acknowledge the contribution of others who have contributed to our research on history text learning. Julia Kushner, Eli Kozminzky, and Robert Mason all participated at various times in joint projects and discussions of history learning. Maureen Marron contributed related studies and analyses. Peter Foltz, in addition to contributions to related history text projects, reviewed a draft of most of the chapters of the book. We especially acknowledge the substantial contributions of Jean-François Rouet to our empirical, theoretical, and methodological efforts to understand the use of multiple texts in history problem solving. Finally, we thank Gareth L. Gabrys for insightful discussions on learning and reasoning.

In carrying out this project, we are indebted to two major sponsors. The Mellon Foundation, through a multiproject grant on "varieties of reasoning" to the Learning Research and Development Center, supported the study we report and some of the additional research we discuss. The Center for Student Learning, funded by the U.S. Office of Educational Research and Improvement, supported related components of our history research, reported elsewhere and discussed in the present volume. For support of the preparation for the book, we are grateful to both the Mellon Foundation and the Center for Student Learning. We are also grateful to the support of the Learning Research and Development Center and its codirectors Lauren Resnick and Robert Glaser.

In the way of personal acknowledgments, the first author expresses his appreciation to Angela Ross Perfetti for postponing her arrival into the world for a few days so that he could finish work on the final chapter. The second author thanks her family for their support and patience. And the third author thanks her family for giving her, among other things, an appreciation of history.

Charles A. Perfetti
M. Anne Britt
Mara C. Georgi

Chapter 1

Stories, Causal Models, and Historical Literacy

On May 4th, 1904, a U.S. Marine Lieutenant raised the American flag over the former French headquarters in what was to become the U.S.-owned Panama Canal Zone. Construction of the Canal began shortly after, and 10 years later, on January 7, 1914, the first ship passed through the Panama Canal.

Borrowing the flashback technique from the movies, we have begun a story either at the end or somewhere in the middle. (It was the end in 1914, and something like the middle in 1976 when the Panama Canal became a potent issue in the presidential campaigns.) The question we address in this monograph is what it means to learn this story. What does learning history consist in? What does it mean to understand a history text?

To anticipate the kind of answer we will suggest for these questions, we must complicate the story of the Panama Canal a bit by providing the flashbacks. Cut to 1849: The California Gold Rush had been underway for 1 year. Pressures for coast-to-coast transportation in North America were growing, resulting in a plan for a transcontinental railroad. A railroad across Panama was built by 1855, but it did not satisfy the appetite for a quick overland route; the idea of building a canal somewhere across the narrow land mass in Central America was kept alive. But other events in the world interacted with the canal idea, and it floundered a bit. There were tensions with Britain—tensions concerning Central America—to be resolved. Then there were the French, who acquired permission to build a canal in 1879 and got started, only to see their efforts collapse in 1889. U.S. interest in the project, which never totally waned, was renewed. By 1898, there was war with Spain, and the slow movement of ships between the two oceans dramatized the value that a canal would bring to military deployments. The end of the war brought a U.S. empire in the Pacific (the United States won the Philippines, Guam, and Puerto Rico and annexed Hawaii in the same year) and further increased the desire for a canal. Although diplomatic obstacles with the British remained, the main obstacle was the location of the canal. Because Panama was a territory of Colombia, the United States needed Colombia's permission to build there. (As an interesting complication, Nicaragua provided another possible canal location.) An agreement was reached with Colombia at the diplomatic level, but the deal was rejected in the Colombian Congress. Revolutionary activity in Panama began to increase, and in November 1903 a successful revolution occurred, much to the advantage of the United States, who could now deal directly with Panama instead of with the stubborn Colombians. About 2 weeks later, a treaty between Panama and the United States was signed. The rest, as they say, is history.

The preceding paragraph is a crude summary of a complex story. Each sentence describes a set of complex events in the Panama Canal story and many events have multiple interpretations. For example, one motivation for a canal was improved transportation. However, this emphasis on transportation highlights commercial and military needs while obscuring other motivations that might have been important, such as an expression of nationalism ("Manifest Destiny"). And some of the sentences hide disputes about actual events. For example, historians agree that the United States provided at least tacit support for the Panamanian revolution, but there is less agreement on exactly how important this support was to the Panamanians.

Despite its simplicity and distortion, we think this Panama Canal story is an approximately accurate outline of the story of the canal from the U.S. point of view.[1] We make the stronger claim: A grasp of something like this story is part of what it means for the ordinary educated person to know the history of the Panama Canal. What the expert knows about this history is likely to be very different—a story with more differentiation and more connections, with more levels of explanation, and more hedges. Even the expert's understanding, however, includes the basic story.

This then is the central assumption of our approach to history as a problem of cognitive psychology. To learn history is to learn a story. To understand history as a nonexpert is to know the story. There is more to both learning and understanding history than this, of course. We claim merely that what one knows includes a story.

In the remainder of this introductory chapter, we first present a broader context for history education and then return to what it means to learn history as a story, concluding with an overview of the remaining chapters. This introduction lays the foundation for a detailed examination of college students' learning and reasoning about two related stories concerning Panama and the United States, the U.S. acquisition of the Panama Canal Zone in 1903 and the 1977 treaties returning the Canal Zone to Panama in 1999.

HISTORICAL LITERACY

We invite the reader to recall the first paragraph of this chapter. Can you remember the dates of the flag raising and the inaugural voyage through the Canal? History

---

[1] There are many stories to tell about any historical topic. In this case, we refer to the Panama Canal Story, recognizing that there is a Panamanian Story, A Colombian Story, and, depending on which events are in central focus, many other stories.

educators lament the learning of history as a list of dates and names, and understandably so. To the extent that an emphasis on dates and names detracts from deeper understandings—understanding explanations of historical events in particular—it would seem to be a misplaced emphasis. We assume that learning about the Panama Canal story is something more than remembering that the first ship sailed through on January 7, 1914.

The contrast between history as a set of dates and names and history as explanations can be reduced, at least as far as the understanding of history is concerned. However, the *teaching* of history faces the additional problems of time and resource limitations and traditions of testing. Some things will be emphasized and some things will be left out, and in many cases it is the attempt to communicate complexity that is omitted. For example, historical causation as the interplay of social forces is often overlooked in the classroom and replaced with a simple story about dates and names. Carretero, Asensio, and Pozo (1991) use the European "discovery" of America to show this contrast. Is the "discovery" story about Columbus and his relationship with the Spanish Monarchy? Or is it a story of 15th century social and economic forces with long-term significance for both the Western hemisphere and Europe? As Carretero et al. point out, the concepts needed to elaborate the second story "pose a rather strong cognitive demand" (p. 29) and make for difficult learning.

In our view, there is nothing incompatible between stories and explanations. To understand history, it is indeed eminently sensible to take both a story approach and an explanation approach. History includes not just stories, but very good stories. And good stories are complex, with rich connections, events that play multiple roles, and multilayered interpretations. Is *The Taming of the Shrew* a simple story about a certain man's (Petruchio) winning and bending the will of a certain woman (Katrina)—a story about individual motivations, problems, and solutions? Or is it a complex commentary on sex roles and stereotypes? "Both" would seem to be a nice compromise answer, but there is more to it than that. The concrete referential information, the characters and what they do (the events), is privileged over the abstract thematic perspective to some extent. The story needs its events, the things that happen and thus cause other things to happen. The thematic perspective depends on the referential narrative. *The Taming of the Shrew* is a story that needs Petruchio and Katrina in order to have anything else to say. There is no story about sex stereotypes without a story about Petruchio, Katrina, and their particular circumstances.

Is the analogy between Shakespeare's story and history's "discovery" story going to work? Can we say then that there is no story about economic and social forces on discovery without Columbus and Queen Isabella? Certainly the importance of social and economic forces for state-sponsored adventures can be told in other ways. And the long-term impact of such forces beyond the year 1500 *must* include more than Columbus. The story of the "discovery" of America is incomplete without social forces, but this story is not possible without the Spanish Monarchs and their sponsorship of this Genoan named Columbus.

Of course, one might correctly argue that the traditional discovery story is either misleading (some other European was first), too simplistic (it is very selective in its usual telling), or laden with values that promote a Eurocentric view of the history of the Americas. These are critical issues about what ought to be emphasized and how the story ought to be told.[2] But if there is to be a discovery story, it has to have some parts of the "discovery."

In short, to repeat a main assumption, we think learning history includes learning a story. It is far from everything that constitutes learning history. It is merely the minimum standard we would be willing to apply to answer the question of whether a student has attained competence in historical topics.

Beyond this minimum, we look to a higher standard—historical literacy. To be able to engage in discourse on history is to be able to do more than tell the story. One must be able to indicate, through speaking or writing, some awareness of what we call the "methods" of history. By this we do not mean specifically the tools and methods of historians, although the idea is in that direction. Rather, we mean developing awareness that, for example, the received story is simple and distorting and that the story had to be recorded in documents of various kinds, which serve as the evidence for the story. Historical literacy also implies an appreciation that evidence counts and some sense of where evidence comes from. Without knowing the sources of evidence, students cannot evaluate the story.

An example of what it means to expect students to have a sense of historical evidence comes from an interesting study by Wineburg (1991) that illuminated some differences between historical experts and novices (high-school students). In examining paintings depicting the Battle of Lexington, students showed little tendency to use information from written historical documents as standards against which to compare the accuracy of the pictures. Asked to choose which picture was the most accurate depiction of the battle scene, the students made limited use of historical documents that could provide critical information, even though they had just read the texts. Historians actively sought information from such documents, whereas students seemed unaware of the privileged status of the documents. As Wineburg concluded, more facts about the American revolution would not necessarily be helpful for such students "when they remain ignorant of the basic heuristics used to create historical interpretations, when they cannot distinguish among different types of evidence, and when they look to a textbook for the 'answer' to historical questions—even when that textbook contradicts primary sources from both sides" (Wineburg, p. 84).

---

[2]We have, of course, chosen a very controversial example to discuss the story concept. There are very legitimate reasons to question the telling of the Discovery story in its traditional short form. The lives of original inhabitants are easily ignored in this story, and the use of the word *discovery* itself can be offensive in suggesting an uninhabited land. Value issues are very much alive in arguments about curriculum, of course, and rightfully so. In our terms, these amount to questions about whose story gets told.

Historical literacy gets expressed through informed discourse that takes account of historical methods, especially the forms of evidence, at some general level. To illustrate by returning to our story of the Panama Canal, it is not that a person with historical literacy knows the details, or even the essence, of the Hay–Bunau-Varilla Treaty of 1903. Nor should the name of the treaty be known necessarily. Rather the student realizes that some treaty must exist spelling out the rights of the United States and Panama in the Canal Zone. Imagine an argument about the Canal. If someone says the "United States has the right to have troops in Panama," the student will be able to ask a question—"Is that what the treaty says?", or "How do you know?" Our definition of a historically literate student is someone with the ability to express his or her knowledge of the world combined with an understanding of a historical story. This knowledge of the world is a combination of specific information from history and some practical knowledge.

The essence of historical literacy, however, combines such knowledge with articulate reasoning. Historical literacy implies an ability to reason about historical topics—to place them in more than one context, to question the sources of a historical statement, to realize that more information is needed to reach a conclusion, and so on. There may be nothing special about historical reasoning, except that it depends on perhaps a little bit of historical knowledge. It may be a manifestation of a general reasoning ability, one informed by specific information but guided by general reasoning principles. But general reasoning principles would not be enough. The kind of reasoning we have in mind is probably a reflection of attitudes toward texts and evidence that is acquired with education. Neither specifically historical nor fully general, this kind of reasoning depends on learning to approach texts and evidence in certain ways, critically and with an attempt to sort out evidence and construct arguments.

We assume that historical literacy, in some form along the lines we have suggested, is a reasonable goal for high-school students, and certainly for college students. This goal is apparently not met at the high-school level (Ravitch & Finn, 1987). Neither is there impressive evidence that students acquire much in the way of "historical facts." Perhaps curriculum decisions appear to trade off "thinking" with "names and dates" in history. We are unaware of any evidence, however, that suggest that students are overly burdened with either one of these components of learning. More typically, students may know neither fact nor interpretation, neither story nor analysis. We think that these components of history go together in historical literacy. We emphasize historical literacy as a high-level goal, without withdrawing our claim that knowing the story is an important part of the picture.

We now consider more fully what it means to understand history as a story.

STORIES AND CAUSAL MODELS

In claiming that history is understood as a story, we have a specific psychological idea in mind: Understanding history is having a mental representation of historical events. To understand the Panama Canal story in something like the way we summarized it in the beginning of this chapter is to learn a sequence of events linked by causal–temporal connections. So, for example, the United States wanted to have a canal *because* faster transcontinental movement would aid commerce and *because* military deployment would be improved. And the United States had to negotiate with Colombia *because* Panama was part of Colombia; but *then* Colombia rejected the treaty and *then* Panama had a revolution and, *as a result*, the United States could negotiate with Panama. In this bit of text, we have italicized some linking predicates—"because," "then," "as a result"—to indicate the informal sense of causal–temporal links. The general idea is that events (e.g., the Panamanian Revolution, the Colombian rejection of the treaty) and states (the U.S. desire for a canal) are linked by causal–temporal connections. To understand the Panama Canal story is to know the relevant events and states and to understand the causal–temporal connections between them.

Causal–Temporal Relations

There is a bit of equivocation in the idea of causal–temporal connections. First there is uncertainty about causality. Was there a causal relationship between Colombia's rejection of the treaty with the United States and the Panama revolution? Or was there just an incidental temporal relationship? Such uncertainty is abundant in history, and the goal of historical scholarship is essentially to reduce that uncertainty. For the nonexpert, however, there is either uncertainty or a belief about a causal relation. That is, someone may believe that the Colombian action was a sufficient condition for U.S. support for the revolution and that this support was necessary for the success of the revolution.

Such uncertainty is specific to a particular case. But there is a second equivocation in the basic idea of causal–temporal relations. Whether one event *causes* another in any strong sense (i.e., whether one event is necessary and sufficient for the occurrence of a second event), may be unknowable in principle in history. Some events seem clearly necessary for others to have occurred: For there to be normal international negotiations with Panama, it was necessary that Panama be independent of Colombia. Most of the more interesting historical episodes, however, appear to fail this test. Was it necessary for the United States to encourage an uprising in order for the Panamanian revolution to be successful? For it to occur? Was the Spanish–American War a necessary cause of renewed interest in the Canal project? Finding sufficient causes is even more difficult and finding necessary and sufficient causes seems virtually impossible in history.

When we speak of causal relationships, therefore, we are speaking loosely, not by the rules of logical inference but according to plausible inferences. The "temporal" in causal–temporal suggests the sense in which this is true. When one event follows another event in time, the temporal relation is taken to be causal–temporal if the circumstances seem to support a causal inference. The first event may have been necessary for the second, it may have been sufficient, or, probably the most common case, it may have been neither. The last case can be considered a probabilistic causal relation. Event 2 was made more likely to occur because of Event 1 in the context of other factors. Causal–temporal relations include all these possibilities. When someone knows a historical topic, what is known is the causal–temporal relations that are the core of the story.

The idea that causal connections are central to story understanding has a rich history in cognitive research. Trabasso and his colleagues in particular have developed the causal analysis of narratives, suggesting that the comprehension of stories depends on establishing story coherence through causal relations (Trabasso, Secco, & van den Broek, 1984; Trabasso & van den Broek, 1985). Some earlier work on story understanding also took note of causal structures in accounting for what readers remember from stories (Omanson, 1982). Previous work on story grammars, following Rumelhart (1975), emphasized story components rather than event connections in their analyses (Mandler & Johnson, 1977; Stein & Glenn, 1979; Thorndyke, 1977). These approaches to stories also imply a role for causal connections as part of the meaning of event categories. The point of departure of more recent work has been the explicit and fine-grain analysis of causal structures.

Trabasso et al. (1984) provided a detailed and explicit model of causal analysis, spelling out tests for necessary and sufficient conditions, and drawing in part on Mackie's (1980) "causal field," a mental representation of events as they occur in certain circumstances, which give rise to causality. The analysis depends on asking critical questions of each event identified in a story: If Event A had not occurred in the circumstance of the story, would Event B not have occurred? (If so, then A is necessary.) If Event A is put into the circumstances of the story, will B occur? (Then A is sufficient.) Applying this analysis to stories yields causal event chains, and the data indicate that what people remember from the stories are the causal event chains. The causal connections are what makes the story coherent and memorable.

The psychological reality of causal structures is also seen when people write summaries of stories (Trabasso & van den Broek, 1985; van den Broek & Trabasso, 1986) and when judgments of importance are made (Trabasso & van den Broek, 1985). The case for causal structures as a mental representation of stories thus appears to be quite strong. It is not completely clear, however, what this means exactly in terms of comprehension. Does a search for causal structures guide comprehension? Or, do such structures merely reflect an on-line process, something that comprehension brings automatically by other means?

Kintsch (1992) presented data showing that a model of text processing (Kintsch, 1988) that merely establishes referential coherence among propositions in the text is adequate to account for recall data, provided certain assumptions about text features are made. Specifically, Kintsch (1992) added the assumption that syntactic cues to important propositions add processing to those propositions. No special status needs to be given to causal connections. However, the causal analysis of

Trabasso and van den Broek (1985) was a better predictor of the contents of summaries. This is interesting because it might be exactly at the level of summarizing where the demands of the writer or speaker are met by the content of causal representations. The summarizer needs to tell the essence of the story. The causal network is the essence of the story. Although we believe that *when* things occur in comprehension is a crucial question for theories of comprehension, this "on-line" issue is less relevant for the topic we address here. Perhaps causal connections are established on-line. Perhaps only explicitly expressed connections are established. In any case, it is sufficient to assume that causal relations have some kind of status as mental representations, not that they are established immediately as each potential causal event is encountered.[3]

The Use of Causal Structures

Our use of causal structures, explained in more detail in chapter 2, is based on the weak assumption suggested earlier. We do not assume that these structures guide comprehension, although they might in some sense. We assume that they represent what a person knows (or believes) when he or she knows some historical topic. In addition, as we detail in the next chapter, we see causal structures as research tools. Not only are they mental representations, they are a means of assessing what students learn when they learn historical material. To assess what someone has learned about the Panama Canal story, we ask what parts of the causal model have been acquired through learning. To ask whether two students have the same knowledge is to ask whether their causal models are the same.

SUMMARY

Knowing history includes knowing stories. There is much more to historical knowledge than stories, however. Historical literacy implies some awareness of the forms of historical evidence and the ability to engage in discourse that addresses evidence. Nevertheless, the richer concept of historical literacy also includes the concept of history as narrative. Narrativity itself depends critically on causal–temporal relations among events. We apply causal analysis to understanding of history texts and claim that to understand historical events is to take account of the causal–temporal relations among them. A mental representation of historical events includes a causal network of some kind.

---

[3]We assume that, as far as the initial stages of comprehension are concerned, there is a more restricted kind of processing occurring, one more dominated by word meanings, syntactic structures, and propositions (Perfetti, 1989, 1990). Inferences are necessary to establish many causal connections, and these may not always be made immediately, although the timing of inferences remains a source of some disagreement (McKoon & Ratcliff, 1986, 1992).

OVERVIEW

In the remaining chapters, we address specific issues of history learning, within the contexts we have discussed in this chapter. We address issues that are important in cognitive psychology as well as issues that seem to be more about education or about history. We need to be clear that, above all, this is a study of the cognitive psychology of learning from text. We report an extended study of history text learning and we refer to other research we have carried out on history learning. We address a number of issues along the way. There are two empirical bases for our observations. First, we report in chapters 3 through 8 on a learning study that resembles case studies as much as traditional cognitive research. This study will demonstrate what it means to learn history as a story. Second, we discuss, especially in the final chapter, an extended view of history learning that goes beyond the story. In terms of the framework we have developed in this chapter, the bulk of what we report concerns history as a story. We also include some complementary observations based on studies we have done that examine history as text-based reasoning.

The following are key points detailed in the remaining chapters:

History Text Learning.   Our study is a contribution to the cognitive psychology of text learning. We demonstrate that readers' representations of certain kinds of texts include causal–temporal event chains.

Extended Learning.   We report a study that requires students to engage in learning over an extended period of weeks, essentially a kind of minicourse. We believe that this procedure produces some interesting observations about learning.

Reasoning.   Both our learning study and additional studies we discuss focus on reasoning as well as learning. We see these learning and reasoning issues as closely linked, and we demonstrate this in general ways.

Multiple Texts.   Students in our study read multiple texts, a condition we think assists learning. Further, we discuss additional studies that place multiple texts and documents in a central position for reasoning about history, and show how students use documents in reasoning.

Individual Differences.   We consider the differences as well as the similarities among students in learning and reasoning.

Text Models.   In addition to suggesting that history stories are represented as causal–temporal models, we argue that we need to extend our ideas about text models to account for multiple text situations. We describe such a model.

History.   Our studies are centered on history, but much of what we address can be viewed as general issues of learning, reasoning, and text use. There are some specifically historical dimensions, including the use of historical documents and observations on history students' reasoning.

In chapter 2, we examine causal models in cognitive psychology and provide a causal–temporal model for our focal story of the U.S. acquisition of the Panama Canal Zone. Chapter 3 presents the methods of the study, an examination of a small number of college students' learning and reasoning in a minicourse on the Panama Stories. Chapters 4 through 6 include the results of Part 1 of our study: the learning results, assessed in terms of the causal model (chapter 4), the reasoning results (chapter 5), and individual differences among our subjects in learning and reasoning (chapter 6). Chapters 7 and 8 present Part 2, learning and reasoning about a second story in U.S.–Panama relations, the 1977 treaties returning the Canal Zone to Panama in 1999, and a hypothetical scenario designed to raise questions about the United States honoring these treaties. Chapter 9 summarizes key results and discusses conclusions from both parts of the study. Chapter 10 discusses related research on text-based history learning and the implications of our work for both general issues of text learning and history education.

Chapter 2

Causal Analysis in History

In this chapter, we describe a causal analysis of a single historical story, the acquisition of the Panama Canal Zone by the United States. The causal analysis has two aspects. First, it is an assumption about the mental representations that are constructed as part of story understanding. Second, it is a methodological tool by which one can assess the parts of the story that a given individual has understood or recalled. We do not independently demonstrate that the kind of structure we describe is, in fact, a mental representation. Rather we assume that it is, drawing on empirical demonstrations that causal structures of this general kind have some psychological status (Trabasso & van den Broek, 1985). It may turn out that some other representation form is a closer fit to some kinds of psychological data, and hence qualifies as a psychologically better model. Until such time as critical data are available, ours is a plausible working assumption about what it means to understand a history story as a causal–temporal structure.

The essential ingredients of the causal analysis are the causally or temporally ordered events that are linked together as a causal story. These events typically include human agents, their actions and motives, and circumstances that situate the events.

Many historical accounts are stories about human agents who seek power, govern nations, achieve political change, or wage war. Other stories are about agents who invent, build, create, explore, discover, and influence culture, religion, and technology. Agents can be individuals, groups, or even abstract entities such as nations, political parties, and religions. No proper story can be told without agents and the events in which they participate. Nevertheless, it is important to emphasize that there are other kinds of historical accounts, focused less on individuals and events and more on impersonal forces, especially social and cultural conditions. Even the most impersonal accounts, however, build on events that organize, over time, a story of some kind. Our analysis is especially for historical stories in which events and human actions are central. It can be applied, with modification, to any historical account that makes reference to events and relationships between them.

For the kinds of historical texts we consider here, learning history consists of learning events and the causal–temporal connectedness of these events. To illustrate, consider a segment from a text describing the acquisition of the U.S.-built Panama Canal:

> The first order of business was to secure the abrogation of the Clayton–Bulwer Treaty. When Secretary of State John Hay began negotiations with the British, he found them surprisingly agreeable; at that time they were fighting the Boers in South Africa and, being isolated in international diplomacy, they sought the friendship of the United States. The results were two Hay–Pauncefote treaties. (Center for Strategic & International Studies, 1967, p. 7).

The text refers to at least three events: removing the obstacle of the Clayton–Bulwer Treaty, negotiations between two nations, and the signing of a new treaty, the Hay–Pauncefote Treaty. The text also refers to an important motivation that links these events: Other problems facing a nation motivate its willingness to negotiate an agreement. This segment, typical of historical texts in this regard, is not merely a list of disconnected events, but rather a reconstruction of events connected coherently by motivations, causes, and enabling relationships. Nations negotiate and sign treaties because they want to gain something from another country. (In this example, Britain was motivated to negotiate with the United States because they wanted the friendship of the United States.) In understanding history, causal relationships between the critical events are assumed; the task is to reconstruct the critical precipitating events that adequately explain the causes of these critical events. Thus, one or more stated events are seen to motivate, enable, or cause the event of interest.

Because causal relations are central in texts describing historical events, we develop a model of causal analysis similar to the kind that has proved useful in describing the causal relations in other types of narrative texts. This type of analysis was developed by Trabasso and van den Broek (Trabasso, 1989; Trabasso, Secco, & van den Broek, 1984; Trabasso & Sperry, 1985; Trabasso & van den Broek, 1985; van den Broek, 1989b) to study simple narrative stories.

CAUSAL ANALYSIS OF NARRATIVE TEXTS

Trabasso and van den Broek (1985) analyzed short narratives with simple story structures. Their analysis separates the text into clausal units that express events. Each pair of clauses is then tested to determine which events are causally related to other events, resulting in a list of all possible causal connections. These connections would then describe the logical relations necessary to understand the story. For example, consider this story from Warren, Nicholas, and Trabasso (1979):

> It was Friday afternoon. Carol was drawing a picture in the classroom. David felt mischievous. David decided to tease Carol. When Carol was not looking, he tied her shoelaces together. Carol tripped and fell down. (p. 24)

First the six sentences are segmented into eight clause-like units (see Table 2.1). The logical relations are determined for each pair of clauses, according to four types of causal connections: physical cause, psychological cause, motivation, and enablement. Clauses 6 and 7 are related to each other through a physical cause connection: Carol tripped as a mechanical response to having her shoelaces tied together by David. The relationship between Clauses 1 and 3 is also defined as causal by Warren et al. (1979), a psychological rather than a physical cause. David's involuntary feeling of mischievousness is presumed to result from the fact that it is Friday afternoon. Clauses 3 and 4 are related by a *motivating* connective: David was motivated to tease Carol because he felt mischievous. Finally, the enabling relation is demonstrated in the connection between Clauses 5 and 6. Because Carol was not looking, she was in a necessary but not sufficient state for David to be able to tie her shoelaces together.

Once all the appropriate connections (signified by links) are made between events (signified by nodes), a network such as the one in Fig. 2.1 is constructed. There should be a clear causal chain from the beginning of the story to the end of the story. Using their system, Trabasso and colleagues can predict what subjects recall, summarize, and view as important in a story. The more causal links an event has, the higher the probability it will be recalled (Trabasso & van den Broek, 1985), included in a summary (Trabasso & van den Broek, 1985; van den Broek & Trabasso, 1986), and judged as important (Trabasso & Sperry, 1985; Trabasso & van den Broek, 1985; van den Broek, 1988). They also found that dead-end events, those not on the main causal chain, are less well recalled (Trabasso & van den Broek, 1985), judged less important (Trabasso & Sperry, 1985), and not mentioned in a summary (van den Broek & Trabasso, 1986).

CAUSAL ANALYSIS OF HISTORY TEXTS

Although this system has proved useful for narrative analysis, some modifications are necessary before applying such a system to history texts. First, this system was used only on relatively short simple stories, whereas history texts are significantly longer and more complex. In larger more complex stories, it is necessary to increase the grain size of the analysis from a clause to an event. Second, the system

TABLE 2.1
Simple Narrative

(1)	It was Friday afternoon.
(2)	Carol was drawing a picture in the classroom.
(3)	David felt mischievous.
(4)	David decided to tease Carol.
(5)	When Carol was not looking,
(6)	he tied her shoelaces together.
(7)	Carol tripped
(8)	and fell down.

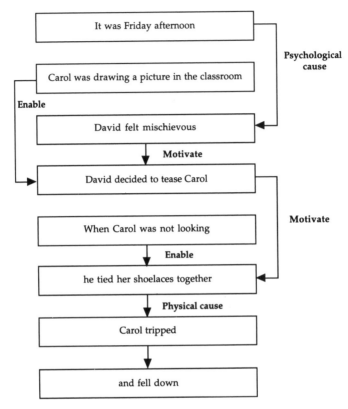

FIG 2.1.   Event network from Warren, Nicholas, and Trabasso (1979). Reprinted with permission from Ablex Publishing Corporation.

developed by Trabasso and colleagues was designed to analyze the logical connections necessary to comprehend a particular text rather than highlight common information in different texts. Their analysis is text specific rather than event specific. In analyzing a text about particular historical events, it is useful to consider one *common template* of the events. In this way, although any given history text may not include all of the events and relations, the commonalities among many texts with respect to these events and relations will be highlighted. Finally, the purpose of reading is generally quite different in the case of history. In contrast to the type of narratives Trabasso and van den Broek used, more importance is typically given to accuracy in comprehending historical events. Thus, in history there is a fairly well defined set of events that comprise the story. Accordingly, a causal model for history texts should assess the fit between the causal event structure of the text and the structure of the actual historical situation. In effect, a causal–temporal model in history is a model of a situation (van Dijk & Kintsch, 1983) rather than a model of a text.

Thus there are two points of departure for our causal structure analysis, further explained in the next section. These result in causal–temporal event structures for analyzing history texts.

Intermediate Grain Size: The Event

The first departure is to make the unit of analysis an entire event rather than a clause. This is primarily a pragmatic modification, one required by the differences in length of text. History texts are significantly longer than the texts used in typical story research. In fact, the texts in our study range in length from 1,701 to 13,110 words. Compare these lengths with those of most of the narrative texts studied, which range from 83 to 420 words (Fletcher, 1989; Kintsch & van Dijk, 1978; Trabasso, 1989; Trabasso et al, 1984; Trabasso & Sperry, 1985; Trabasso & van den Broek, 1985; van den Broek, 1989b). On average, the expository texts studied have been only slightly longer, from 69 to 641 words (Black, 1985; Graesser & Goodman, 1985; Mayer, 1985; Meyer, 1985; Miller, 1985; Thibadeau, Just, & Carpenter, 1982; Varnhagen, 1991).

Although all the models of text analysis assume that these systems are extendible to any text length, we conclude that a more coarse-grained analysis is sufficient for our texts. It is unnecessary to have a detailed, fine-grained analysis of all the explicit and implicit causal relations between every pair of clauses. Although complete clausal analysis is useful for an 83-word, 13-clause text, the many multiclause events of a longer text make this analysis impractical. For example, in order to adequately describe the story of the acquisition of the Panama Canal, one would need to include approximately 40 events including the Spanish–American War, the U.S. negotiations with Colombia, and the Panamanian revolution. Each of these events would itself include many words and many clauses. In effect, each event is a substory.

Here are three examples of substories embedded in the Panama Canal story: (a) how lobbyists went about changing Congress's decision on where to build a canal, (b) how the United States influenced the Panamanian revolution, and (c) how Colombia came to reject a U.S. treaty. In a fine-grained analysis, each of these larger events can be analyzed in the same way as the simple stories from narrative research. For a 13-clause text, Trabasso (1989) represents 15 causal connections. For a representation of a moderately long history text with 40 events and an average of 20 clauses per event, there would be approximately 800 clauses, 30 within-event connections for each of the 40 events (1,200 connections), perhaps 80 between-event connections, and an inestimable number of connections among the 800 subevents within substories.

We are working with long and complex texts, and we are interested in the reader's final representation of the events described in these texts. For this purpose, the reader's representation of larger event-related segments, rather than clauses, is the appropriate level. Of course, we do not assume that a reader does not have access to smaller clause-linked units. Indeed, we assume that understanding texts at this level is the means by which a representation at the event-link level is constructed.

The issue is simply the grain size necessary for the research task and which unit corresponds to that level. For history texts that unit is most reasonably the event rather than the clause.[4]

Representing Similarities: One Common Template

The second departure from previous causal analysis reflects our interest in student learning of the situation, the story common across multiple texts. The Trabasso and van den Broek system was developed to describe comprehension of a particular text, based on the analysis of the clauses of that text. Our goal was a system that could be used to compare learning from any number of very different texts. For example, each text describing the acquisition of the Panama Canal is certain to discuss the events of the Panamanian revolution. Any historical topic will include many such events that are central to the story and, therefore, must be part of any text on the topic. Typically, what varies among texts is the presentation of the events. We wanted a system that could capture the common events even when presented differently in different texts.

For this, we need a more abstract representation of the events themselves, independent of the way an author represents them. Because there are many ways to connect these event units, the causal–temporal connections among events may vary from text to text. We need not merely an analysis of one text but a common template to describe the similarities and differences among the texts. Thus, we developed an idealized template of the events and causal–temporal structures that are central to any historical account of the Panama Canal.

THE ANALYSIS OF EXPOSITORY ASPECTS
OF HISTORY TEXTS

Although a causal–temporal analysis is appropriate for examining the narrative component of history texts, there is a need to evaluate both the specific

---

[4]It is an interesting empirical question whether the predictive ability of the Trabasso analysis is affected by the length of the text read. For example, are the number of connectors and the location on the causal path predictive of what is recalled? Are all possible causal connections between and within substories contained in the subject's representation of the text? Are all subevents within a larger event on the main causal chain if the larger event is? How do memory and processing constraints affect which between-event connections are represented? Are causal connections between larger events differentially represented and are they more likely to be recalled? We assume that the connection of larger event units to each other have priority over connections within these events. The more abstract level representation of the within substory information may be a chunk or unit. A chunk may be easily reinstated and connected to other chunks but within substory events are less easily reinstated and more difficult to connect. Perhaps the event units are better recalled than within substory events or connectors. With these questions in mind, we assume that such a detailed fine grain analysis would not prove any more insightful or beneficial than our intermediate coarse-grained analysis.

propositional information written in the text and the interpretative or persuasive statements that the author interjects. For this reason, history texts need to be analyzed through traditional expository analysis (Bovair & Kieras, 1984; Kieras, 1985; Kintsch & van Dijk, 1978; Mayer, 1985; Miller, 1985).

It is often the intent of the reader of history texts to learn the specific details that are part of the narrative account. Because one purpose of writing about historical events is to inform the reader, an analysis must be sensitive to the propositional knowledge included within the complex event units already described. Our method of determining units of knowledge is derived from the expository analysis of Bovair and Kieras (1984), which is a modification of Kintsch's propositional analysis (Kintsch & van Dijk, 1978). Each clause is segmented into a unit, with the predicate and the arguments of the predicate included in this unit. Any modifiers are represented separately. In history texts, these modifiers are often prepositional phrases, adjectives, and adverbs. Five modifiers that are especially important in representing knowledge from certain kinds of history texts are locations, dates, terms of treaties, proper names, and the credentials of an individual.

Writers of historical texts also often write to persuade the reader that the author's interpretation of the events is reliable. Authors generally include statements that interpret the events described. (This may be less true of history textbooks used in schools; see Crismore, 1984). For instance, one author writing about the acquisition of the Panama Canal may present the events with an intent to argue that the Panamanians, rather than the U.S. government, were responsible for the Panamanian revolution. In order to persuade, the writer may include an interpretive statement such as the following:

1. These nationalists, *contrary to North American myths too long propagated in textbooks*, did not suddenly spring up full-grown at Roosevelt's command (emphasis added).

Many, if not most, history texts include interpretative statements that can and need to be represented. Thus, the author's interpretive statements and comments were included as propositions in our system and are represented in the same way as are modifiers and predicates because they are generally not marked by authors as interpretation.

THE ANALYSIS OF HISTORY TEXTS: CAUSAL– TEMPORAL EVENT STRUCTURES

Our study used four texts that described the historical events involved in the U.S. acquisition of a canal in Panama. From these texts, we constructed a single common template of the causal–temporal event structure. We identified 39 complex events or states, agreed upon by all the texts, that were important to the story (see

Appendix A). An example event is *Panama Revolts* and an example state is *Colombia Owns Panama*. From these events we constructed an idealized template of the story by connecting the events and states with causal links that convey the relationship between two events. Figure 2.2 shows this idealized template. In our case, the most important causal links are *motivate, enable,* and *physical cause,* as defined by Warren et al. (1979). For example, *Colombia Owns Panama→* Motivate→*United States Negotiates with Colombia→Enable→U.S.–Colombia Treaty.* We also included temporal connections, although Trabasso and van den Broek (1985) exclude temporal connections and represent only causal connections. In history stories, it is often the case that the temporal context in which an event occurs may enable a reader to interpret the event. Examples of these connections include: *At the same time, After the war,* and *While the U.S. was making treaties.* In these cases an author connects the two events without making any causal relationship explicit.

A simplification of the Panama Canal acquisition story follows: The California gold rush→Motivate→U.S. interest in a Central American canal. Spanish American War→Result→United States gains new Pacific territories→ Motivate→increased U.S. interest in a canal. (Obstacle:) British have interests in area→Motivate→U.S.–British negotiations→Result→a treaty that allows United States sole rights to build. U.S. Senate debates on a canal location→ Result→Panama chosen. (Obstacle:) Colombia owns Panama→Motivate→ U.S.–Colombia negotiations→Result→Colombian congress rejects treaty→ Motivate→Panama revolts. U.S. supports Panama in revolution→Enable→Panama wins revolution→Enable→U.S.–Panama negotiations→Result→treaty that allows United States to build canal→Result→Panama Canal.

Each text was scored against our idealized template with events common across texts and the particular connections varying. Sentences 2a–2d provide examples from the four texts of four different ways of conveying the same event unit, *Colombia Owns Panama:*

2a. At the time, Panama was a part of Colombia, ...

2b. ... the Isthmus of Panama, which was then a Province of New Granada....

2c. Three years later, the government of Colombia (Panama was then only a geographical expression, a poverty-stricken, pestilential province of Colombia racked by chronic internal disorder)....

2d. Spain ... destroyed Panama's autonomy be attaching it to the Viceroyalty of New Granada (now known as Colombia).

The textual information relevant to each event was then propositionalized according to the system developed by Bovair and Kieras (1984). Clauses were divided into units consisting of a predicate and its arguments, modifiers, and interpretive statements. Only nonredundant modifiers were counted as a unique proposition within any given event. For instance, only the first mention of the

Spanish–American War was scored as a proposition; similarly, only the first mention that it occurred in 1898 was scored as a proposition. Because many events occurred in a single year and understanding the temporal order of events is important in determining what happened and why, the month, day, and year are each considered separately. Four other modifiers—locations, terms of treaties, proper names, and an individual's credentials—were also classified.

For example, Sentence 3 contains five propositions. The predicate *opened negotiations* includes both negotiators (United States and Colombia). The final four propositions result from the importance of dates (*January* and *1903*), credentials (*U.S. Secretary of State*) and names of characters (*John Hay*):

3.   In January 1903, U.S. Secretary of State John Hay opened negotiations with Colombia.

The interpretive statements of the author also were included as unique propositions. An example of an interpretative statement from Congressman X's text is found in Sentence 4 and an example of an interpretative statement from Professor Y's text is found in Sentence 5:

4.   It was a *typically farcical* revolution, one of many in the history of Latin America (emphasis added).
5.   These nationalists, *contrary to North American myths too long propagated in textbooks*, did not suddenly spring up full-grown at Roosevelt's command (emphasis added).

After each text was scored on the idealized template (Fig. 2.2), the explicit connectors were marked. Then the knowledge for each event was calculated. For each event unit the number of propositions was counted, including predicates, connections, modifiers and interpretative statements. Only initial mention of these details was counted for each event. For instance, the credentials of John Hay were only counted once although he appeared throughout the story.

Once the idealized template was constructed, it was used to compare both the texts and the students. Although each text presented the same basic story, there were variations among the parts of the story that were emphasized, and the authors had different interpretations of some events. These text differences were easily noted using the idealized causal model. In addition, subjects' summaries and responses to comprehension questions were scored against the template. From their scores, we determined the common information learned by all the students and the places where the students had difficulty with the story. Individual differences in learning style and the quality and quantity of information learned by each student were also determined using the idealized causal model template. Finally, the causal model allowed us to ascertain what text specific information was learned by the students.

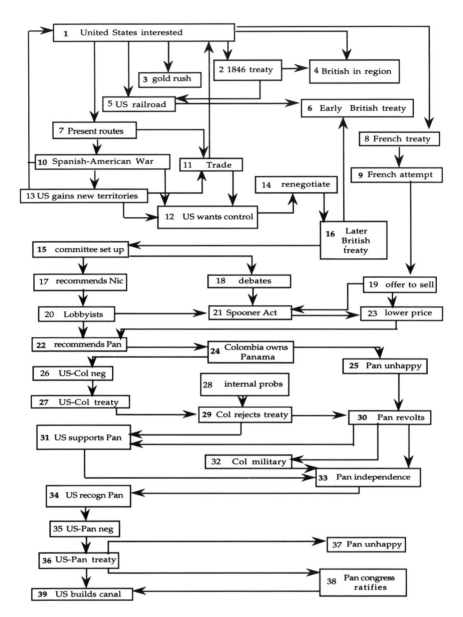

FIG. 2.2.   Causal model template of the history of the acquisition of a U.S. canal in Panama.

SUMMARY

History texts that express causal–temporal event structures can be analyzed according to those structures. Previous research has demonstrated that simple texts can be analyzed according to their causal structures. We have presented a related system of analysis which also assumes that causal–temporal event structures are part of the learner's representation of a narrative text. However, this analysis departs from the previous research in its attention to larger units, events rather than clauses, and its focus on events in the historical situation independently of their expression in particular texts. Thus, our analysis adds two factors to the typical causal–event analysis—the propositional content of texts and the author's rhetorical stance—and thereby provides tools for the analyses of learning from historical texts and observations of both text and learner differences.

Part **I**

The Acquisition Story

Chapter 3

The Learning Study: Goals and Methods

GOALS IN LIGHT OF PAST TEXT RESEARCH

Text reading involves a complex process of cognitive and language processes that, when executed successfully, result in comprehension. And learning from text results when these comprehension processes yield a representation, in the mind of the reader, of some situation described in the text. Thus processes of word identification, parsing, and meaning-based (propositional) encoding lead to basic comprehension of sentences. When combined with prior knowledge and the drawing of inferences, these processes lead to a knowledge-rich understanding—a learning—of text material. This much is a more or less standard view of what it means to read, understand, and learn from a text that is supported by a wealth of research and detailed by processing theories (Just & Carpenter, 1987; Kintsch, 1988; Perfetti, 1985; van Dijk & Kintsch, 1983).

Is there anything special about learning a history text? Perhaps not. Indeed, in the context of the preceding chapters, history learning is an example of story learning, about which much is known through other research (Graesser, 1981; Mandler & Johnson, 1977; Stein & Glenn, 1979; Trabasso & van den Broek, 1985). However, we see three questions or points of departure that arise from examining history texts in the way we have. First, in contrast to other narrative text research, there is more to a history text than the narrative structure itself. As we have argued in chapter 1, the idea of historical literacy entails more than merely learning the story. It involves interpretation and reasoning about both the events of the story and the author's presentation of those events. Although one can imagine such issues as part of narrative understanding in general, narrative research has focused on other issues. The reasoning aspect of history learning is probably quite general, applying to a wide range of texts that provide stories about events, causes, human and social agents, and so on. Examining instances of such reasoning is one of the points of departure of our study.

The second point of departure was anticipated in chapter 2: the length of a text. As we have noted, text research rests largely on studies of short texts read by subjects during brief periods of less than an hour. Many reading situations involve more intensive contact with a text than this. In ordinary school learning, for example, students spend a protracted period of distributed learning, reading pieces of texts over a period of weeks. There is no reason to think that the processes of text reading and comprehension that have been discovered and modeled in text research are profoundly different in more sustained text encounters. The question of learning over extended periods, however, can be addressed only by examining just this kind of text learning. Again, this is not special to history. But, as with the reasoning component, it is something well represented by history texts.

A third point of departure is that text research has been concerned with reading a single text. There are circumstances, including college classroom learning and other forms of scholarship, in which a learner reads more than one text on the same topic. Sometimes, as in a classroom with "supplemental" texts, two books will overlap in content and differ in purpose and depth of treatment. In other cases, the texts may be quite comparable in their depth of topic treatment, differing mainly in perspective or persuasive goals. It was part of our purpose to examine students' learning about a single topic from different texts.

Thus, the goals of our learning study were to track students as they learned from history texts. The study does not address standard questions of text processing. Instead, our three points of departure from text research—learning that includes reasoning, learning that takes place over weeks rather than minutes, and learning from multiple texts—require us to ask different questions. These questions include the following:

1. What is the time course of learning the basic structure of a historical story, compared with learning about the details?
2. When different texts present different perspectives or different facts, what are the effects on learners?
3. How do learners accommodate their prior learning to new information?
4. What kinds of individual differences are observed among a relatively homogenous group of college students in their reasoning styles?

These are a few of the questions addressed in this study.

There is one important aspect of the study that shapes the kinds of answers it can provide to these questions. Because of our emphasis on close examination of a small number of individual students over an extended period, we had to choose qualitative analysis over quantitative analysis for many of the questions. In other history text studies, we have used more standard sampling sizes, but this is a small sample study that lends itself to case study analysis.

The study consists of two parts. Part 1, which is the focus of this chapter and the next three, concerns the students' learning and reasoning about the events that led to acquisition of the Panama Canal Zone by the United States and the subsequent building of the Panama Canal. We refer to this as the Acquisition Story. Part 2, which is discussed in chapter 7, concerns more recent events related to the Acquisition Story, namely the 1977 treaties between Panama and the United States that allow for the Canal Zone to revert to Panama in 1999. A final segment of Part 2, covered in chapter 8, created a hypothetical scenario on the future of Panama as a way of evoking further reasoning from subjects based on what they had learned in the texts.

PART 1 METHODS

Part 1 of the learning study addressed the four general questions listed earlier. To answer these questions, we had to discover which facts and relations were learned when, where confusions arose, what kinds of information were well remembered, and what kinds of information were forgotten.

To discover the course of learning, we observed how the students built causal models by tracking their learning over four texts. We also tried to discover how information from a text affected the model constructed from a previous text. Is new information integrated into the student's causal model? If it is contradictory, does it replace information in the model or is it noted separately as conflicting with events or relations already in the model?

To ensure that there was some possibility for conflicting information or alternative perspectives, we presented the students with two texts—of the four texts in total—written from clearly contrasting perspectives. To track the effects of students' prior beliefs and knowledge on how they handled these alternative perspectives, we obtained measures of relevant political attitudes as well as relevant historical knowledge.

The Texts

Four texts were used in the study, including a first brief text to introduce subjects to the topic. The texts varied in amount of detail provided, length, complexity, and perspective. All four covered the period from the California Gold Rush in 1848 to the signing of the 1903 treaty awarding a strip of land, the Canal Zone, to the United States and allowing the United States to build the Panama Canal. Our causal model covered only this time period.

The first text, given in the lab, was a short (1,656 word) text read sentence by sentence on the computer (and therefore referred to as the Online text). It was an abridged version of the second text plus small excerpts from texts that the subjects did not read.[5] Text 1, written by the experimenters, was designed to be neutral in its presentation of the basic acquisition story. It essentially is a chronology of events relating to the U.S. interest in a canal from the Gold Rush to the signing of a treaty with Panama. Although this text did include the Panamanian revolution, it excluded, by design, any mention of U.S. involvement in Panama's revolution. This

---

[5]The first two texts are reprinted in Appendix B.

exclusion allowed us to track the students' course of learning on the question of the revolution. Because each subsequent text added information about the Panamanian revolution, we could detect whether students expanded their mental model about the revolution based on new information of if they replaced old knowledge with new facts.

Like Text 1, Text 2 was an unbiased account of the events between 1848 and 1903. Text 2 was almost twice as long as Text 1 (3,269 words). It was an excerpt from a 1967 report authored by the Center for Strategic Studies (then at Georgetown University and currently the Center for Strategic and International Studies), written after a period of unrest in Panama to address the ongoing problems between Panama and the United States. It did not completely avoid opinions but it provided a balanced view. Text 2, which we refer to as the CSIS text, questioned U.S. actions in some passages:

> Historians still dispute what role the United States played in the revolution, but the arrival of the U.S.S. Nashville in Colon harbor on the evening of November 2, 1903, and the refusal of United States officials of the Panama Railroad Company to transport Colombian troops across the Isthmus, leaves little doubt that the United States favored the independence of Panama. (p. 8)

In other passages, Text 2 can be interpreted as supporting the United States position that Panama was able to pursue self interest in the treaty with the United States:

> Bunau-Varilla's motives may have been even deeper and darker, especially judging by his actions before and after composing the treaty, but at the time of authorship he had the authority to compose the document as he saw fit. ...(p. 10)

Thus, we defined Text 2 as unbiased because it was largely a factual account of the story, and because its infrequent passages implying opinions were balanced.

The final two texts were persuasive texts, written during the Congressional debate on the treaties signed by Carter and Torrijos in 1977. These treaties, eventually ratified, would return the Canal Zone to Panama in 1999. Each author (referred to as Congressman X and Professor Y) wrote to support one side of the question "Should the United States turn ownership of the Panama Canal over to the Panamanian government?" As part of their argument, each text told the Acquisition Story in a manner consistent with the author's opinions about the 1977 treaties. Thus, the text that argued against the "give-back" told an Acquisition Story in which the United States was innocent of any wrongdoing in its dealings with Panama. The other text, which favored the 1977 treaties returning the Canal Zone to Panama, told an Acquisition Story in which the U.S. was not entirely above suspicion in its dealings with Panama. The texts were by no means equally "biased," however, with the antitreaty text being much more one-sided in its presentation.

In a controlled laboratory experiment, the persuasive texts would have had similar styles and similar lengths. Because finding made-for-the-lab texts is impossible and because we wanted to use existing texts rather than sanitize them, we accepted the differences between our texts as a "natural" difference. The conclusions allowed by such a procedure are limited, but, as we will show, not without some interesting implications.

Congressman X.   The pro-U.S. text was written by a conservative Republican Congressman for the purpose of rallying U.S. public opinion against the 1977 treaties that would return ownership of the Canal to Panama. In the section read by our students, the author described the history from 1848 until the 1903 treaty, sprinkling the story with his opinions about both the Acquisition Story and 1970s events. The nine pages are filled with colorful language and vivid images consistent with his viewpoint. He adeptly uses language and selective facts to convey an urgency that Text 4 lacks. One subject who favored the 1977 treaties commented that Congressman X's text was compelling and made him question the U.S. decision to give the Canal to Panama. One example of X's style follows:

> When revolution broke out, there was no local opposition; control of the railway, hastily granted American recognition, a landing party of forty-two United States Marines in dress whites, and an off-shore U.S. naval presence preempted Colombian suppression of Panamanian independence. It was a bloodless coup with the sole exception of one unfortunate casualty, neither American, Colombian, nor Panamanian; but an unfortunate Chinese who managed to walk into a token artillery barrage—one small bang in a massive chorus of Colombian whimpers. (p. 32)

Professor Y.   The alternative-perspective text was written by a professor of Latin American history. The Acquisition Story text was 17 1/2 pages long and began Panama's history with its discovery by Balboa in 1510. The students were not asked any questions about the history before the Gold Rush and no pre-Gold Rush event was included in our template causal model. Professor Y filled his text with facts, names, and dates. The text appears to be written for an educated audience trying to learn more about the U.S.–Panama negotiations that had led to the 1977 treaties. The section our subjects read ended at the 1903 treaty. No mention of the 1977 negotiations was made nor did the author insert his opinion about those negotiations in this section. Y provided a detailed account of the United States' involvement in the Panamanian revolution but he emphasized the strong feelings of nationalism among the Panamanians:

> [Panamanian] nationalists, contrary to North American myths too long propagated in textbooks, did not suddenly spring up full-grown at Roosevelt's command. The belief that Panama should exist as a separate independent country was neither artificially created suddenly in 1903 nor propagated in Washington before it took hold in Panama City. The Panamanian nationalism of 1902–03 formed only one part of an ancient story, although, as it turned out, the most important chapter. (p. 23)

These two texts provided opportunities to observe the development of a causal model when conflicting perspectives and even conflicting information are presented. In supporting his viewpoint, each author gives facts the other chooses to ignore. (Congressman X does this more frequently). This gave us a chance to learn whether students included facts from both sides of the argument, whether one perspective became dominant in their models and to observe any effects that specific inconsistencies might have on learning. One fact in particular addressed the inconsistency question. Each text gave a travel time for the U.S.S. Oregon's trip around South America. Three of the four cited approximately 68 days but X's text claimed 90.

The Subjects

Six University of Pittsburgh students were each paid $110 for their participation in our "minicourse." They ranged in age from 18–25 years and represented all four undergraduate classes. In-depth profiles of the students are provided in chapter 6. Briefly, our subjects were Eileen, a female senior; Dave, a male sophomore (age 25); Jen, a female junior; George, a male senior; Robbie, a male freshman; Mitch, a male sophomore.[6]

Three additional students from the same population participated as control subjects. They received $15 for their participation in Meetings 1 and 8. Like the six learning students, all the controls were White and all spoke English as their first language. The controls discussed the hypothetical Postponement Bill from the scenario of Meeting 8 without having any knowledge of the early history, the 1977 treaty debates, or the relationship between the United States and Panama.

How They Were Chosen. The students were selected from among 29 students in introductory psychology classes and from an upper-level psychology class of 22 students. Two factors determined eligibility to participate in the learning study: (1) Because of the amount of reading involved, only above average readers were included. (2) Individuals with a strong history background or high knowledge of Panama could not take part. Students first took screening tests that assessed their relevant knowledge and reading ability. The upper-class students were screened on only the relevant knowledge test, and those selected then took the remaining screening tests prior to their participation in the study. The following tests made up our screening procedure:

1. The comprehension section of the Nelson-Denny Reading Test, which contains 36 multiple-choice questions. This measured reading ability.

2. A section of the New York State Board of Regents exam in history. This consisted of 49 multiple-choice questions, mainly about U.S. and European history

---

[6]The students' names have all been changed.

after 1500. The Regents exam is given to high-school juniors at the end of the school year and must be passed (65% or better) before students can be considered competent in history in New York State public schools. This assessed the students' general history knowledge.

3. A Panama knowledge test. This was a 16-question test designed by the experimenters to determine the extent of subjects' knowledge about Panama and the Canal. It included general questions, (e.g., *Where is Panama? Why is the canal important?*) There were also questions about its history, (e.g., *Who built the canal? When was it built?*) There were questions about the 1977 treaties, (e.g., *Who was responsible for the treaties? How will Panama's rights and responsibilities change?*) Finally, there were questions about the U.S. invasion of Panama in 1989 (e.g., *Name the dictator the United States captured. State some reasons the United States gave for its invasion*). Subjects were also asked to place eight countries (Colombia, China, Denmark, Israel, Italy, Panama, Sri Lanka, United States) and the Pacific Ocean on a blank map of the world. This determined topic-specific knowledge.

4. All potential subjects also were asked to rate, on a 5-point scale, their level of agreement on a series of opinion statements. These opinion statements are listed in Appendix C. This was not used as a screening device but we hoped it would provide some insight into the subjects' personalities.

Better than average reading ability, based on the Nelson-Denny scores, was the first requirement for participation. Five of our six subjects scored greater than 30/36 and the sixth subject scored 26/36. The Nelson-Denny scores are normed by year in school, but because of the age range of the students, the percentile ranks of the students would be skewed. For consistency, we used the Nelson-Denny percentile scale for end of first year in a four-year university. Only one student fell below the 92nd percentile in reading ability, scoring in the 62nd percentile.

History knowledge was assessed by performance on the Panama Canal test and the Regents exam. Although some students scored well on both tests, none seemed to possess more than good general knowledge of history. Certainly none knew enough to be eliminated from our study because they "knew too much." The overall subject pool (51 students) averaged 7.36 correct out of 16 possible on the Panama Canal test. Our six subjects scored an average 9.17 and the three controls averaged 10.33. The 26 students taking the Nelson-Denny but not participating in the study averaged 23.0. Our subjects averaged 31.5 on the Nelson-Denny. The subjects taking the Regents history exam but not participating in our study averaged 56.9%. Our six subjects exceeded the necessary 65% passing grade on the Regents exam with an average of 69.7%.

The Procedure

As participants in our minicourse, students agreed to meet with the investigators eight times. Because we wanted to simulate extended course-based learning, at least in part, we required students to read most of the texts as homework assignments. They recorded the time and location of each homework reading.

During the "course" meetings, the students answered questions orally based on the assigned reading. The total time spent in these meetings ranged from 7.67 hours to 12.42 hours, with an average of 9.53 hours. The self-reported reading time totals varied from 4.75 hours to 8.83 hours, with an average of 7.25 hours.

The eight meetings were scheduled 3 or 4 days apart, and lasted between 45 and 90 minutes depending on the session and the individual. The subjects were given a text and instructed to read it before the next meeting and be prepared to answer questions about it. At each session, we asked comprehension questions and reasoning questions, which were answered orally. In addition, most meetings had an additional task, specific to that meeting.

Part 1, the Acquisition Story, required five meetings. Meeting 1 was an introductory session. Both controls and subjects participated in this meeting. Students took a 15-minute comparative history/current events test designed by the experimenters to assess knowledge and the use of that knowledge to answer reasoning questions. This included factual questions about World War II (e.g., *What was the purpose of the Nuremburg Trials?*). An associated reasoning question was *Do you think Nazis should still be put on trial for their participation in World War II?* The reasoning questions were scored separately and are not included in the assessment of subjects' prior knowledge. A sample current events question would be *What is apartheid?* The corresponding reasoning question was *Do you think it should be abolished?*

Because the controls participated only in Meetings 1 and 8, their two meetings were scheduled within 2 or 3 days of each other. The control subjects were given a summary (341 words) of the 1977 treaties as homework reading.

For Meetings 2 through 5, the students repeated the same pattern each session. First, they wrote a 24-line summary of the text following the request *Summarize the events leading up to the building of the Panama Canal.* The students were given 15 minutes for this task, which was intended to prompt their thinking about the Panama Canal story. They were then asked to "think up a level" and write the same summary using eight lines and a maximum of 5 minutes.

The Learning Questions.   The students were asked the same six general questions at each session to assess their comprehension and learning. Each question was designed to tap information from a specific component of the causal model (see Fig. 2.2). Because the students answered orally, we immediately probed an incomplete answer with more specific questions. The questions and examples of the probes are as follows:

1. Outline early U.S. interest in the building of the Canal.
    (p) What role did the U.S.-built Panama railroad play?
    (p) What happened between the United States and Spain in 1898?
2. What was the main purpose of the Hay–Pauncefote Treaty?

(p) What countries signed the treaty?

(p) What was happening in Great Britain at the time that enabled this new treaty?

3. Once a decision was made to build a canal, a commission was set up to find a place to build it. What options were seriously considered at this point?

    (p) What recommendation was initially made?

    (p) What was the Spooner Act?

4. Describe the political relationship between Colombia and Panama.

    (p) Which country was controlled by the other?

    (p) How many times did Colombia face uprisings in Panama?

5. After the decision to build a canal was made, the United States signed two treaties, the Hay–Herran Treaty and the Hay–Bunau-Varilla Treaty. What were they and what were the differences between them?

    (p) Which countries signed each treaty?

    (p) Why did Colombia reject the Hay–Herran Treaty?

6. What role did the United States play in the Panamanian Revolution?

    (p) Why did Panama want its independence?

    (p) What was the status of the Hay–Herran Treaty?

These six questions, which followed every reading assignment, were followed by three questions specific to the text that the students had just read (the current assignment). The purpose of these questions was to encourage the students to read each text carefully.

The Reasoning Questions.   After the learning questions, students answered open-ended questions, which we called reasoning questions. There were five different types of reasoning questions:

Counterfactual

1. What if the revolution had not been successful? What would have happened?

2. Would the revolution have been successful if the United States was not interested in a canal through Panama?

3. What would have happened if the Colombian congress had ratified the Hay–Herran Treaty?

4. Suppose the French had been successful in building the canal?

5. What would have happened if the other Panamanian diplomats had accompanied Bunau-Varilla to Washington?

6. What would have happened if Nicaragua had had a stronger lobbying power in Washington?

Value Judgment

1. Were the U.S. dealings with Colombia fair to Colombia?

2. Were the U.S. dealings with Panama fair to Panama?

3. Was the U.S. role in Panama's revolution justified? Why or why not?

4. Do you believe the United States should have negotiated with Bunau-Varilla or waited for the two Panamanian negotiators?

5. What is your opinion of Bunau-Varilla?

Confrontational
1. Is it just a coincidence that the United States benefitted from the Panamanian revolution? Why do you think the Colombian resistance was so ineffective?
2. Why did the United States let the French build a canal?
3. Why were the Panamanians represented by a Frenchman?
4. Why did the United States get a better deal from Panama?

Source Evaluation
1. Who does the author believe caused the revolution? What does he use to support his view?
2. What do you think was the author's opinion of the negotiations between Bunau-Varilla and Hay?
3. Do you believe the author presented enough of the facts to paint a complete picture?
4. Did the author present a neutral coverage of the events? If not, what do you think the author's attitude was?

Metaknowledge
1. What else would you like to know that was not given in the text?

Meeting 2 started with the students reading Text 1 (the Online computer text). At certain points in the text, we interrupted with text-specific questions. The students then wrote the two summaries. They then provided oral answers to the comprehension questions and to the reasoning questions. The oral procedure promoted more complete responses from the students and also allowed us to clear up any ambiguities.

Meeting 3 was scheduled to discuss Text 2, the second nonbiased text. As in Meeting 2, all six students wrote two summaries and answered comprehension and reasoning questions. Before the reasoning questions were asked, the students answered the three text-specific questions. Finally, the students were given a 30-minute reasoning/analytical section of the GRE to provide a measure of their reasoning ability. Before leaving, students received the third text as homework. This was the first biased text.

Meeting 4 covered this first text written from a specific perspective. Three students read the pro-American text by Congressman X and three read the text by Professor Y. All wrote the two summaries and answered the comprehension, text specific, and reasoning questions. There was no other task at this meeting. Again, students were given a text for homework.

Meeting 5 covered the second biased text. The three students who read Congressman X first now read Professor Y and vice versa. The procedure followed that of the earlier meetings. Students were also asked a few questions comparing the two texts (e.g., *which did you agree with more strongly?*).

Meeting 5 also included some tasks relevant for Part 2, the Return Controversy—the 1977 treaties. These tasks are described in chapter 7.

SUMMARY

This chapter has described the goals and methods of the learning study. The study departs from other text research in its attention to both learning and reasoning, its focus on extended text learning, and its use of multiple texts. Subjects were six undergraduates who had more than adequate reading skill and most of them had moderate general history knowledge consistent with precollege competence. They read assignments on their own and, in meetings with the experimenters, wrote summaries and answered a scripted set of comprehension and reasoning questions after each assignment.

Chapter 4

Learning From the Texts

In this chapter, we describe the course of learning achieved by our subjects. A distinctive aspect of the study was the repeated assessment of learning over four assignments, each involving a different text. The texts differed in ways we describe later. There was a story told by each text, however, and it is the learning of this story that we examine. To the extent that our causal–temporal analysis has identified the coherent heart of the story across the texts, we expect to see the events and their causal connections represented in what students learn and in the summaries they write.

CAUSAL MODEL TEMPLATE

A causal model template, a representation of the important events and causal structures of the Panama Canal acquisition period, was developed as a learning assessment tool (see chapter 2 for a description of the model). The causal template served to evaluate subjects' summaries and responses to comprehension questions.

As we have emphasized, when students learn history, we assume they construct the kinds of causal–temporal connections that represent story understanding (Trabasso, 1989; Trabasso & van den Broek, 1985; van den Broek, 1989b). In the case of the story of the United States' acquisition of the Panama Canal Zone, a very incomplete causal chain reflecting what a student might have learned is as follows: United States wants a quicker route between its coasts→*Motivate*→United States negotiates with Panama to build a canal through Panama→*Enable*→United States acquires rights to a strip of land in Panama→*Result*→United States builds the Panama Canal.

For our purposes, the causal template captures the basic coherent story in 39 higher level units. These 39 units included both events (e.g., *United States recognizes Panamanian independence*), and states (e.g., *Colombia owns Panama*). The event units that covered treaties contained two distinct pieces of information—a treaty existed and the main purpose of the treaty. For example, the event unit *U.S.–Colombia treaty* was represented in the template as (a) a treaty between the two countries and (b) gave the United States the right to build a canal in Panama. Because of this, our 39 units became 44 *events* in our idealized template of the story.

Motifs

The 44 events were sorted into eight thematically related groups, called *motifs*. Appendix A lists the eight motifs and the event/state units in each. The first motif, *Motives to Build*, provides a setting for the story, indicating why the United States wanted a canal: The United States wanted a quicker, safer route between the Pacific and Atlantic Oceans because the present routes were long and dangerous. In addition, various financial and military circumstances reinforced the perceived need for a canal. The second motif, *Early Attempts*, includes two initial attempts at solving the problem of a quicker route: The United States built a railroad across Panama and signed a treaty with Colombia to allow protection and neutrality of any present or future passage across Panama.

The next four motifs can be considered obstacles to a U.S.-controlled canal. The *British Involvement* motif covers the negotiations and resulting treaties between the United States and Great Britain that gave the United States the right to build a canal without British interference. The *French Attempt* motif is France's failed attempt to build a canal in Panama and the eventual sale to the United States of its Panamanian property. The *Find a Place to Build* motif captures the U.S. search for a canal site, including the creation of a committee charged with this task, Congressional debate about alternative sites, and passage of a law enabling the President to begin negotiations with Colombia for a canal through its territory of Panama. The final obstacle motif, *Need Permission*, describes the U.S. attempts to win the rights to build a canal in a foreign country. It includes the events surrounding the U.S. negotiations with Colombia, the fact that Colombia owned Panama, and the eventual rejection of the U.S.–Colombia treaty by the Colombian congress.

The final two motifs involve the surmounting of these obstacles. The *Panamanian Revolution* motif includes details of the revolution and its possible roots in Panamanian nationalism and Panamanian fear of losing a canal. These factors combined to spark a successful Panamanian rebellion and the controversial U.S. involvement in this revolution. The eighth motif, *U.S.–Panama Treaty*, describes the negotiations between the United States and the newly formed Panamanian government that resulted in a treaty giving the United States permission to build, operate, and maintain sole control over the Canal. These motifs, which capture the story at a global level, were used to indicate which parts of the story students learned.

Types of Events

Some events are more central to the story than others. To capture this distinction and to examine differential learning of more important over less important incidents, we classified the 44 events into two categories: Information that was central to the story (*core events*) and information less central to the Panama Canal story (*noncore events*). The core events (in boldface in Appendix A) are necessary to tell the basic story; the noncore events (those not in boldface in Appendix A) add information that elaborates the core events. For example, *U.S.–Colombia treaty* is a core event because it is essential to the basic story; the story cannot be told coherently without it. However, *Colombia busy with internal problems* is a noncore event, because the story can be told without it.

Actions and states consistently covered by multiple texts recounting the Panama Canal story were designated as events by the authors. In addition, two of the authors independently sorted the events into approximately equal numbers of core and noncore units. This resulted in 23 core events and 21 noncore events for the final three texts. Because the initial text did not cover the Panamanian revolution, it had 22 core events and 17 noncore events.

Our expectation was that subjects would learn the core events more quickly than the noncore events because the core events were on the causal chain. For the same reason, they should include more core events in their summaries.

Information Within an Event.   Each event (e.g., *Panama revolts*) included the key event (e.g., a revolution occurred in Panama) and its associated details (e.g., when the revolution occurred). These details are referred to as *supporting facts*. The shortest text contained 39 events and 498 supporting facts.

Responses and summaries were scored using events and supporting facts. Students earned one point for each event and supporting fact presented. For example, *A revolution occurred in Panama on November 3, 1903, and was instigated by wealthy Panamanians*, would be scored as one event (*Panama revolts*) and three supporting facts (*Nov. 3*; *1903*; *by wealthy Panamanians*).

We expected that students initially would learn events, with only a small number of supporting facts to aid their general understanding of the story. This is because the coherence of the story derives from the causal–temporal connections of the events, and learning the texts is driven by these coherence relations. Over time, we predicted that students would learn more supporting facts. However, this pattern would not be expected in the short summaries because the space constraints limited students to providing only the basics of the story.

Before reporting the learning results from Part 1, we describe, in the next section, the critical features of the texts read by the students. These features include the motifs emphasized by each author, the ratio of core to noncore information, the ratio of information about all of the treaties to information about other aspects of the story, and the coverage of the Panamanian revolution. These attributes determine how the Panama Canal Acquisition Story is told and interpreted.

THE TEXTS

The Online text was given to each subject first. This text contained 605 propositions, and focused on three motifs: the *U.S.–Panama Treaty* (20%), *British Involvement* (22%), and *Find a Place to Build* (18%). By design, it gave minimal information about the *Panamanian Revolution* (4%). It was designed to be a summary of the story that at least briefly mentioned all the critical occurrences. It contained only slightly more core (58%) than noncore (42%) information, and slightly more nontreaty information (58%) than information about any of the treaties (42%). The Online text was presented to subjects on a computer screen, one line at a time.

The CSIS text was the second text read. It was slightly longer than the Online text (1,140 propositions), and its main focus was on the *U.S.–Panama Treaty (35%)* and its consequences. It also discussed the *British Involvement* (13%) and the *French Attempt* (15%). Significantly more of the text centered on core information (70%) as compared to noncore (30%), and there was more nontreaty information (66%) than information about the various treaties. As one subject, George, correctly noticed in comparing the CSIS text to the Online text, "Well, a lot of the excerpts on the computer were from the [CSIS] text. Of course, [CSIS] was a lot longer than the computer. I think what you did was type in the important stuff and leave out the small details."

In addition to elaborating events in the Online text, all three of the other texts contained material not in the Online text. The most significant difference was the controversial Panamanian revolution. The CSIS text also mentioned other, less important early treaties and a much later treaty that gave compensation to Colombia after the canal was built. As Dave said, "The [Online text] was just general background. [CSIS] went into more detail. I also think this was written on a slightly higher level. It wasn't just declarative fact. I felt they really wanted you to think things through."

Congressman X's text was longer (2,198 propositions) than either of the first two texts. The main focus was on *Need Permission* (19%), the *Panamanian Revolution* (21%), and *U.S.–Panama Treaty* (20%). As in the CSIS text, X mentioned significantly more core (71%) than noncore (29%) information. The text also had approximately equal amounts of nontreaty information (58%) and treaty information (42%). In addition to information about the Panamanian revolution and other elaborations of information mentioned in the first text, Congressman X mentioned other U.S. administrations' policies on a canal, the compensation to Colombia after the canal was built, and details about an earlier failed attempt by U.S. businessmen to build a canal in Nicaragua. As Mitch said after reading X, "It focuses more on the period right before the canal building and the revolution. It doesn't go into any detail about early on. Just basically concerned with the U.S. Pretty opinionated. He put his ideas in there." The opinion of the author indeed came through to all subjects. As Dave put it, "[X] seems to believe U.S. had virtually no involvement whatsoever in the revolution in Panama. He feels it was the interest of a few Panamanian businessmen and also American interest. Less formally written. He used more colloquialisms like ‹the fat was in the fire›."

The final text, written by Professor Y, was the longest (3,365 propositions). The main focus of Y's text was the *Panamanian Revolution* (39%), with secondary focus on *Motives to Build* (11%), and *British Involvement* (13%). Like the Online text, Y's text did not include more core (49%) than noncore information. But there was considerably more nontreaty information (78%) than treaty information (22%). The treaties played a smaller role in Y's exposition about the U.S. acquisition of a canal in Panama. He developed the personalities, more intricately describing the individuals in the Panama story. As Dave put it, "[Professor Y] went into more detail about people involved rather than just treaties and results. Went further back in history." Or, as Eileen noted, "This text has more names of people involved in the treaties, in the whole project and also the text emphasizes understanding the crisis of the '70s so I think it's written to help people understand the crisis in the '70s." In addition to elaborating on information mentioned in the first text, Y prefaced his text with a long section outlining the early history of Panama, dating back to 1510 and the Spaniards. This included how Panama was "discovered," settled, and exploited for gold, the decline of the Spanish Empire in Panama, and the early influences and relations between Panama and the U.S. (e.g., Monroe Doctrine). As George pointed out, "[Professor Y] also went into detail before American interest in a canal. Gave a bit of a picture of how Panama was, why the Panamanians felt nationalistic. One of the reasons was because they were such a powerful province when the Spanish Empire was still at its height. Panama City was moving millions of dollars of gold and silver every day. That painted more of a picture for me as to what was going on there before American interest. Panama was on the Earth 300 years as far as white man inhabiting the area before America had an interest, really."

LEARNING RESULTS

Our primary assessment of learning is the total amount learned, defined as any correct information produced by the student in the summary, in answer to the comprehension questions, or in response to the reasoning probes. We were interested in what the student learned about the story, expressed in any way during our interviews. For this assessment, we compared what the subject reported with the causal template. We report the results either for each text and student or just a group average. In the cases where we comment on only an individual student or text, it is because that score was outside one standard deviation from the mean.

Initial Reading

Students learned the story of the Acquisition of the Panama Canal fairly well from the first reading. After reading the Online text, the average subject's total learning was 41% (i.e., on average, 41% of the events and supporting facts given in the Online text were mentioned by a subject on at least one opportunity—in a summary, or in response to a comprehension or reasoning question). During this initial reading, students focused on learning the events: They learned 73% of the core events and 64% of the noncore events. In addition, they learned nearly half (48%) of the causal–temporal connections between the events. Thus, subjects were quick to learn the central points of the Acquisition Story.

Compared with the high rate of event learning, subjects learned a smaller percentage of the total supporting facts, 15% of core and 12% of noncore supporting facts. This percentage comparison may be misleading because of the substantially greater number of supporting facts (297 core and 201 noncore) than events (22 core and 17 noncore) found in the first text. It seems correct to conclude, nevertheless, that after one reading of a short history text, students learned most of the events and connections between those events and somewhat less of the supporting information.

Subsequent Readings

Multiple readings of the Panama Canal story, as told by different authors, resulted in quick mastery of the events and a more gradual learning of the supporting facts. From the first reading subjects learned the core events (16 of the 22 core events). By the second reading, they increased the number of core events learned to 19 and by the third reading they had learned practically all of the core events (21 of 23).[7] Although they learned core events quite well from the start, subsequent readings helped to solidify this learning. Noncore events, on the other hand, were not learned better over subsequent readings. Students learned a fair number of these initially (11 of 17 noncore events), but the number of noncore events remained constant over subsequent readings: 12, 11, and 13 (of 21 possible) after each reading. Thus, learning of noncore events remained stable at approximately 60% over the course of the study.

By contrast, the students continued to learn supporting facts across all four assignments, as illustrated in Fig. 4.1.[8] After one reading they learned 46 supporting

---

[7]Recall that the first text had one less core event than the other three texts and four fewer noncore events.

[8]Because the total number of supporting facts is so large, we report numbers of facts learned rather than percentages.

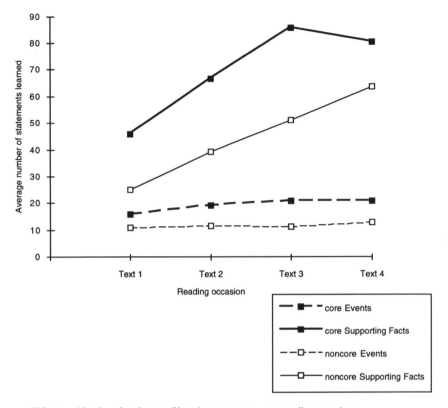

FIG. 4.1.   Number of each type of learning statement across reading occasions.

facts (of 297 possible) about the core events and 25 supporting facts (of 201 possible) about the noncore events. The students learned more of both types of supporting facts over additional readings. In fact, after the second text, the number of supporting facts learned increased from 46 to 67 for core events and 25 to 39 for noncore events. As Fig. 4.1 indicates, learning of facts increased linearly for both core (about 20 supporting facts through Text 3) and noncore (about 13 supporting facts per assignment). Although the final assignment did not increase the learning of core supporting facts, the increase in noncore supporting facts continued (51 to 64). Overall, the students very quickly learned the most important events and over multiple readings they more gradually elaborated on this picture. Indeed, after four readings they were still learning noncore supporting facts.

What types of detail did students learn? Figure 4.2 shows the number of core and noncore supporting facts across assignments. The solid lines show the supporting facts that were available in the first text, labeled "initial" information. The dotted lines, labeled "noninitial" information, show information not available in Text 1 that was contained in Texts 2 through 4. As Fig. 4.2 shows, subjects learned new supporting facts from Assignments 2 through 4, rather than merely

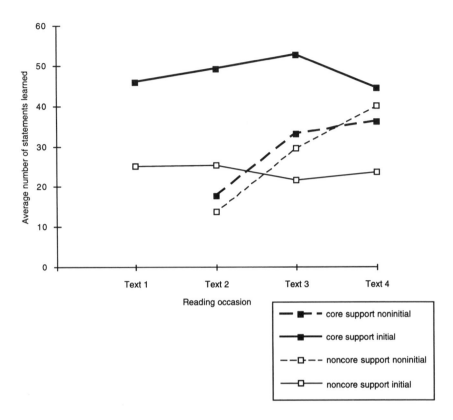

FIG. 4.2. Number of core and noncore supporting information statements across reading occasions. "Initial" refers to information that was available in the first text, and "noninitial" refers to information that was only mentioned in subsequent texts. For this reason, the two noninitial lines only begin at Text 2.

increasing their learning of facts that were initially available. Thus, students appear to have learned the basic story from the first text, which focuses on the more important core events and their supporting facts. Then, over additional readings, they continued to report the same basic story, but added details not previously encountered.

This "novel detail" effect occurred despite the fact that most of the initial supporting facts (from the first text) were also contained in the subsequent texts. Students appear to have focused on new details that supported critical story components (e.g., information on relations between Panama and Colombia and the Panamanian revolution). There are at least two classes of explanation for this novel detail effect. New information might be learned because it is novel, hence attention attracting, or it might be learned because learners see it as important for the story. Although we cannot distinguish these two alternatives from the present study, it is interesting to consider the possibility that learning of details is selective. Students may notice and recall details that give life to the broad story components.

Motifs

Overall, the students learned information from each of the eight motifs, but their learning was strongest for three motifs: the *U.S.–Panama Treaty*, *Motives to Build*, and *Panamanian Revolution*; *Early Attempts* and *Finding a Place to Build* were the least learned motifs. However, this motif learning pattern differed slightly following each text. Which motif was covered the most thoroughly (or the most briefly) depended on the text.

After the first reading, the students' total learning was concentrated in the U.S. *Motives to Build* and *U.S.–Panama Treaty* motifs. They also learned about the *British Involvement* and *Find a Place to Build* motifs. The first text focused on three of these motifs, excluding only the *Motives to Build*. We believe that students learned a lot about *Motives to Build* because this motif is critical in the causal structure of the story. Even though the text did not focus on the U.S. reasons to build a canal, subjects learned these reasons, we think, because they were helpful in establishing causal coherence for the story as a whole. Thus, after an initial reading, the students had learned why the United States believed a canal was necessary, the two major obstacles to the U.S. goal, and the eventual surmounting of these obstacles.

After the second reading, subjects continued to refer to three motifs—*Motives to Build*, *British Involvement*, and *U.S.–Panama Treaty*—and they added information about the *Panamanian Revolution*. Although elaborative details about the Panamanian revolution were not available in the first text, students quickly learned this information at the first opportunity. Interestingly, the second text did not focus on the Panamanian revolution. Instead, it covered the treaty between the United States and Panama, and the involvement of both Britain and France. It is likely that the revolution was correctly seen as important in the causal–temporal sequence, and was learned despite its relatively light treatment by the text.[9] Finally, after this second text, subjects learned all they were going to in the *Motives to Build* motif. Typically they learned just the core events. Their learning of this motif can be characterized as just enough to lay a foundation for the story.

After the third assignment, subjects learned mainly the *Panamanian Revolution* motif, but they also continued to refer to *Motives to Build* and one of the obstacles (*British Involvement*).

---

[9]Of course there is an alternative explanation for learning information that is not an object of text focus. Students can selectively attend to new information at the expense of information that was already familiar from the preceding text. We can only offer speculations on these matters. Our study did not have the identification of learning mechanisms as its goal.

By the final reading, students still mentioned the *Panamanian Revolution* motif, but the issues in the *Find a Place to Build* motif became important again. Most subjects were still learning more information about the *Panamanian Revolution* by the final reading and learning was most accelerated for this motif.

Learning over successive assignments is partly a matter of specific texts, as well as learning the story told by all texts. In general, we cannot attribute learning to specific texts, because the sequence of texts was fixed, except for the last two. (Recall that one half of the students read Congressman X and then Professor Y, whereas the other half read these in the reverse order.) After Congressman X's text, students reported information about the *Panamanian Revolution* motif and also referred to the *Motives to Build* and the *British Involvement* motifs. They continued to tell the early part of the story—why the United States wanted a canal and the obstacle posed by the British—despite the fact that the text did not focus on these parts of the story. Instead X's text focused on the *Need Permission* (the need for the U.S. to obtain permission to build a canal), the *Panamanian Revolution*, and the *U.S.–Panama Treaty* motifs. From reading this text, subjects learned the most about the *Need Permission* motif. Congressman X went into great detail about the Hay–Herran Treaty between the United States and Colombia, and Colombia's eventual rejection of the treaty.

After reading the text by Professor Y, the students reported much information about the *Panamanian Revolution* motif because Professor Y's story is centered more on the Panamanian and Colombian relations that led to an eventual revolution by the Panamanians. Information from the other seven motifs was reported much less frequently. Also noteworthy is that the *Early Attempts* motif was learned mainly following Professor Y's text, whether students read it third or fourth. This text connected the earlier attempts at an isthmian crossing to the revolution in Panama, making the *Early Attempts* motif much more salient.

Students' Summaries

The results reported to this point include data aggregated from students' responses to comprehension and reasoning questions and their summaries. In this section, we discuss just the information given in the short summaries. The short summaries reflected the students' perception of the most important parts of the story. Recall that these short 8-line summaries followed an initial 24-line summary. Subjects thus were first able to organize what they had learned in one writing task, then required to prune it by $\frac{2}{3}$. It is this second, shorter summary that we take to reflect a high level of abstraction across the causal–temporal model.

The students produced adequate short summaries even from the first assignment. This first reading (Online text) produced the shortest summaries (mean length of 73 words). Summary length following the second assignment increased and remained relatively constant thereafter: 90, 92, and 89 words across the final three assignments. (Appendix D contains the short summaries written by the six students following Congressman X's text.)

Summarization provided an opportunity for abstraction, which, in its extreme form, can eliminate reference to specific events. Such "hyperabstractions" were sometimes part of our students' summaries. For example, one subject (Dave) wrote that "The canal was born out of a long session of international political bargaining," an abstraction that collapses a complex chain of events without referring to any. Some hyperabstractions may reflect a lack of specific knowledge, whereas others may reflect a sophisticated summarizing strategy. In either case, the number of such hyperabstractions was highest following the first text; there were 10 instances across the six subjects. The number of hyperabstractions remained relatively constant (7, 6, and 6) across subsequent assignments. This reduction in hyperabstractions is consistent with subjects' general learning. The decrease in hyperabstractions between Text 1 and Text 2 corresponded to a large increase in the number of supporting facts learned by subjects.

These hyperabstracted summary statements were most common for references to U.S. interests in a canal (the *Motives to Build* motif). Of the 29 hyperabstractions, 14 referred to these interests. For example, Jen wrote that "the U.S. began to seriously discuss the need for a canal" and Robbie wrote that "U.S. was always interested in canal across isthmus." Both of these statements convey the U.S. interest without referring to a specific event. Another common hyperabstracted reference, given 12 times, concerned the diplomatic activity the United States had with other countries. For example, Dave wrote that "Considerable legal and political maneuvering was required to initiate such a situation." Mitch wrote "along with the treaties (some ratified, some not) the U.S. made with various countries around the world."

Proportion of Learned Information Summarized. It is the critical characteristic of a summary, the requirement to be selective in including information, that makes it interesting as an assessment of students' learning of the core of the story. To get a measure of this selectivity, we calculated the proportion of each type of information (core events, core supporting facts, noncore events, and noncore supporting facts) included in the summaries. The proportion was calculated as follows: After each text, we determined a baseline score for each student. The baseline score was the total amount learned within each category. The *proportion summarized* was the ratio of the total earned in the summary to the subject's baseline score. For example, after the first reading Eileen produced 5 core events in her 8-line summary while reporting 16 core events across all opportunities. (This 16 is her total core event learning for that session—summary, comprehension and reasoning answers.) Thus, Eileen's proportion of core events summarized was 31% ($\frac{5}{16}$). That Eileen was able to get 31% of her total knowledge of core events into an approximately 73-word summary suggests that she chose only information that was important to the Panama Canal story.

Figure 4.3 shows that Eileen's proportion summarized was typical of our subjects. After the first text, the proportion summarized for core events (36%) was higher than the proportion summarized for noncore events (19%), core supporting facts (13%), and noncore supporting facts (7%). We consider this an indication that the students were able to select the information that was central to the story. (It is also a validation of our causal analysis' distinction among core events, noncore events, and supporting facts.) Subjects' summaries included only the details needed to clarify the core events. Even after only one text our subjects wrote good, concise summaries.

More striking, however, is the relative stability of the summaries across the four sessions. Students immediately wrote core event summaries and continued to do so with little variation in the kinds of information included. Moreover, they continued to produce concise Event-based summaries despite learning more supporting facts. Even summaries written after the subjects had accumulated impressive amounts of detail contained mainly core events with negligible noncore events and supporting facts. Thus, students quickly learned the basic story and their summarized understanding of the story was not diminished by learning more information.

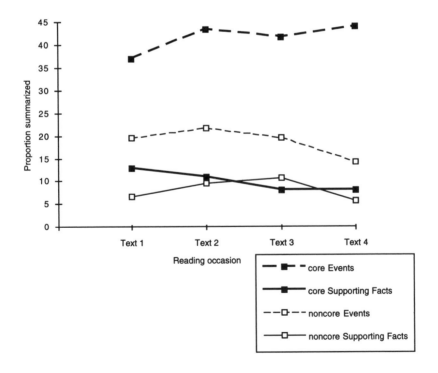

FIG. 4.3.   Proportion of learned events and supporting facts summarized across reading occasions.

CONCLUSIONS

The course of learning can be characterized as rapid or gradual and as complete or incomplete, depending on the level of the story. For the core event structure—the story events and their causal links—learning was both rapid and complete. Students learned most of what there was to learn about the core events from the first text, and about all there was to learn by the second text. Early learning appears to be event-driven. Subjects acquire the basic story, filling in the details at a slower pace.

This state of affairs is, we suggest, a normal consequence of comprehension goals that are served by story coherence. The event structure is the causal–temporal glue of the story that provides this coherence. Students' attempt to understand the story results in an event-based representation made coherent by the links among the events. This interpretation of event learning is consistent with the assumptions of Trabasso and van den Broek (1985; Trabasso, Secco, & van den Broek, 1984; van den Broek, 1990) concerning the importance of causal representations in understanding. What subjects learned was a causal–temporal chain of events that made the Panama Canal Acquisition Story coherent. They learned this readily from a single reading of the story in a relatively impoverished text. We emphasize again, however, that the comprehension mechanism by which readers achieve causal coherence is a complex matter, beyond what we address here. Well-written texts, as these were, go a long way to providing the kind of causal coherence that characterizes students' learning (Kintsch, 1992), even as readers themselves engage in strategies to promote coherent representations.

The learning of supporting details appears to take a slower and perhaps less complete course. Facts that supported core events were acquired from the beginning, but increased with each assignment until the last. And students appeared to have still been learning about noncore supporting facts at the end.

There are several important points to emphasize about these observations. First, we emphasize that the course of learning cannot be described as "events-first, facts-second." Every student learned important supporting facts from the very first opportunity. Details are clearly important, neither ignored nor delayed in their learning. Causal–temporal structures may not be so much the heart of a story as its skeleton or frame. The heart of the story is the events and their most important details together.

Why then the slower learning of details? Two reasons, we think. First we must keep in mind that there were more supporting facts to learn, so there remains room for improvement even after the events have been mastered. Second, learning details entails learning events: Consider the student who learns that Secretary of State Hay was the United States' author of the Hay–Herran Treaty and that this treaty provided for specific concessions to Colombia in exchange for rights to Colombian land in Panama on which to build a canal. In the course of demonstrating such knowledge of supporting facts, such a student also demonstrates knowledge of two key events in the story, *U.S. Negotiates with Colombia* and *U.S.–Colombia Treaty*. Thus, there is not a disassociation between event learning and fact learning. The two are interdependent. Consistent with this interdependence is that subjects learned more about details that supported core events than details that supported noncore events.

Another important aspect of detail learning is that texts play a role. Our texts did not necessarily provide the same set of details, although there was substantial overlap. Part of the story of detail learning is that students learned new facts from each text they encountered. Their learning was rich, an initial representation of events and supporting facts that was augmented by new event-relevant details in subsequent learning.

Summarization provides some contrast with this picture of learning. Summaries were remarkably stable. At the same time that students were acquiring an impressive amount of supporting facts that connect the fabric of the story, they showed an ability to focus on the core events when they wrote summaries. Students' familiarity with the summary form presumably played a role here. Summaries are supposed to relate the main thread of the story, and that is what our subjects' summaries did. Their focus on core events confirms our assumption that the causal event structure of a history story is psychologically salient, while also supporting our specific analysis that distinguishes among core events, noncore events, and supporting facts associated with those events.

Chapter 5

Reasoning About the Canal

In addition to the general course of students' learning, we were interested in how students reasoned about problems, both problems intrinsic to the Acquisition Story and problems of text interpretation. In this chapter, we report how subjects responded to our probes of their reasoning over the first part of the history of the Panama Canal. We were especially interested in how students applied what they had learned. Our examination of student reasoning can be considered a study of informal reasoning in a subject matter domain. A surge of research interest in informal reasoning has been targeted at argumentation (Kuhn, 1991; Stein and Miller, 1991; Voss, Fincher-Kiefer, Wiley, & Silfies, 1993), subject matter learning, and thinking skills (Baron & Sternberg, 1987; Perkins, 1985; see Voss, Perkins, & Segal, 1991, for a collection of papers on subject matter reasoning and critical thinking skills.) Our point of departure is our more detailed observation of student learning and the potential for linking reasoning and reasoning change to learning. We aim, among other things, to demonstrate effects of learning on the structural properties of reasoning, by linking student reasoning to components of the causal–temporal model. We aim also to examine the influence of texts on the stability of reasoning.

Our procedure was to ask open-ended reasoning questions after students had read each text and completed the summary and comprehension tasks. We presented students with a variety of problems and asked them to engage in informal reasoning about the Acquisition Story they had learned to that point. We developed five broad types of informal reasoning questions:

Counterfactual questions asked the students to imagine a change in some event in the story and to speculate on the consequences of this counterfactual assumption. Such questions require the students to consider and manipulate aspects of their causal model. *Value judgment* questions asked students to consider a situation in terms of some implicit values (e.g., whether some action was "fair"). *Confrontational* questions forced students to address a puzzling aspect of the story which was not explicitly explained in any of the texts. *Source evaluation* questions asked students to comment on the perspectives and bias of the author, part of an important heuristic in historians' attempts to evaluate contradictory claims

(Wineburg, 1991). Finally, *Metaknowledge* questions asked students about any gaps they might perceive in their knowledge, given what they had learned from the texts.

In our instructions to the students, we emphasized that we would ask questions without right or wrong answers and that, instead, our interest was in what they thought about certain aspects of the Panama Canal story. Because our reasoning questions varied in form, the range of possible responses from the students did also. Students answered all reasoning questions orally so we could further probe interesting or incomplete answers.

COUNTERFACTUALS

Counterfactual questions were intended to force the student to use his or her causal model to speculate about the consequences of (counterfactually) altered events. We examined the structure and content of the students' reasoning, and the extent to which it reflected the use of knowledge. The counterfactual questions are repeated here from chapter 3:

1. What if the revolution had not been successful? What would have happened?
2. Would the revolution have been successful if the United States were not interested in a canal through Panama?
3. What would have happened if the Colombian congress had ratified the Hay–Herran Treaty?
4. Suppose the French had been successful in building the canal?
5. What would have happened if the other Panamanian diplomats had accompanied Bunau-Varilla to Washington?
6. What would have happened if the Spooner Act was not passed by the U.S. Senate?
7. What would have happened if Nicaragua had had a stronger lobbying power in Washington?

To illustrate how a student might use a causal model in such a task, consider the first counterfactual question: *What if the revolution had not been successful? What would have happened?* In an attempt to speculate on the influence of a failed revolution in Panama, one must recall what other events were connected to this questioned event. A causal–temporal model, as described in chapters 2 and 4, would prove useful in tracing connected events. By locating the questioned event in the causal–temporal model, a student could determine its temporal and causal connections to other events. Temporal relations, having weaker causal status, should not have the same impact on subsequent events as motivating or enabling relations (e.g., the revolution enabled a U.S.-built canal in Panama). A student can use a model of the events to propose alternative event scenarios (*claims*) with the options of hedges (*qualifiers*). Further, the student may consider only one alternative outcome or propose several possible outcomes that would follow from assuming an altered event. These alternatives could be either a well elaborated chain of events or merely a list. Finally, a claim may be accompanied by *reasons* for accepting it.

To show the range of student responses, Table 5.1 contains all responses following Congressman X to the question *What if the revolution had not been successful?* Consider Eileen's reply: First, there is a claim that the United States may have had a more difficult time negotiating with Colombia. Eileen supported this claim with a reason ("because we were involved a little bit in the revolution") and further supported this reason with a second reason ("refusing to transport Colombians across railroad we controlled"). This line of counterfactual reasoning led her to claim that, without the revolution, the United States would not have a canal. She included multiple qualifiers to modify both her claims ("Maybe, I don't

TABLE 5.1
Each Student's Answer After Reading Congressman X's Text to the Reasoning
Question, "What if the revolution had not been successful? What would have
happened?"

Eileen: We would have had much tougher time with working out the treaty with Colombia because we were involved a little bit in the revolution—in refusing to transport Colombians across railroad we controlled. Maybe we wouldn't have a canal. I don't know.

Dave: The treaty with Colombia ratified and the canal would've gone through Panama anyway. Other areas—Costa Rica or Nicaragua—would've been looked at and possibly a treaty signed with them and a canal built through their territory.

Jen: I think the U.S. still [would] be building a canal through Colombia—with Colombia through Panama. Even though the treaty would've been changed and Colombia would have to agree to it. If the revolution failed, then Colombia would negotiate a new treaty with U.S.

Mitch: Since the Hay–Herran Treaty was rejected by Colombia, I guess they would have to either give up on Panama and since the Spooner Act they would have to negotiate with Nicaragua. Or they could renegotiate another contract with Colombia.

Robbie: I think that the U.S. would've dealt with Colombia. I think there'd still be a canal across but I think it would have gone more towards the Hay–Herran Treaty than Hay–Bunau-Varilla Treaty. I think Colombia might even got [sic] a little more because they weren't going to sign it. We would've had to give them more money or less land, maybe a little more power to them.

George: Chances are more likely that a canal would have been built in Nicaragua instead. I don't think the U.S. was going to be dealing with Colombia any more. Especially after ... even if the U.S. tried to intervene and lost, it would be like Vietnam again back then. [An interviewer asked "What do you mean by that?"] Well, the U.S. decided to try and intervene in Vietnam and after 10 years got their asses kicked and the Vietnamese have no interest in dealing with the Americans considering they tried to help a rebel faction in their country. I think the same thing would have happened in Colombia. The Colombians wouldn't have wanted to deal with the Americans so I think the Americans probably would've had no chance to build the canal in Panama and probably would've built the canal in Nicaragua.

know") and her reasons ("a little bit"). As Eileen's response indicates, students were quite willing to play this game of speculation.

In the next section, we first describe the structure of the students' responses to the counterfactual questions in terms of their ability to construct alternative possibilities (claims), how often they provided support for these assertions (reasons), and finally, whether their assertions were hedged (qualifiers). This analysis of the Counterfactual questions is a modification of Toulmin's (1958) system for representing arguments. We then examine more closely the *alternative event chains*, focusing on the number of different options expressed and the length of these chains. We address whether the students argue that the altered event would influence the course of history or that things would have proceeded in much the same way with or without that event. Finally, we examine the student's use of knowledge in counterfactual reasoning.

Structure of Counterfactuals

Claims. Given a counterfactual assumption, students were able to make claims about altered event outcomes. On average, students made 2.5 claims per response. (Eileen made the fewest claims, averaging 1.6 per response; the remaining students averaged about 2.8 claims per response.) The number of claims was influenced by both text and reading occasion. The mean number of claims increased from the first assignment (2.2) to the last (2.8), reflecting the role of increased learning on the ability to manipulate the causal model. On average, the students made the most claims after Congressman X's text (2.8 claims).

Examples of claims for the "failed-revolution" counterfactual are given in Table 5.1. Eileen began by claiming that negotiations with Colombia would be more difficult and concluded by asserting that the United States would not have a canal. Dave argued that the United States would have had a canal but questioned its location, suggesting Colombia, Costa Rica, or Nicaragua. Like Dave, Jen also claimed that the United States would have a canal and that a treaty with Colombia was still an option. She believed the treaty would be different, but that "Colombia would negotiate a new treaty with (the) U.S." Mitch made three claims: "give up on Panama," "negotiate with Nicaragua," and "renegotiate another contract with Colombia." Robbie made one main claim, "the U.S. would've dealt with Colombia," which he fleshed out in detail. Our final student, George, asserted that the United States would still have a canal, but "probably would've built the canal in Nicaragua."

Reasons. Students provided reasons to support 29% of their claims, or, on average, 1.1 reasons per response. (Students gave multiple claims for most responses, tracing a path of possible outcomes before they reached a final decision.) Robbie was the least likely to provide reasons, averaging only one reason for every two questions. George supported his answers most often, averaging about two reasons for every one question (1.9 reasons per answer). The number of reasons increased after the second reading and remained relatively stable thereafter. The students mentioned an average of only .64 reasons per response after the first reading and 1.2, 1.4, and 1.3 after the final three readings, respectively. There was no influence of the text on the number of reasons provided.

Table 5.1 depicts variability in students' tendencies to provide reasons. In contrast to Eileen, who (as already noted) provided two reasons in connection with her initial claim, both Dave and Jen provided only claims, with no reasons to support them. Mitch supported his claims with reasons and, as was typical of many of his other answers, he focused on legal issues: "Since the Hay–Herran Treaty was rejected by Colombia" and "since the Spooner Act, they would have to." Robbie gave a very good reason for claiming that the United States would have had to concede more to Colombia in any revised treaty, noting that the Colombians had rejected the original treaty. We see also the use of historical analogy, Vietnamese–U.S. relations following the war in Vietnam, as part of George's reasoning on this counterfactual.

Qualifiers. Students often revealed the tentativeness of their speculations by including hedges, or qualifiers. On average, students provided one qualifier per answer, ranging from Robbie and Jen, who provided only .6 and .7 qualifiers per response, respectively, to Eileen, who provided 1.2 qualifiers per response. As with the number of claims, there was an influence of text and an increase in hedges with reading occasion. Students' responses after the first assignment contained an average of .8 qualifiers, increasing to a mean of 1.1 following the third text. The fewest qualifiers (.8) occurred after the Online text and the most qualifiers (1.1) occurred after Professor Y's text.

Students used qualifiers for many of their claims and for some of their reasons. We illustrate this again with the first counterfactual (see Table 5.1.) Typical of Eileen's style, she included a couple of qualifiers: one qualifying a reason ("a little bit") and one qualifying a claim ("Maybe—I don't know"). Other students also included qualifiers in their answers. For example, Dave said "…possibly a treaty signed…", Jen commented that "Colombia would have to agree to it," and George believed "Chances are more likely that…".

Challenging the Hypothetical

An alternative approach to a counterfactual is to challenge the plausibility of the counterfactual assumption, and occasionally students did so. For example, two students appeared to reject the counterfactual premise of the first question concerning the revolution. Mitch said after reading Professor Y, "I don't think it had a chance of not working with U.S. backing. It couldn't fail." George was the other student to challenge this premise. After reading the CSIS text, he asserted that "Since the U.S. was in there, Colombia didn't have a chance," and after reading

Professor Y he stated quite plainly that "America didn't plan it so it wouldn't be successful, and obviously it was successful."

Every student challenged a counterfactual at least once, but most challenged on only one occasion. Five challenges came after Professor Y's text and two came after each of the other texts. Robbie and George were the only two students rejecting the plausibility of our counterfactuals more than once. Robbie refused to accept the premise of the reasoning question *Would the revolution have been successful if the United States was not interested in a canal through Panama?* On three different occasions he claimed that the revolution had nothing to do with the canal. After the second reading Robbie said "I don't think the Panamanians who were revolting could care less about the canal. They were concerned about how their life was going, how their country was going. They were revolutionizing [*sic*] against that, not for the canal."

Summary.   The typical response for a counterfactual was an elaboration of an altered event chain. Students usually developed alternative event sequences, but occasionally challenged the counterfactual premise.[10] Students were able to consider multiple options and most backed their claims about such options with at least one reason in every response. Over assignments, students acquired increasing ability to produce enriched scenarios. By the second assignment, they provided more claims, reasons, and qualifiers, and continued to increase the number of claims and qualifiers (although not reasons) after the final two assignments. After Congressman X, the students produced more claims, whereas after Professor Y, they provided more reasons and qualifiers. Thus the more complex and detailed text, that of Professor Y, led to both more hedging and more support for the students' alternative event sequences. The more urgent and more one-sided text, that of Congressman X, led to a greater number of claims by the students.

---

[10]Only rarely did a student respond to a counterfactual situation with an unscorable response or an error. One kind of error was a response *inconsistent* with other known events. In the question about the Panamanian revolution, such an error was made by some students who claimed the United States would negotiate and sign the Hay-Herran Treaty with Colombia. The error is the failure to note that two months previously Colombia had rejected that treaty and that the rejection was a factor in the revolution. Thus, it is not plausible that the United States and Colombia would merely sign this treaty. (Of course, if students acknowledged the obstacle of the rejected treaty by saying that it would make negotiations more difficult, then claiming negotiations with Colombia would follow was not considered an error.) Although these inconsistency errors were uncommon, they occurred in all the counterfactual questions at least once. A second, even more rare form of error, was a response that violated the counterfactual premise. Eileen's first response to the counterfactual *Would the revolution have been successful if the United States were not interested in a canal through Panama?* included the claim that "the U.S. would've been interested in helping Panama win because [the] treaties were much better for us." The claim that the United States would want better treaties violates the premise of the question. That such errors were very rare indicates that the students were able to represent the counterfactual situation.

Content of Counterfactuals

Counterfactual reasoning can reveal some glimpses of students' implicit "theories" of the causal connections in the story. A story of history consists of multiple, intertwined events. Altering one event, in some situations, may be seen as altering the course of subsequent events significantly; in other situations, event alteration could be seen as more local in consequence, not affecting other events as substantially. Thus, the counterfactuals allowed us to examine the extent to which our students saw the alterations we provided as "changing the course of history." A student might suggest that a certain outcome would have occurred even with the removal of some significant event; alternatively, the student might suggest the outcome would have been altered. We refer to the first as *outcome-preserved* responses and the second as *outcome-altered* responses.

Across the different hypothetical situations, students gave more outcome-altered responses than outcome-preserved responses. Thus, students generally thought things would change more often than they believed things would remain the same. The degree of alteration expected by the students was highly variable, however. Some students located an effect only on the most contiguous events on the causal model; other students noted more far-reaching effects by tracing either forward or backward on the causal model.

A simple strategy for a counterfactual would be to determine which connection in the causal model should be severed, and then consider the immediately preceding or immediately following events. To illustrate again with the first counterfactual on the revolution, the student would consult a representation of the events similar to that in Fig. 5.1 and sever the connection between *30. Panama revolts* and *33. Panama gains independence*. A response would then consider that the following events (e.g., 33 and 34) would not have occurred. In a more complex strategy, the student would examine the motivating and enabling relations associated with the altered event, and then make predictions based on these relationships.

The Complexity of Outcome-Altered Responses. To quantify this difference between simple and complex strategies for the outcome-altered responses, we constructed a measure of the distance between the event altered by the counterfactual question and some other event that the student believed would be altered as a result. This distance score can be considered an index of the complexity of the student's causal reasoning path. It was defined by three event designations, illustrated in Fig 5.1:

1. The event altered by the counterfactual, the *severed event*. In Fig 5.1, this is event *30. Panama revolts.*
2. All events mentioned by the student in responding to the counterfactual, which were marked on the causal–model template (the shaded boxes in Figs. 5.1–5.3).

3. The event that the student said would change, the *altered event*. For calculations of distance, each step (motivating or enabling link) between the severed event and the altered event earned one distance point.

For example in Fig. 5.1, if a student mentioned that the United States supported Panama in its revolution, then one distance point was awarded. If the student also mentioned the Spooner Act, that would earn 4 more points for a total of 5 distance points.

Next, we examine students' responses to the first three counterfactuals, focusing on the extent of outcome-altered versus outcome-preserving responses, the nature

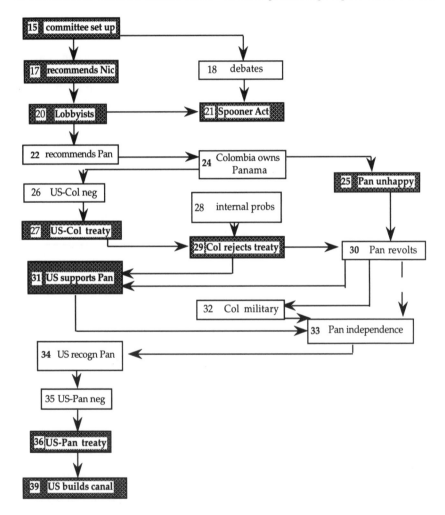

FIG. 5.1. Causal model for the question, "What if the revolution had not been successful?"

of the counterfactual reasoning, and the complexity, measured in distance along the causal–temporal model, of the outcome-altered responses. The part of the causal–temporal model relevant for these three questions is shown in Figs. 5.1–5.3.

What if the Revolution Had Not Been Successful? What Would Have Happened?

The Panamanian revolution played a critical enabling role in the American acquisition of a canal in Panama because it enabled the United States to bypass Colombia (which had rejected a treaty allowing the United States to build a canal) and deal directly with the new Panamanian government. A student reasoning about the missing connection between events 30 and 33 must examine the events immediately preceding and contributing to the critical point (*25. Panama not happy being ruled by Colombia*; *29. Colombian congress rejects treaty*; and *31. United States supports Panama in revolution*), and those events following and dependent upon the critical connection (*34. United States recognizes Panamanian independence*; *35. United States negotiates with Panama*; *36. U.S.–Panama treaty*; and *39. U.S. builds canal*).

Students tended to conclude that the outcome would have been different had the revolution failed: 46 of the 60 (77%) responses fell into the outcome-altered category. Eileen and Mitch had the highest proportion of outcome-altered responses (89% and 88%, respectively), whereas Jen had the lowest (50%). Thus, students confirmed the causal importance of the revolution to the story.

The majority of students focused on how the United States would have acquired permission to build a canal had the revolt failed. Some responses suggested the location of the canal would remain in Panama and only the treaty would be different. Robbie, for example, said "U.S. would have still dealt with Colombia, we'd still have a Panama Canal but we wouldn't have as much land…" Other students reasoned that there would be no canal in Panama, or that the United States would look to other locations such as Nicaragua.

For about one third of the outcome-altered responses, the students also told why they thought things would be different, especially that the U.S. involvement in Panama's revolution and Colombia's earlier rejection of the U.S. treaty would affect how Colombia negotiated with the United States. (See Eileen's and Robbie's responses in Table 5.1.) Students also occasionally gave reasons to support their outcome-preserved responses by challenging the hypothetical (i.e., the revolution couldn't have failed), supporting these challenges by citing American involvement in the revolution.

The outcome-altered reasoning showed some complexity for most students. On average, students earned 5.1 distance points and mentioned two different events (shaded boxes in Fig. 5.1) per response. Thus, on average, the students referred to about three links before the severed event, *30. Panama revolts*. However, some students considered mainly events very close to the severed event. The outcome-altered responses of Jen and Robbie were the simplest, an average of only 1.3 and 1.5 distance points, respectively (i.e., these students mentioned only events one or two links from the counterfactual event). In contrast, Mitch and George gave the most complex outcome-altered responses, scoring an average of 8.3 distance points each and mentioning three events that were approximately three links from the critical, severed event.

Complexity was affected by both the assignment order and the text. The first text, because it did not discuss the revolution in detail, resulted in the simplest response chains (average of 2.6 distance points). The final text resulted in the most complex answers (8.0 distance points), reflecting the fact that by the final text the students had read three different versions of the revolt. By text, the responses were most complex following Congressman X's text (7.7 distance points) and least complex following the Online text.

Would the Revolution Have Been Successful if the United States Was Not Interested in a Canal Through Panama?

This question again addresses the Panamanian revolution, but with a focus on U.S. interest in a canal. The relevant portion of the causal–temporal model for this question is shown in Fig. 5.2. The most direct way to represent this counterfactual is to eliminate Event *31. United States supports Panama in revolution*, severing both the connections between 30 and 31 and the connections between 31 and 33. A student reasoning about the counterfactual event could examine the events that lead to a revolution in Panama (e.g., *25. Panama not happy being ruled by Colombia* and *29. Colombian congress rejects treaty*).

As in the previous problem, students gave primarily outcome-altered responses, concluding that the revolution probably would have failed: 31 of the 43 (72%) outcomes fell into the outcome-altered category. George had the highest proportion of outcome-altered responses (91%) and Robbie had the lowest (20%). Robbie's very low rate of outcome-altered responses resulted from his rejection of an implicit link in the counterfactual question: Robbie consistently argued that because the U.S. played only a negligible role in the revolution, the lack of American interest in a canal was irrelevant to its success.

There were again text differences: Responses after the Online text had the lowest proportion of outcome-altered responses (57%), whereas Professor Y's text had the highest proportion (85%).

Students who claimed an altered outcome generally argued that the uprising would have failed because there would have been no American intervention. Students either agreed with Eileen that "[the canal] was the primary reason for the revolution" or they believed that U.S. military assistance prevented Colombia from quelling the revolt. Jen, Mitch, and George all noted that the Colombians were thwarted by the United States in their attempts to put down the rebellion.

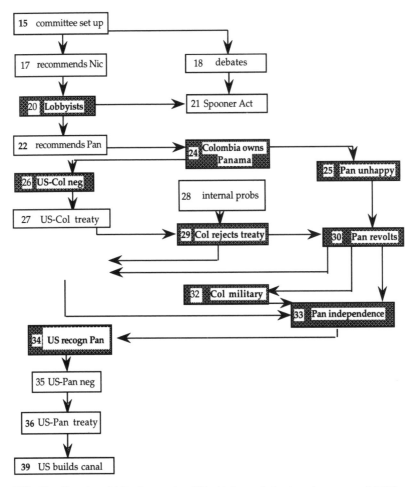

FIG. 5.2. Causal model for the question, "Would the revolution have been successful if the United States was not interested in the Canal through Panama?"

Students' outcome-altered answers were less complex for this question than for the previous one. On average, they earned only 2.1 distance points, with 1.5 different events (shaded boxes in fig. 5.2) per response that were typically only one causal link away. As in the last question, Mitch and George gave the most complex outcome-altered responses, scoring an average of 4.0 and 3.8 distance points, respectively.

The assignment order and text influenced the complexity of answers as measured by the distance score. Again, the final text resulted in the most complex answers with an average of 5.8 distance points. However on this question, Professor Y's text resulted in more complex answers (average of 5.5 distance points) than the other texts.

When students answered with an outcome-preserved answer—the revolution would have been successful anyway—they often qualified their belief by saying that the Panamanians would have gained independence eventually, but perhaps, as George noted, "not in 1903."

What Would Have Happened if the Colombian Congress Had Ratified the Hay–Herran Treaty?

This question also deletes an event in the causal–temporal chain. As shown in Fig. 5.3, shortly after the Colombian congress rejected the Hay–Herran Treaty (Event 29), Panama rebelled (Event 30). The link could be merely temporal, but a stronger causal link—that the Panamanians were angry that Colombia was depriving them of a canal opportunity and this caused them to take up arms or that they were encouraged by U.S. interests to do so—could also be made. The model also illustrates that following the rejection of the treaty, the United States played a role in the revolution (Event 31).

Of the six counterfactuals, this was the only one producing more outcome-preserved responses (45) than outcome-altered responses (37, or 45%). (The other five counterfactual problems averaged 75% outcome-altered responses.) Eileen and Mitch had the highest proportion of outcome-altered responses (64% and 62%, respectively), and Robbie had the lowest (23%).

Like the first two counterfactuals, there were text differences: The Online text had the lowest proportion of outcome-altered responses (37%), and Congressman X's text had the highest proportion (52%).

In the outcome-altered responses, students thought either that the revolution would not have occurred or that the United States would have supported Colombia rather than Panama. In providing reasons for their opinions, students who thought that the revolution wouldn't have happened tended to say that the Panamanians would have been satisfied with the canal opportunity; if they thought the United States would have backed Colombia in the uprising, it was because the United States would have protected its interests in the canal project.

Outcome-preserved responses gave priority to the location of the canal. Robbie stated the obvious following three of the texts: The United States would have the canal under the terms of the Hay–Herran Treaty. Sometimes the response was outcome-preserved because the students responded that Panama would still have rebelled.

Students' outcome-altered answers were moderately complex for this counterfactual. On average, they earned 3.3 distance points, referring to 1.5 different events (shaded boxes in fig. 5.3) per response that were about two links prior to the severed event. The most complex outcome-altered responses were again given by Eileen and George, who averaged 4.3 and 4.0 distance points, respectively. As in the first question, Jen's responses were the least complex, only 2 distance points per assignment.

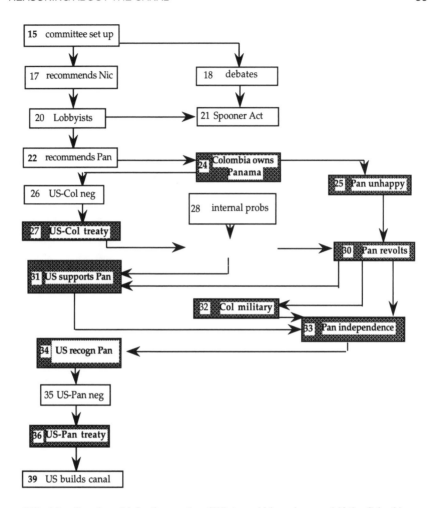

FIG. 5.3. Causal model for the question, "What would have happened if the Colombian congress had ratified the Hay–Herran Treaty?"

There was generally little influence of assignment on this question. The responses after the first text were the least complex, averaging 2.3 distance points, with modest increase in complexity by the second text, and little increase from Texts 2–4, which averaged 3.6 distance points. Although text influence on this question was negligible in general, an interesting influence was seen from Congressman X's text. Consistent with X's argument that the revolution was the result of Panamanian financial goals, both George and Eileen believed there would have been no revolution because the Panamanians simply wanted a canal and the Hay–Herran Treaty satisfied that desire.

The Role of Learning in the Counterfactuals

All subjects used what they were learning in reasoning about counterfactual questions, and this knowledge use increased after each reading.[11] For all counterfactual questions, 48, 63, 79, and 87 knowledge points were earned for each of the four reading assignments, respectively. Congressman X's text yielded 71 points and Professor Y's text, which contained more information, resulted in 95 points.

Students used knowledge in both their claims and reasons. For claims, this was primarily knowledge of events (e.g., Nicaragua was an option for building a canal) but also included supporting facts (e.g., the specific terms of the Hay–Herran Treaty). Knowledge use in reasons also included events (e.g., the United States supported Panama's revolution); however, supporting facts, such as the United States landed 42 marines in Colon just after the Colombian ship arrived with 500 men, were used more frequently.

The student who learned the most (George) also used the most knowledge in his reasoning answers. His knowledge use in the counterfactuals was dramatically higher than all the others (80 points vs. an average of 39 for the other five students). Next highest was Mitch (54) followed by the other students (Dave, 38; Eileen, 36; Jen, 35; Robbie, 34).

Occasionally, a lack of knowledge restricted students' ability to answer the counterfactuals. For example, the question *What would have happened if the Spooner Act was not passed by the U.S. Senate?* created a problem for students, because they had not learned much about the Spooner Act until at least the third assignment. (This question produced many unscorable responses: thus it was not included in the results reported for counterfactuals.) Second, they may have needed more specific knowledge assumed, but not supplied, by the texts. As Eileen put it, "I don't know enough about how acts affect treaties and I don't know that it was necessary, if it was necessary to have an act saying that the president should acquire a zone. I guess it was necessary that the act say what it did." There is no claim here about what would have happened. Only Mitch and George could both recall the heart of the Spooner Act and draw a conclusion to explain its failure.

Summary of Counterfactuals

Responses to the counterfactual questions suggest that students use a causal model in considering how outcomes might have been altered, given a change in some event. Evidence for the "psychological reality" of the causal–temporal model comes from students' ability to provide outcome-altered responses when a putative causal event is removed from the story. Moreover, there are multiple indicators of

---

[11]As noted in earlier chapters, a knowledge point was earned for each event or supporting fact cited by a subject in a reasoning response.

the effect of learning on counterfactual reasoning. Responses showed an increase, over assignments, in the number of claims (alternative outcomes), the number of qualifiers (hedges) associated with claims, the complexity, measured by event distance on the causal model, and the use of knowledge. All of these suggest an influence of learning on reasoning.

VALUE JUDGMENTS

Our interest in value judgments reflects an assumption that deep engagement with history texts, indeed with any story, usually involves evaluations of events and characters' actions. Learners interpret events and actions, in part, through implicit values. Sometimes the role played by values is highly visible and central to even the most casual interpretation of the event. (Think of a student's response to learning about the Holocaust, for example.) Other times, the values are less visible, but nonetheless significant in affecting the learner's interpretation. Learning about the American revolution, for example, may invoke implicit patriotic and nationalistic values. Our assumption was that the Panama Canal story would not evoke as much value-laden reasoning as would current and recent history with more personal involvement of the subjects. Thus we could observe its more subtle dimensions.

We asked students their opinions, based each time on what they had learned, about five different situations relating to the U.S. acquisition of a canal in Panama. The questions are repeated here from chapter 3:

1. Were the U.S. dealings with Colombia fair to Colombia?
2. Were the U.S. dealings with Panama fair to Panama?
3. Was the U.S. role in Panama's revolution justified? Why or why not?
4. Do you believe the United States should have negotiated with Bunau-Varilla or waited for the two Panamanian negotiators?
5. What is your opinion of Bunau-Varilla?

We report the value question results by first describing the argument structure and the use of knowledge in students' responses as a whole. We then discuss each question individually, focusing on the extent to which subjects showed a consensus in their judgments and the stability of their judgments across readings. To illustrate the kinds of responses we obtained, Table 5.2 presents George's answers to the first question.

Structure of Value Judgments

Value judgments were analyzed with a modification of Toulmin's (1958) system presented by Hample (1977) for the purpose of structurally representing an arguer's value judgment or belief. In this system, an argument consists of a claim, a reason, and a warrant, often implicit, which is the connection between the claim and the reason. Consider the following argument: *The United States was not fair to Colombia. It helped Panama win its independence.* Here the claim is that the United States was not fair. The reason is that the United States helped the Panamanians. The warrant is that helping a colony gain independence is not fair to the mother country. Notice that the warrant, or the connection between the claim and the reason, is not explicitly stated. In Hample's model, the warrant is the part of the argument that contains the reasoner's values or attitudes. Thus, warrants should be particularly interesting in our value judgments. In this section, we look at the structure of our students' responses in terms of their claims, reasons, and warrants.

Claims.   The student's basic answer to a question was taken as the claim. On these opinion questions, claims have both a valence (i.e, positive or negative) and a definiteness (i.e., definite, hedged, or neutral). Thus, claims were coded on a five point scale: YES (definite and positive), YES-BUT (hedged and positive),

TABLE 5.2
George's Answers to the Reasoning Question, "Were the U.S. dealings with Colombia fair to Colombia?"

Online: (NEUTRAL)

Apparently the Colombians didn't think so. *They rejected the treaty.* Since I don't remember why the Colombians didn't think so, I can't say if they were getting a fair deal. It sounded like they were getting a good amount of money and the *Colombians had just as much jurisdiction as the Americans did.*

CSIS: (YES)

Well, if that treaty had been signed, I'd say probably it would be more than fair to Colombia. (The U.S.) having *no sovereignty over the land they were signing for, having a time limit on the treaty, 100 years.* If they'd signed it, *we would've paid Colombia $15 million in gold coins and 9 years after that $250,000 annually. Colombian, U.S., and mixed courts.* So I'd say yes, if the treaty was signed it would be more than fair to Colombia, if not unfair to the U.S. [An interviewer asked "was the way they handled Panama fair to Colombia?"] No, that was very unfair.

Congressman X: (YES)

I think they were. I think that's another reason why *the Colombian people didn't like the treaty because they figured it was unfair to them. The U.S. wasn't going to have sovereignty over the land. The Colombians were going to have judicial rights over the land* and they were getting money for it. They had an *expiration date on the treaty.* I think they were using the U.S. over the barrel because they knew the Americans needed the canal.

Professor Y: (NO)

No, from reading that article the U.S. really gave Colombia the shaft, especially when it came to Panamanian independence. At first, I think America tried to be fair with *the Hay–Herran Treaty. Having it spit back in their faces really pissed off Roosevelt* and *John Hay* as well as *Taft who was the Secretary of War* at the time. Which is why they decided that Panamanians were ripe for a revolution and *we're going to make our damned effort to see that they succeed.* Which is what they did.

Note. Knowledge (Events and Supporting Facts) is in italics.

NEUTRAL (presenting both sides or not taking a stand), NO-BUT (hedged and negative), and NO (definite and negative). For example, George's answer following the initial text in Table 5.2 was considered NEUTRAL, because it did not explicitly state his own opinion. Instead George mentioned the Colombian perspective and his limited knowledge. His second and third responses are examples of a YES answer, supported by reference to treaty negotiations. His answer after Professor Y's text is an example of a NO claim.

Value judgment probes proved interesting in exposing a tentativeness and instability in students' reasoning. Subjects changed their minds over the four sessions. In fact, only Mitch changed his opinion on fewer than half the opportunities. Three of the six students altered their opinions at least 75% of the time. For an example see Table 5.2, where George changed his interpretation of the question in his final response. When he judged U.S. actions as fair, he focused on one component of the story (the treaty); when he judged U.S. actions as unfair, he focused on a different component (the Panamanian revolution). This shifting ground phenomenon was characteristic of the value judgments, which were designed to probe evaluations of complex situations. Responding to such a question suggests defining which parts of the situation are important enough to mention (e.g., the treaty or the revolution) and to use as a guide for evaluation.

Examining the responses from the first four value judgments, we find that on most occasions students did take a position on the value judgment (only 16% were NEUTRAL).[12] Most of these positions were stated as definite claims (57% were YES or NO). Students varied in the certainty of their claims. Robbie and Mitch held strong opinions, giving definite answers 88% of the time. George was least definite and most likely to hedge by mentioning support for a counterclaim. Only 27% of his answers were definite. Eileen and Jen were most likely not to state an opinion.

The strength of the claims varied slightly with texts and assignments. As students learned more, they gave fewer neutral answers (26%, 22%, 13%, and 4% across the four readings) and more hedged opinions (13%, 30%, 35%, and 35% across the four readings). The seeming paradox of decreasing neutrality plus increasing hedges is readily explained by what the students learned. They became more opinionated, but, with more learning, also more sensitive to the complexity. Students were also less likely to give a neutral opinion following the two biased texts (9% for both Professor Y and Congressman X) than following the more neutral texts (26% for Online and 22% for CSIS).

Reasons.   More often than not, students supported their claims with at least one reason, averaging 1.4 reasons per response. George justified his opinions most often (1.7 reasons per answer) and Eileen justified her opinions least often (1.1 reasons per answer). There were assignment differences; the first text prompted the

---

[12]The final question, "What is your opinion of Bunau-Varilla?" was formally different from the others and is considered separately later in the chapter.

fewest reasons (0.9) and the final assignment prompted the most (1.3). There were more reasons after Professor Y's text than any other.

The Unstated Warrant. More often than not, students did not state the warrant, the connection between the reason and the claim. Instead, the reasons were often descriptions of situations or events, with an implicit value assumption about the situation. A typical example is Eileen's response after CSIS: "No (the United States wasn't fair to Colombia) because they were having trouble working on (the) treaty with Colombia so they helped revolutionaries in Colombia stage a revolution in Colombia to get a better deal." Eileen fails to say what about the situation she describes makes it unfair; her warrant is implicit. Indeed, because a single reason can be used to support opposite claims, a value-based warrant must be inferred to understand the relationship between the reason and the claim.

When the connection between claim and reason was explicit, it was sometimes a general principle. We were able to identify three such principles in students' value reasoning. One is *the ends justify the means*; Dave, for example, said "Yes they were justified in that the ends justify the means. They wanted a canal cheaply and wanted full control. Supporting the revolution definitely provides those ends." A second principle is that *might makes right*. As Mitch put it after reading Professor Y: "Yes [the United States was justified]; they got an equal share. Colombia was not a strong power. They couldn't control their own colonies. They had to ask the U.S. for help four times. The U.S. could've done anything they wanted to." The third is a *national rights or nonintervention principle*. Dave, who consistently favored nonintervention policies, demonstrated this principle after reading CSIS: "It's not the right of U.S. to intervene in internal affairs of another country."

Occasionally the explicit warrant could be considered a pragmatic reasoning schema, applied to a relatively narrow perspective of the question of fairness. A common schema relevant for fairness uses the perspective of a business transaction. For example, after reading the Online text, Dave said "I would say pretty fair in business deal sense. Somebody made a better deal and U.S. took it." Another perspective views fairness in terms of consent, or the a-deal-is-a-deal principle. Robbie's reading after Congressman X exemplifies this: "I think when two high officials talk like that everything is fair. Fair is fair. If they didn't like it they didn't have to sign it. So I think it was fair, definitely."

Because most warrants were not explicit, we had to depend on the content of the reason to classify them. We found that most responses could be classified in six categories:

1. *Ends justify the means*: any reason that justified an action because it helped attain the final goal. Generally, students who gave reasons in this category felt that the United States wanted a canal and so could do anything to do it.

2. *Legal*: an action judged fair if it was not against the law but judged unfair if it violated a law or treaty. Reasons had to specifically include that a law was upheld

or broken to qualify as a legal justification. Otherwise they were classified as ethical.

3. *Ethical*: a more vague definition of fair. Students who said an action was "right" or something "should have" been done gave ethical justifications.

4. *Deny/minimize role*: a reason that justified fairness by explaining that the United States didn't really do anything. This was generally used by students to explain why the U.S. role in Panama's revolution was justified.

5. *Practical/economic value*: an action deemed fair if there was proper compensation or if that action was the only one that could be taken. Students who gave reasons in this category generally compared the worth of the canal to the amount of money given to the Colombians and, later, the Panamanians and then decided if it was a fair exchange.

6. *Intervention* (nonintervention, altruistic intervention, or self-benefit intervention/imperialism): an action judged as fair or unfair based on whether or not the United States intervened and why it intervened. Nonintervention or altruistic intervention were generally rated as fair treatment and self-benefit intervention/imperialism was rated as unfair.

Over the various value questions, students' responses fell unevenly into the various categories: however, all the categories were used by at least one student. In fact, all the students used between four and six justification categories. *Legal* reasons were more often provided than others but the *practical* and *ends justify the means* categories were also used frequently.

Knowledge Use in Value Judgments

Students used what they learned in justifying their expressions of values. Table 5.2 illustrates George's use of knowledge for the question of fairness to Colombia, with events and supporting facts used by George in italics. After the first text, George cited facts to represent what he had learned rather than to support a claim. By his second response, George used information to support an opinion, namely that the United States was fair to Colombia because the Colombians were gaining from the treaty. As evidence of Colombian gain, he mentioned several terms of the U.S.–Colombian treaty.

The general trend in knowledge use for the value questions was the same as for the counterfactuals: (1) Learning led to increasing use of knowledge; an average of 28, 64, 50, and 103 points across the four assignments. Thus, as students learned more, they used more knowledge in providing value judgments. Increased learning also brought more hedged opinions and more reasons. (2) Professor Y's text resulted in more knowledge use than did Congressman X's text, 86 points compared with 67. Indeed, knowledge use following Congressman X was essentially the same as knowledge use following the shorter CSIS text (64 points.) (3) Among individuals, George used much more knowledge than other students; 80 points, compared with a more typical 30–50 points (Eileen, 37; Dave, 31; Jen, 32; Mitch, 49). However, unlike in the Counterfactuals, Robbie used noticeably less knowledge (only 16 points across 4 questions and 4 texts!).

Robbie's low knowledge use in the value judgments appeared to reflect his persistent misunderstandings of the relationships among Panama, Colombia, and the United States, and especially, the Panamanian revolution. These confusions were especially detrimental in the value probes because three of the five questions dealt directly with this aspect of the story.

In the next section, we examine students' answers to the five value judgments individually. The focus changes from the structure of the reasoning and the use of knowledge to the stability of students' judgments and the extent to which there was some consensus among students. The stability question is especially interesting, because learning from multiple texts creates a condition conducive to some instability. Students' opinions can be altered, potentially, by shifts in perspective among the authors as well as encounters with new information.

Were the United States Dealings with Colombia Fair to Colombia?

The fairness question here is a salient and implicit part of the story. There are two key elements in the story: The first is the U.S.–Colombia negotiations on Panama that resulted in the Hay–Herran Treaty, rejected by the Colombian Senate: Was the treaty fair? The second is the U.S. actions in the Panamanian revolution. One action in particular—refusal to let Colombia use the U.S. owned railroad—might be interpreted as unfair to Colombia.

Consensus.   Students generally responded YES, the United States was fair to Colombia. Across the four texts, approximately 79% of subjects' responses were affirmative or affirmative with hedges. At least 4 of the 6 students answered affirmatively, sometimes with hedges, after all texts, and no more than one student ever judged the United States as unfair.

Stability.   Responses to this fairness question were marked by instability. On two thirds of the opportunities for change, a student changed his or her opinion (12 of the 18 times the question was asked after the first occasion). Only one student (Mitch) held an unaltered opinion across all four sessions. Table 5.2 illustrates (for George) the changeable character of the opinions. In this example, both the opinions themselves and the information used by the student in justifying his opinion shifted over successive assignments.

It appears that text arguments were partly responsible for the students' malleability. Five of the six students responded YES, the United States was fair, after reading Congressman X, whose text included a defense of U.S. actions in the area. In comparison, four students gave different opinions following Professor Y's text, which was more balanced on this issue. Three of these opinions rated the U.S. actions as less fair, consistent with the author's more critical attitude. As shown in Table 5.2, George shows this opinion shift from Congressman X to Professor Y.

Were the U.S. Dealings with Panama Fair to Panama?

The question of fairness to Panama forms a link between the Acquisition Story and subsequent U.S.–Panama relations, including the 1977 treaties. Indeed, the final two texts read by the students made this link: Congressman X's argument against the 1977 treaties was based in part on the premise that the U.S. dealings with Panama 75 years earlier had been fair. Accordingly, it is of special interest to learn how students responded to this fairness question. There are several elements to the ethical problem. Probably the most central is that the terms of the treaty by which the United States acquired canal rights from Panama could be judged less favorable to Panama than the terms the United States had offered just a few months earlier to Colombia, prior to the Panamanian revolution. An added element was the motivation of Bunau-Varilla, who represented Panama in negotiations with the United States. It is possible to view him as an opportunist, whose interest in personal gain was exploited by the United States in the negotiations. (See the question on Bunau-Varilla later in this section.)

Consensus. Unlike the Colombia question, there was not a clear consensus on fairness to Panama. After every text, there were at least two students who judged the United States as fair and at least two who judged the United States as unfair. For both judgments, hedges were common, and after three of the four texts, one or another student was unable to decide about fairness. Over all texts, 46% of subjects' responses indicated fairness, and 42% indicated unfairness, with the remainder undecided or neutral. By the end (i.e., after the fourth text), four students (Dave, Mitch, Robbie, and George) had come to conclude that the United States was fair or mostly fair to Panama, and two others (Eileen and Jen) believed that the United States was unfair or mostly unfair to Panama.

Stability. Of all the value judgments, opinions were most unstable for this question. In this case, 83% of the probes resulted in a student altering his or her most recent opinion (15 of 18 opportunities). All students altered their position at least twice. Between Texts 3 and 4, which represented opposing positions on this issue, two subjects changed substantially from a positive (YES or YES, BUT) to a negative judgment (NO or NO, BUT). Moreover, 5 of the 6 students shifted their opinion at least slightly between the two texts, moving 1 point on our 5-point scale (e.g., from YES to YES, BUT). Three of the five students who changed their opinion believed that the United States was fairer after reading X than after reading Y, consistent with Congressman X's more pro-American stance. Contrary to the text differences, however, two of the five students gave answers that rated U.S. actions more fair after Y than X.

Was the U.S. Role in Panama's Revolution Justified? Why or Why Not?

This question also gets at attitudes concerning U.S. relations with Panama. Although the question presupposes some role for the United States in the revolution, it leaves it to the student to define the role. Students would be expected to use what they learned in determining the nature of U.S. participation in the Panamanian rebellion in order to make a judgment.

Consensus.   As with the fairness-to-Panama question, there was not a clear consensus. Opinion was divided, with 42% of the responses indicating that the United States was justified, 29% indicating the United States was not justified, and 29% indicating a neutral or undecided position. Because the first text had little on the revolution, subjects tended to be appropriately neutral in their response.

Stability.   Once again, opinions were quite unstable, changing on 10 of 18 (56%) opportunities. All students except one (Robbie) altered their opinions at least once. There were some text effects. After the second text, which considered the possibility of a U.S. intervention in the revolution objectively and without detail, three of the six students were neutral on the question. After the last two texts, only 1 of 12 responses remained neutral or undecided. There was also a difference between the texts of Congressman X and Professor Y. Three of the six students shifted in the direction of the author, indicating a greater belief that the U.S. role was justified after reading X than Y. After Congressman X, only one student believed the United States was not justified, and this answer was hedged. After reading Professor Y, opinions were evenly divided and two subjects gave unhedged opinions that the United States was not justified.

Do You Believe the United States Should Have Negotiated with Bunau-Varilla or Waited for the Two Panamanian Negotiators?

This question probes a specific event that is part of the fairness theme. Philippe Bunau-Varilla, a French national whose complex role in the acquisition story goes back to the de Lesseps project for which he was chief engineer, became a central figure in the drive to locate a canal in Panama (rather than Nicaragua), and later inserted himself into the Panama–U.S. treaty negotiations. He also held a strong financial interest in the Panama project. On November 16, 1903, two representatives of the new Panamanian government were in New York, on their way to Washington. Bunau-Varilla, an appointed Panamanian representative with a definite personal stake in the canal venture, rushed to revise a treaty draft to present to U.S. Secretary of State John Hay before the two representatives could arrive. As captioned by a 1970s film made in Panama, the resulting treaty was "The treaty that no Panamanian signed." Our question aimed at the ethical perspective students might bring to bear on this issue.

Consensus. The consensus opinion on the question was YES, the United States should have waited. Approximately 61% of subjects' responses over the four texts were affirmative or affirmative with hedges; 26% were negative (but never hedged), and the remaining 13% were undecided or neutral.

Stability. Generally the students were unstable in their opinions, showing alterations on 56% (10 of 18) of the opportunities. However, two students (Mitch and Jen) were very consistent, expressing the same opinion after every text. There was some text influence on opinion. After the short Online text the consensus was strong, but shifted considerably after the longer but still neutral second text. The shifts between the two opinionated texts were modest, with three students expressing the same opinion after both Congressman X and Professor Y. Of the three students who changed opinions, only one shifted in the direction consistent with the author (i.e., more inclined to think the United States should have waited for the two Panamanian negotiators after reading Professor Y than after Congressman X).

What Is Your Opinion of Bunau-Varilla?

This question further taps the value themes surrounding the character of Bunau-Varilla and his important role in defining Panama–U.S. relations.

Consensus. Because this was not a yes–no question, consensus has a different meaning. Responses could be classified into three categories: Students concluded that Bunau-Varilla was (a) good to the United States, (b) good to himself, or (c) smart. Of course, students might suggest that Bunau-Varilla was both smart and good to the United States or good to himself. Two students could be classified as predominantly in each of the three categories. An overall consensus view might be characterized as suggesting that Bunau-Varilla was a clever manipulator of events whose actions benefitted himself and the United States.

Stability. Students' responses were more stable for this question. Four of the six students gave essentially the same opinion after all four texts. Because most students gave the same answer after all four texts, there is no evidence for a text effect on their answers.

Summary of Value Judgments

In making value judgments, students demonstrated both a strong influence of learning and considerable instability. Knowledge citations and hedges both increased over assignments, and on more than half the occasions, students changed their immediately preceding judgment. Students reached consensus on one half the value questions and there was some variation in their opinions for the other half. The students frequently supported their claim (i.e., their basic judgment on the value question), with one or more reasons. *Legal* reasons were the most common. Warrants linking reasons to claims were often only implicit, and explicit warrants were generally a principle such as "the ends justify the means."

CONFRONTATIONALS

Confrontational questions were intended to force students to deal with implicit problems and contradictions that were exposed in the texts. The "confrontational" character of the question varied from explicitly forcing the students to respond to an argument that one might make about the U.S. role (Item 1) to merely asking whether implicit contradictions in the story were noticed (Item 2). The focus of our analysis is on the reasons students provided and their use of knowledge.

We asked students to explain four different situations relating to the U.S. acquisition of a canal in Panama, repeated here from chapter 3.

1. Is it just a coincidence that the United States benefitted from the Panamanian revolution? Why do you think the Colombian resistance was so ineffective?
2. Why did the United States let the French build a canal? (The confrontation here is that stated U.S. policy was against a foreign-owned canal in the region.)
3. Why were the Panamanians represented by a Frenchman?
4. Why did the United States get a better deal from Panama?

Structure of Confrontationals

Responses generally began with a claim followed by reasons justifying that claim. As a group, these questions produced more variation among students than did the value judgments. Most questions showed little or only subtle text influence on the kinds of reasons provided. There were small text differences in the number of reasons, ranging from 1.9 reasons per question after the first text to 2.9 reasons after the third text. Students supported their answers with an average of 2.5 reasons per confrontational question. George, as in other questions, produced the most reasons (3.1); Eileen gave the fewest (1.8 reasons per question).

Knowledge Use in Confrontationals

Students used knowledge in their explanations of confrontationals as they did in other question types. The general pattern of knowledge use mirrored that found for other questions: (1) Learning led to increased knowledge use. The total knowledge used in the four Confrontational questions increased at each assignment: 24, 63, 106, and 122 points. Thus, with increased learning, students used more of what they learned in their explanations. (2) Students used more knowledge after Professor Y's text (134 points) than after Congressman X's text (94 points). (3) George again used the most knowledge in his responses (99 points). A group of three students showed an intermediate level of knowledge use—Dave (53), Jen (53), Mitch (56). Robbie again showed much less knowledge use (28), but was joined by Eileen (26).

In the next section, we examine the kinds of reasons students gave in responding to confrontational questions. As in the value questions, we focus on consensus and stability. Stability, however, has a different sense than in the value judgments, referring to the quality and quantity of reasons provided by the students.

Is it Just a Coincidence That the United States Benefitted From the Panamanian Revolution? Why Do You Think the Colombian Resistance Was So Ineffective?

These questions were intended to force the students to deal with a central ethical issue in the story. The second part of the question is especially confrontational in that it requires the student to develop a competing explanation of Colombian military ineffectiveness. The implicit alternative is that the United States benefitted because it intervened. Notice that the first question appears to invite a negative response.

Consensus. Students generally suggested that the United States benefitted more from design than coincidence. There was only one exception (Robbie) and that was restricted to the first text, which had nothing about the revolution.

Stability. Students' opinions that the United States gained more from design than coincidence were relatively stable over assignments. Although more reasons overall were given after Professor Y than Congressman X, there is no clear evidence of text influence on students' responses to the "coincidence" question.

For the part of the question concerning Colombia's military ineffectiveness, there was a marked increase in the number of reasons provided. The number of reasons given increased over assignments on 12 of 18 possibilities. After the last two biased texts, students produced about twice as many reasons as after the first two (40 vs. 21). Differences between the X and Y texts were negligible (18 and 22 reasons, respectively).

However, the kinds of reasons given did show text influence. We expected that subjects would fault Colombia's military efforts after reading Congressman X, whereas, after reading Professor Y, they would tend to fault U.S. interference or to credit Panamanian nationalism for Colombia's failure to defeat the revolution. Indeed, 56% (10 of 18) of reasons given after students read X faulted Colombia and 64% (14 of 22) reasons after students read Y referred either to U.S. influence or Panamanian nationalism. However, even after reading Congressman X, subjects sometimes included U.S. interference as a reason. All students who gave multiple reasons for Colombia's failure included U.S. interference in at least one reason.

Why Did the United States Let the French Build a Canal?

This question confronted the students with a superficial contradiction on a less central part of the story. The mid-19th century part of the story included a U.S. policy, as stated by President Rutherford Hayes for example, prohibiting any foreign canal project in the region. The French project in the 1880s would seem to have violated this U.S. policy.

Consensus.   Three categories accounted for most of the reasons given for why the United States allowed the French project: (1) It would benefit the United States (The United States would use it, eventually control it, or learn from France how to build one.) (2) The United States knew that the French would fail. (3) The United States had no option. (Legally it could do nothing, and it was occupied with other things.)

Stability.   There appeared to be no influence of a specific text's arguments on the kinds of reasons given by the students because reasons were not differentially produced after X vs. Y. Students produced more reasons in their answers following the last two texts, compared with the first two (33 vs. 26).

Why Were the Panamanians Represented by a Frenchman?

In considering this question, a student might cite a narrow, legalistic reason (i.e., that Bunau-Varilla was appointed by the Panamanian government), a richer historical reason that refers to Bunau-Varilla's history of involvement in Panama, or the simpler skeptical view that Bunau-Varilla was in that position because the United States placed him in that position.

Consensus.   Subjects cited all these reasons, reflecting the complexity of Bunau-Varilla's role in several parts of the story: his early association with the French project favored him for this role, his role in the revolution, his legal status as an appointee of the Panamanian government, and his backing by the United States.

Stability. Although there were multiple explanations for Bunau-Varilla acting as Panama's representative, each student tended to provide the same reasons after each text. There was, however, a tendency to provide more reasons after the last two than after the first two texts (35 vs. 24 reasons).

Why Did the United States Get a Better Deal From Panama?

This question confronted subjects with an important part of the story ending. The treaty granting the United States control of a canal zone was more favorable to the United States than the treaty offered to Colombia. This discrepancy, along with the circumstances in which the treaty was signed (the Bunau-Varilla questions), were at the core of sentiment against the fairness of the treaty.

Consensus. Students' responses were basically variations on a single theme: Panama was forced to accept lesser treaty terms. The students elaborated this theme by saying that Panama was too weak to exercise any leverage in negotiations and that the United States manipulated this situation to its advantage. Students sometimes added that the United States used Bunau-Varilla to advantage in arranging an attractive treaty, or that Panama needed U.S. protection from Colombia, or that Panama was too naive to make a better deal.

Stability. There was no evidence of text influence on the kinds of reasons provided by the students. Except for one subject (Dave), there was no overall increase in reasons over assignments, nor between the first two (25 reasons) and last two texts (22 reasons).

Summary of Confrontationals

Compared with the value judgments, the confrontational questions produced much more stable replies. Opinions changed less frequently, reflecting a limited influence of text. Student responses generally showed some consensus and usually included reasons to support claims. As in the other types of reasoning questions, students included more knowledge in their responses as they read more texts.

SOURCE EVALUATION

Source questions were aimed at students' awareness of the points of view of the authors. The four texts varied in a number of ways—their level of detail, the distribution of text focus on the various events of the story, and the authors' rhetorical goals and arguments in service of those goals. The general conclusion from this group of questions is that the students were frequently affected by the authors' arguments despite not always explicitly taking note of the texts' bias.

Who Does the Author Believe Caused the Revolution? What Does He Use to Support His View?

The students generally detected the authors' views on the revolution. Authors X and Y agreed that the United States did not foment the Panamanian revolution, but they did not agree on how to explain the revolution. Congressman X claimed that the revolution was caused by a small group of wealthy Panamanian businessmen who wanted the financial gains a canal would bring. Professor Y, on the other hand, credited the revolution to a long history of Panamanian nationalism and grievances against both Colombia and the United States. Thus, although both authors argued that the United States was not culpable, their differences in explaining the revolution could be significant in shaping readers' opinions about other parts of the story. By arguing that the greed of a minority motivated the revolution, Congressman X could imply that Panama got what it deserved. By arguing that traditional patriotic motivations led to the revolution, Professor Y could allow the reader some sympathy for Panama.

All students except one (Robbie) were influenced by at least one of the authors. After the biased texts, three students' answers directly reflected the opinion of the author they most recently read. Eileen, Dave, and George all blamed wealthy Panamanians for the Panamanian revolution after they read Congressman X. After reading Professor Y, they noted at least one of the following: the meeting between Bunau-Varilla and Roosevelt at which they discussed U.S. actions in the event of an uprising in Panama, earlier Panamanian uprisings against Colombia, and the U.S.-controlled railroad's refusal to transport Colombian troops to the rebellious Panama City. In each case, the student is demonstrating a more complex view of the revolution than what they offered after reading Congressman X.

Jen appeared to be affected only by Congressman X's text. She accepted X's claim that the United States was innocent of any illegal intervention because there was "...no evidence that the U.S. played a role in [the revolution]" even though she told us that the United States prevented the movement of Colombian troops.

What Do You Think Was the Author's Opinion of the Negotiations Between Bunau-Varilla and Hay?

This question was intended to tap the students' views of the opinion of the author concerning the critical final episode of the story, in which Bunau-Varilla rushed to present Secretary of State Hay with a treaty while Panamanian representatives were detained in New York. Hay had written a treaty almost exactly the same as the treaty he had offered to Colombia earlier in 1903. Bunau-Varilla modified that treaty, giving the United States more land and control of the zone "in perpetuity" instead of the fixed 100 year-lease offered to Colombia.

Professor Y treated the negotiations, especially Bunau-Varilla's actions, with healthy skepticism. Although not explicitly critical, Y noted that Bunau-Varilla ignored orders to wait for the other two Panamanian negotiators and made reference to some questionable behavior by Bunau-Varilla. Congressman X dismissed criticism of Bunau-Varilla's unilateral actions by arguing that the Panamanian government ratified the treaty. In addition, X praised the treaty as being clear and concise, as opposed to more current (1977) "devious, Kissingeresque agreements."

The students had trouble answering this question because they tended to give opinions about the individuals doing the negotiating instead of the process Hay and Bunau-Varilla went through. That is, the students usually just repeated their (generally unfavorable) response to the earlier question *What is your opinion of Bunau-Varilla?* In fact, Eileen was the only subject to consistently respond to the question properly, although others occasionally commented on the negotiations. After Congressman X, Mitch gave an answer that reflected X's habit of commenting on current politics when he said "[X] was comparing it to Kissinger. When you read a treaty by him, it's not understandable. I think [X] liked the way [the treaty] was done and that the U.S. got a good deal."

Do You Believe the Author Presented Enough of the Facts to Paint a Complete Picture?

This question attempted to get at students' perception of the author's completeness. Although novice learners could not be expected to know whether relevant parts of the story have been omitted, they can make implicit comparisons between texts and they can compare information in the text with their schema-based expectations.

In 15 of the 24 cases, the students agreed that the author painted a complete picture. Appropriately, their judgment of completeness was lowest after the short first text, which three of the six subjects judged to be incomplete. Professor Y's text was judged to be complete by five students and Congressman X's text was judged to be complete by four subjects.

Students' reasons for judging the text incomplete fell into two general classes: (a) *fact*—judgments that facts were missing, was the most frequent; and (b) *bias*—judgments that the author was biased, was common for one of the texts. When citing lack of facts, students revealed a general assumption that stories are necessarily incomplete. For example, after Text 2 George said "I'm sure there were other things going on." Three subjects reported bias in Congressman X. Dave questioned X's coverage of the story, Mitch stated "he left a few things out" and, although George felt that X presented enough facts, he believed X's story was not an objective report of the events. No students, by contrast, spontaneously identified any bias in Professor Y.

Did the Author Present a Neutral Coverage of the Events?
If Not, What Do You Think the Author's Attitude Was?

In our view, the texts varied from solidly objective (Text 1) through strongly subjective and argumentative (Congressman X). We assumed this important source characteristic would be visible to students. Bias could be, and was, attributed to these texts in connection with colorful language, omission of facts, and detectable rhetorical goals. Additionally, students found a text biased if it interpreted events to support a specific point of view or if it displayed an attitude toward the events described.

In fact, some students volunteered observations about bias before being asked, especially concerning Congressman X's text, which was seen as biased by four subjects. George said "I got a good flavoring of Americanistic [sic] propaganda while I was reading...I think he doesn't have an objective view." Mitch remarked "[X] left a few things out. I remember reading through it and knowing information that changed about the story." Dave also noted that there were gaps in X's story, and believed that X was biased because of these omissions. Two subjects (Robbie and Jen) thought that Congressman X's text was neutral. However, Mitch summarized well the view that most students had about Congressman X: "He was pretty much trying to show that the U.S. was the good guy".

By contrast, all six students agreed that the first text, the Online text, was neutral. Jen added an interesting statement to justify her belief "I guess [the first text] was neutral by not giving all the facts." Most of the students also agreed that the second text was basically neutral but they recognized that the text was written by Americans. Two students echoed George's feeling that "you can tell it was clearly written by an American." Robbie said "I think he was biased to the U.S. ...He explained it not biasedly [sic] but you can tell he's American."

Professor Y's text was rated neutral by two students and a third was not quite sure. However, even students detecting bias in Y's text indicated only a mild bias. Robbie's response was quite typical: "I think he was as neutral as possible. I think he had a slight attitude towards the U.S." Mitch's justification of his answer was an interesting way to judge neutrality: "I guess he was neutral. He threw his opinions in but he let it be known that those were his opinions".

Summary of Source Evaluation Questions

Students were certainly aware of source characteristics in a general sense. In all of the source evaluations, the majority of students' responses indicated they were sensitive to differences between the texts. Author differences in explanation of the revolution, the amount of information presented, and bias were noticed. Students appeared to be sensitive to text selectivity as well, judging the earlier texts less complete than the later ones, and 60% of their texts as sufficiently complete overall. When the students felt they needed more information, it was because they believed that facts had been omitted or that the text had a definite bias. Congressman X's text was judged more biased than Professor Y's, although two students seemed to have not detected this difference.

METAKNOWLEDGE

In learning the twists and turns of a story, and being confronted with controversy, learners can come to appreciate the limits of their understanding. We asked *What else would you like to know?* to discover students' views of their limitations.

A knowledge gap can result from incompleteness in the text and from a confusion about some part of the story. Students reported knowledge gaps of three kinds: (a) in their knowledge of the basic story, (b) in their understanding of the historical context, and (c) in their ability to evaluate a controversy.

Students recognized their knowledge gaps, even volunteering their need for more information before we asked this question. Eileen, for example, often said she thought some part of the story was missing. Dave and Jen also said at least once that they needed more information. Dave provided two examples. After Text 2, he was interested in Bunau-Varilla: "More about the character of Bunau-Varilla. What was it, ego? Did he want money? Was he looking for U.S. influence?" After Congressman X he said "The big gaps I see are: the French involvement…and Nicaragua."

Responses in the *basic story* category indicated the students were trying to learn more about the Acquisition Story. Requests such as Mitch's "more about the revolution" were more common after the first two texts. However, sometimes a confusion about a part of the story lingered. After three of the texts, Robbie asked for clarification on the French involvement. First he wanted to know "How France got involved." After Text 2, he told us, "I'm still hazy on how France got in there." After Professor Y he again asked, "How did France get involved?" It was only after the fourth and final reading that he seemed to understand the French connection.

Occasionally, students wanted information that concerned the *historical context*, rather than the story itself. For example, George asked, "What happened between 1850 and 1879?" after the first text. Although he didn't need this information to understand the U.S. involvement in obtaining rights to build a canal, such context would be important in understanding the fuller story. After the final reading, George called on his own historical knowledge to answer his question: "The only thing it didn't mention was what was going on with American interests in the 1860s and that's understandable because the Civil War was going on. Americans didn't have much of an interest in anything after the war besides rebuilding the South."

Given the controversies around the acquisition story, we expected that a third category of knowledge gap, knowledge that might be used to *resolve controversy*, would be significant for subjects. Students indeed indicated a need for such knowledge, despite the considerable amount of text that had been devoted to knowledge relevant to the controversies. For example, Dave responded, "Prove to me why [Bunau-Varilla] did the right thing for Panama even though it looks so skewed in U.S.'s favor." And Jen, wondering about the controversial U.S. involvement in the Panamanian revolution, asked, "If Panamanians had wanted their independence did the U.S. really push them?"

Summary of Metaknowledge

Even after four assignments of about 40 pages, most students showed some appreciation of the gaps in their understanding of the story. The gaps included holes in the basic story, a lack of historical context, and insufficient information to resolve a controversy. All of the students requested additional information about at least one aspect of the story.

CONCLUSIONS

Students showed a willingness to engage in conversations about the Panama story. We do not claim this willingness is surprising. We asked them questions and we expected them to respond. We do suggest, however, that the image of the passive college student unable to think about what he or she reads is one that is easily altered. In appropriate circumstances, it is clear that students, facing a topic for which they have neither expertise nor intrinsic interest, will wrestle with problems of interpretation, text, and values.

We observed some especially interesting reasoning patterns. Perhaps the most interesting is the tentativeness with which students approached value questions and the instability that marked their opinions. Opinions were often hedged. And they were often reversed after more reading. Interestingly, the most unstable opinion came on the centrally argued interpretation of the Panama Canal Acquisition Story: Was the United States fair to Panama? In answering this question, students altered their opinion in one direction or another on better than four in five opportunities. All six students were affected by this vacillation.

In retrospect, such fickleness might be expected. First, the question itself is open to wide interpretation. What does "fair" mean? In general? In international relations? Certainly, subjects can slightly modify their "definition" of fairness from one time to another. Second, this is a question that, in one form or another, was central to the long-standing controversies surrounding U.S.–Panama relations. It is reasonable that college students, previously innocent of significant knowledge of the controversy, should partly recapitulate the two sides of the controversy, rather than embody one side consistently.

There is an even more interesting possibility, however. Students may have allowed themselves to be influenced by information. Their changes in opinions corresponded not merely to different times, but to different texts. The texts themselves appear to have induced conflict and reflection on elements that might contribute to forming an opinion. This effect does not seem to be a simple susceptibility to propaganda. If subjects merely echoed the opinions of what they had most recently read, we should see a clear dovetailing between text and opinions. However, the text influence was not always simple. Five students changed opinion between their reading of Congressman X and Professor Y. Although three of those were more likely to believe the United States was fair after reading X, consistent with his rhetorical goals, the other two shifted toward this opinion after reading Professor Y, whose text can be characterized as more balanced, providing more information and less ideology. Its influence in this direction would seem to be a matter of information rather than rhetoric. To oversimplify a bit, some of the instability in opinion may come from learning the story rather than learning an argument about its interpretation. Knowledge begets uncertainty.

Knowledge indeed is the second interesting component of the reasoning demonstrated by our students. As shown in the previous chapter, there was significant learning over the four assignments, rapid at first for the main events of the story, somewhat more gradual for the important details that define the events. We saw that subjects used this knowledge in reasoning, although they were not asked to explicitly. Some students used knowledge to a limited extent, but all used it. And the general trend was that the citation of knowledge followed the same pattern seen for the learning of supporting facts. As more facts were learned after the second text, more facts were included in responses to the reasoning probes. On most questions, there was an increase in the use of knowledge from the second text to the third text. Also, there was a tendency, when there was a difference, for more knowledge to be included after the more informative text of Professor Y.

Our suggestion is simply that students use what they are learning in reasoning, even about questions that probe values. This relationship is certainly not necessary. Strong opinions can be held in the absence of knowledge where there is a strong personal or religious investment in an opinion. But when the opinions can be plausibly related to knowledge, they are. Part of this trend can be attributed to the students' compliance with academic discourse. In a history essay exam, they would presumably do the same. They would appreciate that a request for an opinion is a request for an informed opinion. What we see in addition is the parallel increase in knowledge and the use of that knowledge in reasoning.

This conclusion is supported by the analysis of counterfactual reasoning, where we were able to quantify not only the use of knowledge but the complexity of reasoning. Students used knowledge in these questions, and increasingly so over learning episodes. Moreover, as they learned more, they were able to provide more claims and more qualifications or hedges to these claims. Furthermore, as indicated by the distance measure applied to the causal–temporal event structure, increased learning led to more complex reasoning. Students, with more learning, used more of their causal–temporal model in considering the impact of altered events. Thus, counterfactuals demonstrated a quantitative influence of learning on reasoning that is both substantive and structural. Substantively, students increasingly cited knowledge in responding to questions. Structurally, learning led to more complexity in reasoning.

As a third conclusion, also from the counterfactuals, it is interesting that subjects typically responded to counterfactual reasoning probes with an altered-outcome view of events. Views of historical inevitability were in the minority, and when they were voiced they were based on specific assumptions of power differentials. The United States, in these cases, was seen as able to assert its will even in altered circumstances. But the trend was clearly toward thinking that if events had gone differently, other events would have gone differently as well. And the events that would be altered can be seen to lie on the causal chain that we claim is the heart of the story. Thus, seeing this kind of counterfactual reasoning is a form of validation for the causal analysis.

Finally, we must conclude that our students were very alert to the source characteristics for the story. They were able to separate the situation from the text. Their spontaneous comments on the texts demonstrated their awareness of authors' bias. And their answers to our questions about sources showed accurate perceptions of what authors believed about the events they were describing. We think this is an important development in mature text learning, and we do not assume that it comes readily. Many students may have trouble separating a model of the situation from a model of the source arguments.[13] It may be that multiple texts make this distinction more clear: The texts refer to the same situation and share descriptions of its events. Accordingly, their differences as texts, sources with rhetorical goals, can become more visible.

---

[13]See Rouet, Perfetti, Britt, and Favart (1994) for a discussion of source argument models.

Chapter 6

Individual Learners and Reasoners

In general quantitative ways, we have seen how a small number of students, reading from several texts, learned and reasoned about the Panama Canal story over a course of weeks. The students, however, were individuals, each with a distinctive background and a characteristic approach to the learning and reasoning tasks. Although individual differences are always present in learning, they are typically invisible, either because the research design is blind to them, the number of subjects is too large, or both. In our case, the number of learners was small, and our sustained interactions with them over weeks of instruction made their individual differences more visible.

Of course, individuals, including our subjects, were different in many ways, so we are quite selective in examining individual differences. We focus on those differences that are informative for understanding the general course of learning and reasoning. Individual variation is assured and is of little interest in itself. What is of interest is *how* individuals differed in their learning. If the texts present a story with the kind of temporal structure we suggested, then all or most students should acquire this same basic structure, rather than some idiosyncratic representation. Individual differences should lie in other features—their rate of learning, their final level of learning, their attention to details, and other factors that reflect individual talents and approaches to this learning situation. For example, students might differ in how they summarize—more or less detail, more or less representation of core events, more or less influence from the most recently read text. Individual differences might also be traced to background knowledge.

In reasoning, we focus on individual differences in complexity of reasoning, the influence of texts, and the students' approach to value questions. There is less reason to expect any particular commonalities among individuals, beyond their uniform compliance in responding to our questions. But there is ample reason to wonder whether some students showed more resistance to text influence than others, for example, and whether individuals differed in their basic approach to value questions. We are not guided by strong prior convictions on these reasoning issues, but we assume that individual backgrounds, knowledge, and beliefs, as well as what an individual has learned, play a role.

In what follows, we first describe the individual backgrounds of our students; then we examine each student's distinctive characteristics as he or she learned and reasoned while studying the history of the Panama Canal. We report the same kinds of information on all subjects: their academic background, relevant history knowledge, social-political opinions, current events knowledge, and their news habits. We also characterize each student's style of participation in the project—the time they spent reading the assignments and sometimes the circumstances of their reading. In describing their learning patterns, we characterize for each subject the pace and style of their learning—their reading times, their learning of events over time, their learning of supporting facts over time, and the character of their summaries. (Appendix D presents the summary written by each student following Congressman X's text.) Finally, we characterize each student's reasoning, his or her distinctive characteristics in reasoning about the problems we posed, and how the different texts influenced that reasoning. For the latter, we focus on the key parts of the story concerning the revolution.

EILEEN (TEXT DRIVEN AND CAUTIOUS)

Eileen, a psychology major with a minor in biology, was distinctly "text driven": Her responses to our questions focused on what the text said, and were very sparing of opinions and speculations based on the texts. Her initial knowledge of the Panama Canal was fair: She answered 48% of the Panama questions correctly. She knew a bit about the acquisition of the Canal Zone and could locate relevant countries on the map test (Panama, Colombia, the United States, and the Pacific Ocean); however, she had very little knowledge about the 1977 treaty negotiations and the 1989 U.S. invasion of Panama. She had average general history and geography knowledge. She had taken two history classes in her 4 years in college.

Eileen had some knowledge of World War II, although she underestimated the numbers of people killed in the Holocaust.[14] Her opinion of Hitler was that he "tried his best to solve a problem in his country that needed to be solved but had some prejudices that included evil actions." Like most students, she was unable to

---

[14]We presented students with an additional series of history questions on World War II, the Holocaust, and current events in world politics. Most subjects had some limited knowledge about these topics and we report an individual's knowledge only when it is remarkable in some way. We followed these knowledge questions with opinion questions related to the Holocaust and to current events in world politics. The opinion questions of interest are: (a) What is your opinion of Hitler? (b) David Duke recently sent a book to his constituents arguing that the Holocaust did not exist. What do you think of this?, (c) Japanese-Americans were forcibly relocated within the U.S. during World War II. They were placed in internment camps in unpopulated areas of the country. If you were alive in 1942, would you think this was rational? Does it seem rational today?, (d) What do you think about Eastern European countries' move to democracy?, and (e) With all the changes we've seen in the last year, do you think the Soviet Union is still a large threat to the United States or do we face bigger problems?

identify David Duke, and, when informed about Duke's book denying the Holocaust, said that "history only exists in people's minds. I don't know what he is trying to do." Eileen, as illustrated in this example, usually avoided conclusions. However, on the question of Japanese internment during World War II she thought it "seems so terrible. [We] know they're Japanese. If they were Russians or someone who looked like us it wouldn't have happened. [It was] sensible because of the fear then but not right." As for the Soviet Union, she thought it was "not a large threat. A bigger problem is the environment and the growing population..."

Eileen reported that she watched television news and read *Time* magazine once every 2 weeks. Like all the other subjects, she had never been politically active, and had never belonged to a political organization. Like most subjects, she only occasionally discussed politics with friends. Eileen considered her political views to be average compared to her peers. She did not have strong opinions on political and historical issues. On 22 opinion statements ranging from foreign to domestic policy, she produced no "extreme" opinions.[15]

Eileen was above average in reading skill, as were most other students. In carrying out the reading assignments, she tended to spend considerable time on each text and to learn the details well. She read the first (Online) text slowly, 143 words per minute, and read treaty names especially slowly.[16] She spent a very long time reading Text 2 (CSIS) and an average time reading the other texts. She was one of only two students to report that she consistently reviewed a text prior to coming to the lab to discuss it.

Learning and Summarization Profile

Table 6.1 is a quantitative summary of each individual subject's learning over the four assignments. It shows learning of events and supporting facts and decomposes the latter into facts available from the first text onward (initial supporting facts) and those additional facts from later texts (noninitial supporting facts).

Eileen's learning was quantitatively average. Her learning of noninitial supporting facts came largely from the second text, with minor increases after subsequent assignments. Both her fact learning and her event learning began modestly, and accelerated rapidly after the second text. She learned additional

---

[15]We asked students to rate their opinions on many different topics: general U.S. policy in Central America, specific U.S. policy in Panama, U.S. domestic policy, and U.S. foreign policy. The opinion statements are in Appendix C. An "extreme" opinion is not extreme in the usual normative sense, but merely refers to a rating at either end of the bipolar rating scale. The two opinion statements under "personal beliefs" were not included in this evaluation of the students' opinions.

[16]The Online text, which was read in the lab, was presented one line at a time. The students controlled the rate of presentation by pressing the space bar. When a new line appeared, the previous line disappeared. To determine the distribution of subjects' reading times, we segmented the text information into story ($N = 57$), treaty terms and negotiations ($N = 23$), dates ($N = 11$), treaty names ($N = 7$), U.S. policy information ($N = 6$), and Panama revolution ($N = 5$).

TABLE 6.1
Each Student's Event and Supporting Fact Learning by Text

	Events	Supporting Facts	Initial Supporting Facts	Noninitial Supporting Facts
Eileen				
Text 1	25	62	62	
Text 2	31	125	83	42
Text 3	32	137	82	55
Text 4	34	115	60	55
Dave				
Text 1	25	75	75	
Text 2	30	108	61	47
Text 3	34	151	57	94
Text 4	31	137	74	63
Jen				
Text 1	24	63	63	
Text 2	29	82	59	23
Text 3	29	108	73	35
Text 4	35	127	68	59
Mitch				
Text 1	32	56	56	
Text 2	32	102	75	27
Text 3	35	146	56	90
Text 4	32	134	77	57
Robbie				
Text 1	23	44	44	
Text 2	31	63	55	8
Text 3	28	76	50	26
Text 4	33	103	56	47
George				
Text 1	32	126	126	
Text 2	31	153	113	40
Text 3	35	202	127	75
Text 4	36	220	73	147

supporting facts after Texts 2 through 4, but she also maintained reference to previously learned (Initial) supporting facts. Eileen's learning was free of confusions and errors, and it included an impressive mastery of names, dates, treaty terms and relations among countries. She correctly referred to nearly all 16 dates and six treaties contained in the texts at one time or another.

Eileen learned substantial amounts from all motifs; best learned were U.S. *Motives to Build* and *U.S.–Panama Treaty* and least learned were *Early Attempts* and *Find a Place to Build*. Compared with other students, she learned a great deal about the *French Attempt*.

Eileen's 8-line summaries were longer than most others, averaging 106 words per summary. They included an average number of supporting facts, most of which were initial facts (average per summary = 12) rather than additional facts (average = 3). Because her summaries continued to refer primarily to initial supporting facts, they were stable over time and not influenced by the most recent text.

Eileen's summaries were a strong reflection of what she had learned, containing 21% of her total acquired information. As one would expect with a good summary, Eileen's contained more core events (47% of the core events learned) than noncore events (23% of the noncore events learned). As can be seen from her sample summary (Appendix D), her summaries also included supporting facts, especially names, dates, and terms of treaties.

Reasoning Profile

As a reasoner, Eileen showed three distinctive qualities: She was reluctant to give her own opinion, she gave simple responses, and she was highly influenced by the texts. Evidence that she was a cautious reasoner, one who would respond only with adequate information, appeared throughout her reasoning responses. Of the 20 reasoning questions, she declined to answer 8 after the first text and 4 after the second. She often explained that she didn't have enough information to answer the question, a reasonable reservation after the first two texts, which were not explicit on these topics. Even later, however, having read more informative texts, she sometimes preferred to respond by "according to the text..." rather than risk an uninformed opinion. As another sign of her cautious approach, Eileen included more qualifiers in her counterfactual responses than the other students.

Eileen's rather simple reasoning style was characterized by short responses usually containing a single option. Compared with other students, she provided fewer reasons to support her value judgments and confrontational answers, and she used less knowledge in the confrontationals.

The texts noticeably influenced Eileen. She frequently changed her response in the value questions, shifting closer to the author's position. In a rather different sense of text sensitivity, she was the only student who consistently wanted more information when asked whether the author gave enough details "to paint a complete picture." We can characterize Eileen as being quite sensitive to comprehension monitoring. Her close reading of a text made her more alert to the incompleteness.

One example of text effects is seen in Eileen's answer to the question of whether the U.S. intervention in the Panamanian revolution was justified. She responded affirmatively after reading Congressman X and repeated his argument that the Bidlack Treaty allowed a U.S. military presence; after reading Professor Y she was not sure the Bidlack Treaty supported the military landing. Although she did not reverse her opinion on this question, Y's text appears to have caused her to question

X's argument. In another instance, Eileen attributed the Panamanian rebellion to wealthy Panamanians after she read Congressman X, who had argued that the uprising had been planned by businessmen hoping to make a profit from a canal.

Another question about the Panamanian revolution illustrates the learning effects in Eileen's reasoning responses, which tended to become more complex over assignments.[17] Asked what would have happened had the Panamanian revolution been unsuccessful, her response after the first text was that there would have been a canal governed by the Hay–Herran Treaty (the treaty between the United States and Colombia rejected by Colombia). After the second assignment, she thought there would be a different treaty and explained why. After Congressman X, she added the possibility that there might be no canal. Finally, after her last reading, Professor Y, she gave three different options for how things might have turned out differently.

In summary, Eileen was a text-driven effective learner. Her learning was impressive on treaty names, and dates. Her summaries captured essentially core events, with relevant supporting facts, drawn primarily from her initial learning. She was cautious in reasoning as well as in learning, sticking closely to what she had read. Her reasoning developed in complexity as she learned more. Although she was influenced by texts, she was keenly aware of what the text contained and what it lacked.

Table 6.2 lists some characteristics of each student's learning, summary writing, and reasoning responses.

DAVE (KNOWLEDGE-DRIVEN BUT INFLUENCEABLE)

Dave had above average history and geography knowledge, although he had no college history courses. Unlike the other higher knowledge subject (George), Dave seemed to have gained his knowledge through a practical interest in political and current events. In answering our questions, he was the most willing to speculate based on general knowledge. He was the oldest subject (25), although only a sophomore, majoring in information science with a minor in communications. His Panama knowledge was higher than average in every respect. In addition to knowing something about the acquisition of the Panama Canal and being able to locate relevant countries on the map test, he was the only subject to know much about more recent Panama–U.S. events.

Dave was the only student to correctly identify David Duke. He thought Hitler was a "charismatic leader but deranged individual who was able to rise to power only due to the severe social, political and economic stress of pre-World War II Germany" and that David Duke's book denying the Holocaust was "bullshit. Too

---

[17]Complex responses are those that provide more than one option to a reasoning probe or contain justifications or evidence for an opinion.

TABLE 6.2
Characteristics of the Students' Learning, Summary, and Reasoning Responses

Learning	Summary	Reasoning
Eileen		
Gradual strong event and supporting fact learning	Core event summarizer	Cautious
Detailed	Lengthy	Simple
Accurate	Informative	Text influenced
Text driven		No consistent definition of fair
Dave		
Gradual strong event and supporting fact learning	Not a core event summarizer	Complex
Not detailed	*U.S.–Panama Treaty* motif strongest	Fair defined as nonintervention
U.S.–Panama Treaty motif strongest	Not detailed	
Focused on negotiations	Text influenced	
Jen		
Slow event and supporting fact learning	Core event summarizer	Simple
Not detailed	Short	Stable
		Fair defined as pragmatic/economic and nonintervention
Mitch		
Early event and gradual supporting fact learning	Not core event summarizer	Complex
Not detailed	Short	Stable
Less accurate	Vague	Fair defined as legal
	Least informative	
Robbie		
Slow event and supporting fact learning	Core event summarizer	Simple
Not detailed	Confused	Stable
Confused and inaccurate		Fair defined as legal
No mastery of any motif		
George		
Strong event and supporting fact learning	Core event summarizer	Complex
Detailed	Learned all motifs	Fair defined as legal
Thorough	Stable	Used knowledge
	Lengthy and informative	

many eyewitnesses, actual physical things like graves and buildings. He's a dangerous man. The only people more dangerous are the people who believe him." As for Japanese–American internment camps, he said "no [internment was] not rational, but I can see how it happened. The country and the world were in a panic. I can see how it happened but it doesn't make it right. That's a black eye in recent American history. Maybe recent Japanese immigrants should've been watched but not do that to all Japanese-Americans, war time emergency or not, No definitely not." He believed that "the U.S.S.R. is no longer a major threat, as its economic and food problems would prevent it from financing a war or continuing an arms race. Larger, global problems include the environment and regional disputes that may lead to war."

Dave seemed very interested in knowing what was going on in the world around him. He watched national television news daily, and read the local paper and *Insight* magazine. Dave accurately believed his political views to be somewhat more liberal than his peers. He was the only subject who strongly believed that it was his obligation to be well informed about local and global events and concerns. (All others moderately agreed with this statement.)

Dave had the most coherent ideology of the group, and he was the most skeptical of U.S. actions. He held firm opinions, indicating strong opinions on 7 of the 22 opinion questions, primarily on items concerning domestic policy. These included sponsoring "tasteful" art, gun control, capital punishment, Bill of Rights freedoms, and health services for all. His positions could be classified as socially liberal.

In carrying out the homework assignments, Dave spent a longer than average time reading, usually in his living room or on the campus lawn. Like Eileen, he followed his initial reading with review prior to the lab session. His reading rate for the first (Online) text was average (160 words per minute), and, as for most students, was slower on treaty names. He spent an especially long time reading the texts of Professor Y and Congressman X. Dave was the only student to read the treaties, which we provided but did not assign as required reading.

Learning and Summarization Profile

Quantitatively, Dave's learning was average. He continued to learn additional events after the second and third assignments. Like all the other students, his best performance was 75%–80% of the total events that could have been learned. Dave's learning of initial supporting facts was better after the first text than most other students. He continued to learn additional (noninitial) supporting facts after every text, while retaining the initial supporting facts each time. A noteworthy aspect of Dave's learning of supporting facts was, in contrast to Eileen's, the absence of treaty names—only one mention of a treaty name over four sessions. Neither did he learn more dates over subsequent readings.

Dave did not make many errors. He did, however, have two rather consistent confusions that had not cleared up by his last reading. He confused the early and late treaties between the United States and Britain, a confusion partially due to his failure to learn the treaty names. His second confusion was also a problem for other students: distinguishing among the Frenchman Bunau-Varilla, the French government, and a privately owned French company (New Panama Canal Company) that included Bunau-Varilla as an owner.

Dave learned a lot about some motifs by the first or second assignment, then changed focus to learn those motifs he had not learned. (Initially, he learned about *Motives to Build*, *Early Attempts*, and *Find a Place to Build*, later focusing on the *U.S.–Panama Treaty*.) He learned the most about the *U.S.–Panama Treaty* and the least about the *French Attempt*. Relative to other students, Dave learned more about the *Early Attempts* and the *U.S.–Panama Treaty*, and less about the *French Attempt*. After each reading his knowledge of the *Panamanian Revolution* increased until it was very high after the final text.

Dave's short summaries were of average length (85 words) and contained the fewest number of hyperabstractions (i.e., statements void of reference to specific events). His summaries, however, showed less focus on core events than did those of other students, only 27% of the core events he had learned. His reference to noncore events was about average (17% of noncore events learned). His inclusion of core supporting facts, 8% of what he had learned, was typical of the group; however, he included a higher percentage of noncore supporting facts (14% of what he learned).

Dave's summaries focused on the *U.S.–Panama Treaty* motif and reflected text differences in the treatment of the treaty. After reading Professor Y's text, Dave's summary included the claims that the negotiations were biased against the Panamanians and that this led to anti-American sentiments in Panama. Although Dave's summary after reading Congressman X's text focused on the same motif, *U.S.–Panama Treaty*, it referred to the benefits of the treaty and the canal to Panamanians. Dave's summaries were devoid of dates, and names of treaties. Unlike Eileen, he showed more interest in the negotiations and political maneuvering to complete the treaty than names and dates.

Reasoning Profile

Dave's reasoning showed two distinctive characteristics. First, he was a complex reasoner, providing multiple options in his responses to reasoning questions. Specifically, he offered more *outcome-altered* possibilities in the counterfactuals than any other student. Because outcome-altered responses require the students to change some part of their causal model, providing multiple options demands a good mastery of the story and some sophistication in constructing plausible outcomes, attributes Dave displayed more than most students. In addition, Dave sometimes provided multiple perspectives on a problem. One example came after he read Professor Y and responded to the question *Was the U.S. role in Panama's revolution justified?* Dave demonstrated his awareness that value questions require perspective taking, something not shown by most students: "That depends on whose point of view...from a straight American viewpoint, yes they were justified in that the ends justify the means....But if you look at it objectively and fairly, no, if you agree that each nation has the right to run its own affairs with minimum intervention by other nations."

Dave's second distinctive characteristic was his tendency to judge whether something was "fair" in terms of national rights, a right to be free of outside interference. His response to the justification of U.S. involvement in the revolution, cited earlier, exemplifies this tendency. Given this concept of fairness, Dave generally justified his value judgments with responses in the nonintervention category. Unlike the other students, he never used ethical justifications.

Dave was especially affected by the text arguments in the eight reasoning questions that concerned the Panamanian revolution segment of the story. His responses following Congressman X were almost always different from those following Professor Y. In three of these revolution-related questions, his responses were consistent over the first three texts, only to be altered after reading Congressman X. For example, Dave responded that the U.S. role in the revolution was not justified after the first and second texts, and again after Professor Y; after reading X he believed the United States was justified. To be clear, the typical influence exerted by X on Dave was less than this example of complete reversal. Still, in seven of the eight questions about the revolution, there was at least a slight shift in Dave's opinion in the direction of Congressman X.[18] We could detect a very direct influence of X in Dave's comment that if Panama had been able to win its freedom without U.S. intervention, it "would've been independence of a swamp." This not only echoes Congressman X's argument that U.S. political and economic backing is what made Panama a successful nation, it also echoes X's description of Panama before 1903: "a geographical expression, a poverty-stricken, pestilential province of Colombia racked by internal disorder." Interestingly, Dave seemed to be affected more by Congressman X than by Professor Y, despite a closer match of views with Y. Nevertheless there were examples of influence from both authors in Dave's responses to reasoning probes.

In summary, Dave was a student with higher than average knowledge of history, an interest in current events, and liberal opinions. He was an effective learner who tended to focus his summaries on one motif, the interpretation of the U.S.–Panama treaty. His reasoning was complex and showed richer perspectives on the questions, and reflected a view of fairness based on nonintervention.

JEN (AVERAGE MINIMALIST LEARNER)

Jen was a 20-year-old junior psychology major with a minor in English literature. She had average history knowledge and had taken one college history course. Her

---

[18]An example of a more subtle influence of Congressman X on Dave comes in his response to the question *Were the U.S. dealings with Colombia fair to Colombia?* Although he consistently stated that the United States was fair to Colombia in most respects, he had also expressed doubts about this judgment after Texts 2 and 3. After reading X, he dropped this hedge.

initial Panama knowledge was average (38% of the Panama questions answered correctly). Although she could locate topic-relevant countries on the map test, she knew very little about the canal acquisition period and even less about the more recent events in Panama. Her geography knowledge was poor.

She was one of only two students to accurately estimate the number of people killed in the Holocaust. About Hitler she said "he was an insane man who felt insecure about himself as a leader. He wanted to play god and he tried by wiping out 6 million Jews." She believed that Duke's book "is ridiculous. Being Jewish I'm biased, but I feel that 6 million Jews died and he's saying it is a mistake is preposterous." About internment camps, "the government believed it was rational because they felt that Japanese-Americans would turn on the U.S. No [not sensible] these people had every right to be free. That is why they came to America." When asked about what she thought about Eastern European countries' movement towards democracy she said, "I think it is wonderful. My ancestors are Russian and my grandmother has told me stories that are unbelievable. If the Soviet Union and surrounding countries are able to experience democracy then they should be given a chance." She felt that "if the Soviet Union becomes a democratic state it will be easier for the leaders to sit down and discuss the future of the arms race, which I feel is the biggest problem right now." As illustrated by her comment about her grandmother's stories, she often added a personal connection to her answers.

Jen's opinions were moderate, with only one extreme opinion on the 22 opinion statements (the abortion question). She considered her political views average compared to her peers. She reported that she got news from watching television news and reading the *Wall Street Journal* about three times weekly.

Jen's reading pattern can be characterized as compliant. She did what was required, but not more. She read the assignments in a campus building, spending an average amount of time, and did not review assignments before our meetings. Her reading of the Online text was fast (199 words per minute) and, as was typical, slower on treaty names. She spent an average amount of time reading all other texts. The only atypical aspect about her reading pattern was the timing. Whereas most others either read or reviewed assignments within 1 day of the scheduled lab meeting, Jen read her assignments an average of 3 days prior to the meeting.

Learning and Summarization Profile

Jen's learning was quantitatively average. A gradual learner, she steadily increased the number of supporting facts learned after each subsequent text: Nevertheless, Jen learned less additional information than most subjects. Her initially learned facts, by contrast, were well retained. Jen did not learn dates and, after her best reading, she had learned only half of the six treaty names. However, she did learn details about the terms of the treaties from the second assignment onward.

Jen showed a few minor confusions that were cleared up by the third assignment. After the first text, for example, she believed that the critical Hay–Herran Treaty between the United States and Colombia was between the United States and Nicaragua. She also thought the treaty the United States signed with Britain to eliminate British participation in any future canal had been signed with France. Such confusions are to be expected when a student fails to learn names and dates. There were too many treaties to remember them simply as, for example, "the one with Britain." Along with Eileen, Jen also showed a slight confusion about the terms of the treaty between the United States and Panama. The texts compared the treaty signed between the United States and Colombia to the U.S.–Panama treaty and noted that the Panama treaty was more favorable to the United States. Eileen and Jen incorrectly generalized this advantage by saying that the United States paid less money to the Panamanians than the U.S.–Colombia treaty required.

Jen's learning was incomplete as well as gradual, and she was still learning about most of the motifs at the end. She learned the most about the *Panamanian Revolution* motif and the least about *Early Attempts*, the *French Attempt*, and *Find a Place to Build* motifs. Compared with other subjects, Jen showed no superior learning of any motif, but for one motif, *Early Attempts*, she learned the least.

Jen's summaries were shorter than most others, averaging 74 words per summary, but they included an average amount of information, about 15% of what she learned. Her summaries were mainly unelaborated events, more core events (45%) than noncore events (22%). Her summaries rarely included facts, only 7% of the core supporting facts and 4% of the noncore supporting facts that she had learned. Her statements on treaty information were vague and expressed colloquially. No summary referred to any treaty by name, allowing confusion between the two U.S. treaties with Colombia and the two with Britain. Her short summaries were stable across readings.

Reasoning Profile

Jen, like Eileen, was a simple reasoner. On one of our measures of complexity, the distance score for counterfactual questions (chapter 5), Jen had the lowest score of any subject.[19] Moreover, her responses to counterfactuals rarely used qualifiers. Her reasoning was simple in another sense: She seemed unaware of the texts' biases. She believed that the texts by Congressman X and Professor Y were neutral, although there was evidence that she was influenced by arguments made by both authors.

Like Dave, Jen seemed to identify fairness with nonintervention, with some consideration of financial aspects. Her justifications for the value judgments generally were classified as either nonintervention or pragmatic/economic.

---

[19] Although one of Jen's characteristics was simplicity, she gave a response of increasing complexity when discussing whether the Panamanian revolution would have been successful without U.S. aid. After the first text, she felt the rebellion would have been unsuccessful, because the United States would not have helped Panama if Panama had nothing to offer the United States. After the second text, she added an alternative canal location to her response, and after Professor Y, she added a third option.

Another characteristic of Jen's reasoning was its stability. She gave rather consistent opinions in the value judgments and she seemed to be content with the material given by the texts. She rarely asked for more information, and, in general, showed no interest in reevaluating either her understanding or her conclusions.

Jen, however, was influenced by the texts; this effect was especially seen in the eight reasoning questions dealing with the Panamanian revolution. After three of the texts, she believed the United States was not fair to Panama and cited Bunau-Varilla's involvement as a reason. After reading Congressman X, her judgment on the fairness question was less certain, and she failed to mention Bunau-Varilla at all. In another reasoning question Jen responded, after all texts except Congressman X's, that the revolution would not have been successful without U.S. interest in a canal. Her response after reading Congressman X conformed with his view that the United States was not involved in the revolution. As noted earlier Jen did not seem to see text bias in X, and she gave no indication that she believed that X caused her to change her mind.

An influence of Professor Y also occurred, although less often. After reading Professor Y, Jen reasoned that Panamanian nationalists caused the revolution, consistent with Professor Y's argument on this point. She also believed that the Panamanians would have ultimately gained independence because independence was such a strong desire, also consistent with Y's argument. Reading Professor Y also prompted more thorough responses from Jen in discussion of the revolution. For the counterfactual *What if the revolution had not been successful?*, Jen gave a more comprehensive response that referred to Panama rather than the more typical response that considered only a U.S. perspective.

In summary, Jen's relevant knowledge was typical and modest, her opinions were moderate, and she appeared not to do more than what was required. Her learning was gradual, but incomplete, and showed a lower than average acquisition of additional details with successive assignments. Her summaries were event-driven and unelaborated. Her reasoning was generally stable, although occasionally influenced by texts, apparently without her awareness.

MITCH (AVERAGE LEARNER, POOR SUMMARIZER, COMPLEX REASONER)

Mitch was a 19-year-old sophomore with no declared major. His history knowledge was average, although he had taken two college classes in ancient history. His specific Panama knowledge was average (43% of the Panama questions answered correctly). He could locate the topic-relevant countries on the map test, but he knew very little about the acquisition period and even less about more recent events in Panama. His geography knowledge was also average.

Mitch underestimated the magnitude of the Holocaust. He thought Hitler "was warped (Aryan superiority) but it was incredible the way he turned Germany from

a broken country into a threat to world domination." He could not identify David
Duke, but when informed of his book said "I don't know what he is trying to
do....Pretty much an insult to everyone's intelligence to say that something like
that never happened. It's documented, you can see the buildings." As for the
internment camps, he said "could have been justified but I don't know if it was
rational." He thought that "the U.S.S.R. was only a threat after World War II, but
today there are larger scale problems to worry about, ozone layer, pollution,
apartheid, and third world poverty."

Mitch's opinions were mainly moderate, tending toward more socially liberal,
and he rated himself somewhat more liberal than his peers. He showed strong
opinions on only three of the 22 opinion statements, two of which could be
considered socially liberal responses (abortion and "tasteful" art); the third
concerned foreign policy (United States not obligated to protect world from
communism). He watched television news or read the local newspaper three or
more times a week.

Mitch read the first text slowly (141 words per minute) with exceptionally
slower reading times on treaty names and relatively faster times on story
information. For most subsequent texts, he reported an average amount of time
spent on the assignments, which were read in his living room immediately prior to
the lab session.

Learning and Summarization Profile

Mitch's learning was average, quantitatively. However, unlike most other students,
he learned nearly all the events he was going to learn after the first reading. His
learning of details was similar to Eileen's, initially slow but dramatically increased
over the next two texts. He learned a lot of additional (noninitial) supporting facts
after Professor Y. Like Jen, he learned only half of the six treaty names and very
few of the 16 dates.

Mitch had slightly more errors and confusions than most of the others. His
confusions, like those of Jen, often centered on the participating countries. He
thought that the U.S.-built railroad was in Nicaragua (not a minor error) and that
Colombia was once a British colony instead of a Spanish one. Mitch also had
problems with dates that persisted throughout. For example, he thought that the
Panamanian revolution occurred in 1904 (rather than 1903), a less trivial error than
it might appear. The timing of the revolution is very important for understanding
causal and enabling factors, because the revolution enabled the United States to
sign a treaty with Panama in 1903. However, Mitch did grasp the basic story,
including the basic causal–temporal links, despite incorrect details. He appeared to
have not noticed contradictions between his inconsistent beliefs. Thus, he believed
(correctly) that Colombia failed to suppress the Panamanian Revolution because
Colombia was unable to use the U.S.-controlled railroad in Panama while also
believing incorrectly that the U.S.-built railroad was in Nicaragua. Either these were

two different railroads for him, or it was not important to him to build a coherent story.

Mitch learned most about the *Panamanian Revolution* motif and the least about the *Early Attempts* motif. Relative to other subjects, Mitch was average in the extent to which he learned the motifs.

Mitch wrote the shortest summaries (average of 66 words). They were low in information, only about 8% of what he learned. Although his summaries contained primarily events rather than supporting facts, they were highly selective as event summaries, containing only 27% of the core events and 13% of the noncore events that he had learned. Details were sparse, only 5% of the core supporting facts and 2% of the noncore supporting facts that he learned. Mitch, in short, distilled the story into a very brief and not very good summary.

Mitch's sparse summaries were not a case of inadequate knowledge, but rather an approach to summary writing. He wrote concisely, vaguely, and with hyperabstractions (more than any other subject). The summaries were essentially lists of events with no elaboration on the connections among events. They not only lacked both dates and treaty names, they gave bare mention to the Panamanian revolution, and provided no details on the U.S.–Panama treaty. Like most students, Mitch's summaries showed little specific text influences. To the extent they were summaries at all, they were summaries of the story.

Reasoning Profile

Mitch, like Dave, showed complex reasoning; like Jen, his opinions were stable over time. He differed from both, however, in approaching fairness as a legal concept. Complexity was seen in his distance scores for the counterfactual questions, which were the highest among the students. He also had the largest proportion of outcome-altered to outcome-preserved replies in the counterfactuals. Outcome-altered responses, as we have noted, require the students to think about the story and change some of the events to suggest viable alternatives.

Mitch showed more stability than other students in reasoning about value questions. He was the only student not to change his opinion more than half the time. Not only was he less swayed by texts, he showed no evidence of either text-specific information or text argument in half of his responses. Mitch gave stable and unequivocal opinions. Many of the value judgments had definite claims (a 1 or 5 on our 5-point scale). He seemed satisfied with his ability to make a judgment with the information he had learned. Unlike Eileen, he never declined to give an opinion because he lacked facts.

On the concept of fairness seen in his reasoning, Mitch was a "legalist." In his justifications of fairness judgments, something was fair if it was allowed by law. Fairness was not an ethical consideration. However, neither was it "the ends justified the means."

In the questions dealing with the Panamanian revolution, Mitch showed some text influence. However, unlike most other students, he seemed more likely to be influenced by Professor Y. In response to two questions after reading Y, he referred to the connection between Bunau-Varilla and Roosevelt in the Panamanian revolution, a connection covered only in Professor Y's text. In another question he explained why Colombian resistance to the Panamanian revolution was ineffective by describing, using Y's characterization, the type of people living in Panama. Mitch noted "[Y] said they were refugees and boxers. They were feisty people. They were constantly rejecting authority."

We cannot be sure why Mitch was more influenced by Professor Y than by Congressman X, but the fact that he read Y first, coupled with a mistrust of Congressman X might have played a role. Mitch perceived himself as more liberal than his peers, and this may have an international as well as a domestic dimension, although we have evidence only for the latter. There is evidence that he had doubts about X's text. He thought that "[X]...omits little things to make it seem more on the up and up."

In summary, Mitch, a sophomore with moderately liberal opinions and average relevant knowledge, was an effective learner. Although his learning produced confusions, these were cleared up by the end. His summaries were poor, only vague reflections of what he had learned. His reasoning was influenced more by Y's text than X's, in contrast to most students. His reasoning was complex and quite stable over time.

ROBBIE (NO KNOWLEDGE, SIMPLISTIC OPINIONS)

Robbie was the youngest subject, an 18-year-old freshman with no selected major. He had no prior knowledge of Panama (14% correct on the Panama questions), no significant general history knowledge, and had not taken a college history course. Robbie had trouble with rather ordinary terms important in everyday historical and political discourse, and he frequently asked for definitions of these terms (e.g., *imperialism, apartheid*). A major misunderstanding of the definition of a revolution hampered his understanding of the events until the fourth reading. He understood "revolution" as an exact synonym for "war," interfering with his ability to understand that Panama was fighting only to gain independence from Colombia. He was the only subject who could not locate Colombia and Panama on the map test, consistent with his extremely low geographical knowledge. Robbie had no knowledge about events in Panama since the canal was built.

Although Robbie's World War II and Holocaust knowledge was comparable to others, his generally low knowledge extended to current affairs. He was the only subject who did not know about the highly publicized 1989 Chinese student demonstrations in Tiananmen Square and their suppression by the Chinese government. He was also the only student who could not define *apartheid*. He thought Hitler was "a crazy dude. I don't understand how people could follow him in such loyalty." As for Duke's book (he hadn't heard of Duke) "he's on drugs, he's crazy. I don't know where he's at. It is just an absurd statement." On internment camps, "No, they would have to investigate certain people before they could move [them]. If they live here [in the United States], I think it's obvious that they wanted to be American-well not be American but agree with our point of view. Not at all [sensible]—can't move a bunch of Japanese-Americans looking for a few spies. That's irrational." His belief about the Soviet Union as a current threat was: "I feel that the Soviet Union is always a big problem. But the big problem is if the Soviet Union and Germany get together against the U.S."

Robbie could be said to have "raw" reasoning ability rather than knowledge: He had the highest score on the analytic section of a GRE that we gave the students as part of Session 3. However, his reasoning was naive and moralistic, seldom reflecting critical attitudes toward issues raised in the texts. He was nonopinionated, but in a manner different from Eileen and Jen. Whereas Eileen and Jen had moderate opinions on most of the questions (2s and 4s on our 5-point scale), Robbie appeared to have no opinions (3 on the scale) on 15 of the 22 questions. He indicated strong opinions against restrictions on abortion, against outlawing capital punishment, and in favor of a policy under which the United States would launch an invasion to protect U.S. citizens living in another country. We may infer that his lack of knowledge made it appropriate for Robbie to not hold strong opinions.

Not only did he show little knowledge of current events, but Robbie was the only subject who reported seldom discussing politics with friends. He also was the only student to get his news exclusively from television, although he implied even television news was not a habit. (He watched the news, he said, "if something big happens.") Robbie considered his political views to be somewhat more liberal than his peers, an assessment not necessarily consistent with his opinion ratings.

Although Robbie scored lower on the reading comprehension test than any of our other subjects, he was an average reader compared to college student norms. His reading rate for the Online text was average (183 words per minute), but, unlike other students, his rate did not change substantially on treaty names. Instead, Robbie spent time reading about the treaty terms and treaty negotiations. He read the section on the Panamanian revolution more quickly than average, and was a bit confused about this event afterwards. Among the subsequent assignments, his reported reading times were unusually short for Professor Y's and Congressman X's texts. He generally read in his girlfriend's living room immediately prior to the lab session. Although he appeared interested in participating and learning, he spent considerably less time than others in conversation with the interviewers and considerably less time than others reading the homework assignments. At the debriefing, at the end of the study, Robbie volunteered that he enjoyed knowing so much about the Panama Canal. He could now tell his parents, he said, about a topic he learned in detail.

Learning and Summarization Profile

Robbie started slowly, but his event learning was eventually average quantitatively, increasing dramatically after the second reading. Like Jen, Robbie was a slow and gradual learner of supporting facts, although his final level of fact learning remained the lowest of all subjects. Again like Jen, Robbie's overall slower learning was due to his failure to acquire additional details. His learning of initial supporting facts was better but still below average. Robbie was not good with dates; he made only two references to dates over the four sessions. His references to treaty names were negligible until the final assignment, when he mentioned 4 of the 6 treaties by name. Similarly, he did not learn the terms of the treaties until his final reading.

Robbie's learning showed the most confusions. More than any subject, he had difficulty grasping the relations among the United States, Colombia, and Panama. These confusions were partially a result of his not understanding the idea of a revolution (see also McKeown & Beck, 1990). His failure to understand diplomatic relations and treaties may also have led to confusion.

Robbie did not master any of the motifs. Rather, he had to continue learning parts of nearly all of them on each assignment. By the last reading he had learned a good deal about all eight motifs, most about the *Panamanian Revolution* motif and least about *Early Attempts* and *Need Permission* motifs. His trouble with the *Need Permission* motif appears to reflect his failure to understand that Panama was Colombia's possession. His learning about the revolution was characterized by a steady increase in the number of details. After a slow start, by the fourth reading he had learned many of the supporting facts of the revolution.

Robbie's short summaries were average in length (80 words per summary), and contained an average amount of information. His summaries also were about average in their inclusion of learned information, an average of 16% over the four summaries. Relative to what he had learned, Robbie's summaries contained a high proportion of the core events (45%) and a small proportion of the noncore events (16%). The proportion of learned supporting facts was low, 12% of learned core supporting facts and 6% of learned noncore supporting facts. Robbie was primarily a core event summarizer.

Robbie's basic 8-line summaries were the most stable over the four occasions. However, his summaries increased in accuracy, and he included more treaty specific information as he progressed. In his first two summaries, Robbie showed no clear understanding of the treaties. From statements such as "Great Britain has control first," "We had some control but could not build a canal," and "France also had control of the property," it is not clear that Robbie understood the fundamentals of treaties and negotiations. By the second reading, he gained some control over the treaty situation, but remained a bit confused about who was making treaties with whom, and what a treaty provided for the two countries. His summaries covered most of the motifs, rather than selecting one or more for focus. Like Jen, Robbie made brief unelaborated references to the Panamanian revolution.

Although we do not report long summaries for our subjects, we show the four successive long summaries for Robbie in Appendix E to illustrate his increased learning of treaty information that we observed in Robbie and referred to in the previous paragraph.

Reasoning Profile

Robbie can be characterized as a simple reasoner (joining Eileen and Jen) with stable opinions (joining Jen and Mitch). Also like Mitch, fairness for Robbie was a legal matter. In fact, Robbie's reasoning can be characterized as the least complex of any subject. The reasoning ability reflected in his high score on an analytic section of the GRE did not transfer to our reasoning problems. In the counterfactual questions, Robbie provided the fewest reasons, used the fewest qualifiers, and produced very low distance scores. He also gave the fewest number of outcome-altered or outcome-preserved options. In the value judgments, he used less knowledge than any of the other students.

Stability was a second hallmark of Robbie's reasoning. Like Mitch, he produced definite claims in most of his value judgments. Robbie was typically unaffected by the authors, providing similar opinions after all texts. For example, he consistently expressed the opinion that the revolution occurred because Panamanians were unhappy with their lives, and not because they wanted the benefits of a canal, despite variations between texts in this argument. In another case, he responded consistently (until the final text) that he believed the outcome of the revolution would have been the same if the United States had not intervened. On these and other questions, there was variation in text treatments that led to instability in student opinions. Robbie's consistency in light of text differences is a puzzle. He was neither high in knowledge nor in ideology. His learning was incomplete and confused. His consistency in reasoning may have reflected limited learning rather than steadfastness.

On the occasions when Robbie showed less stability, he demonstrated what can be summarized as an A-B-A pattern, in which he first stated an opinion, reversed it after reading Professor Y, and then reverted to the original after reading Congressman X. One speculative account of this pattern, given what we know about Robbie, is that Professor Y's text was a bit difficult for him and so after Y he was unable to interpret Y's arguments or incorporate them into his model of the events. Instead, he merely repeated what he had just read and then, at the next reading, forgot those arguments. We know that Robbie was the only student who preferred Congressman X's text to Professor Y's. Only he and Jen thought that X's text was neutral. He liked X's text better because "it seemed like an easier language for me" and, at a different point, he said "I got a lot more out of this one." For a student who was as unfamiliar with history as Robbie, it seems sensible that he would prefer a shorter story with vivid images instead of a more academic, detail-filled text.

On the concept of fairness, Robbie viewed an action or person fair if nothing illegal was done. He seemed unencumbered with any more complex notion of fairness and his responses never contained any reference to values that could be considered moral or ethical. Further, unlike Mitch (another legalist), Robbie seemed to consider events fair if the ends justified the means.

In summary, Robbie was a freshman with no relevant knowledge and negligible awareness of current events. His learning, although successful to a considerable extent, was gradual and difficult. He failed to master all the events of the story, learned new facts slowly, and showed serious confusions about key relations in the story. Although it is reasonable to link these facts to his low knowledge, there are also indicators in his study habits that he might not have worked hard at the later assignments. He wrote very stable core event summaries that increased in accuracy. His reasoning answers were less complex than the other students but more stable. Texts sometimes had an influence, but not often. His reasoning about fairness was amoral.

GEORGE (HIGH KNOWLEDGE, COMPLEX OPINIONS)

George was a 23-year-old senior psychology major with a minor in history. The only subject with any general history knowledge, George had completed six different college history courses (including two terms of American history) and had taken Advanced Placement American and European history classes in high school. His Panama knowledge was well above average (73% correct on the Panama questions), and he was the only student to have visited a Central American country. Although he had some knowledge about the acquisition period and could locate the relevant countries in the map test, George knew very little about more recent events in Panama. His general history and geography knowledge was also higher than average. (George was the only subject to score 100% on the map test, and George and Dave were the only students to score over 75% on the general history test.) Like Dave, he used prior knowledge and analogies to answer our questions throughout the study. His response style was thorough, tending toward the verbose. George seemed to want to tell the complete story without being interrupted by our questions. He rarely needed a probe to complete an answer.

George was also the most knowledgeable subject about World War II, and he provided the generally accepted estimate of the number of people killed in the Holocaust. His answers to opinion questions were complex, showing some understanding of different periods and people, and of complex political situations. He thought Hitler was "a brilliant economist in the rebuilding of depressed Germany in the 1920s and 1930s. However, I feel that he went crazy with the power that he had, and did some very evil things." Although he could not immediately identify David Duke, he proved knowledgeable and loquacious when Duke's book was mentioned: "Oh, that guy. That was rather funny, he even admitted it [being the Grand wizard of the KKK]. I'm sure that got a lot of people frightened…Well considering that he has a basic Nazi point of view, I'd say he honestly believes that it didn't exist. The Nazis didn't believe it existed when they were doing it. I mean they thought they were doing the world a favor killing off all the Jews and what they considered lesser people. So I'd have to say yes, judging from the man's point of view he honestly believed that the Holocaust didn't exist." George was also able to discuss internment camps, and post-Soviet Europe with some complexity.[20]

Prior to the study, George was the only student to indicate a strong opinion on any of the Central American/Panama opinion statements, strongly disagreeing both with the U.S. decision in 1977 to turn the rights to the Canal over to Panama and with the statement that the United States should turn over the Canal regardless of changes in the Panamanian government. Among the other 20 opinion statements, George was "extreme" on three, all on domestic policy. In general, he was more conservative than the other students and rated himself as much more conservative than his peers. In the penultimate session he commented "I'm a conservative at heart. I also come from a heavily Republican area." George reported watching television news, reading *Time* and *U.S. News and World Report*, and generally following news on a daily basis.

George's reading pattern was fairly typical of the group of subjects. His amount of reading time was average and his Online rate was average (169 words per minute), slower on treaty names and comparatively faster on the Panamanian revolution. For subsequent texts, his reading times were average, except for the text by Congressman X for Part 2 of the study. He always read just once, the day prior to our lab session, generally in his living room.

Learning and Summarization Profile

George learned much more than any other subject. (The magnitude of his advantage can be seen in Table 6.1.) He learned both events and supporting facts in impressive numbers from the beginning. By the second reading he had learned more supporting facts than other subjects had after four readings. Especially noteworthy is his

---

[20]On the internment question, George said the following: "Chances are more than likely I would've said yes (back then). It may sound terrible but if I lived in California and Hawaii was 1,500 miles away and Japan bombed them, you'd have to look on a more paranoid point of view. The Italian-Americans and German-Americans didn't get locked up. But they were here a lot longer. I guess on a simple issue they seemed more American because they were caucasian instead of mongoloid. In 1941–42 I'd probably would've said yeah we should lock them up and keep an eye on them. (But today) I think it was terrible. These people lost their livelihood and their property. They were a very decorated unit in the war. We came down on the descendants of that group and used them as scapegoats. Which is basically, I think, what the government was looking for."

To the question asking if the U.S.S.R. is still a threat, George replied, "The U.S.S.R is not a big threat to Eastern European countries, but it still has ICBMs aimed at U.S. We should help the U.S.S.R. but still be wary of them. The main problem to the U.S. is that we'll end up picking up the tab for this."

In response to our question about apartheid and whether it should be abolished, Eileen, Dave, Jen, and Mitch all thought it should be abolished. Robbie did not know what it was. George's answer was, "I don't know if it should be abolished or not, either way, it is none of our damn business."

combination of quick initial learning and sustained learning. Even after exceptional learning through the first two assignments, George continued learning throughout the last two. He acquired additional supporting facts after every reading, while retaining the initially learned facts of the story. (His final impressive learning of facts at the end came from Professor Y's text.) George's learning of dates and treaty names was well beyond that of any other subject except Eileen and his overall learning was superior to all students.

George not only learned much of the story, he did so with few errors and confusions. His three minor errors were cleared up by the third text. One confusion, a rather common one found in another study (Britt, Bell, & Perfetti, 1990), was a failure to distinguish between two French figures in the story, de Lesseps, the leader of the French canal project in the 1880s, and the more central Bunau-Varilla, whose complex role in representing Panama was important in the final resolution of the Acquisition Story. George, like the subjects in our earlier studies, at first blended these to make one very important figure. George's other confusion, shared by two other students (Jen and Eileen), was an incorrect inference about U.S. payments to Panama under the terms of the U.S.–Panama treaty. Unlike Jen and Eileen, who inferred incorrectly that this treaty required the United States to pay less to Panama than it would have had to pay to Colombia (under the failed U.S.–Colombia treaty), George inferred that the U.S.–Panama treaty did not require the United States to pay Panama any money at all. In all these cases, the confusion is an inference made by subjects about a specific treaty term (favorable payment terms) from other treaty comparisons (generally favorable to the United States in the Panama treaty).

George, of course, learned a lot about all the motifs, first learning about the *U.S.–Panama Treaty* motif, then the *Motives to Build*, *British Involvement*, and *Need Permission* motifs, with continued learning about the other motifs throughout the assignments. He learned the most about the *Panamanian Revolution* motif and the least about the *Early Attempts* and *French Attempt* motifs. Relative to other subjects, he learned most of the motifs better: He learned more than any other subject about the *Motives to Build*, *British Involvement*, *Find a Place to Build*, *Need Permission*, and *Panamanian Revolution* motifs.

George's summaries were longer than most others, averaging 104 words per summary, and they contained an above-average amount of information from the second assignment onward. His summaries contained many dates, treaty names, treaty terms, and other specific details. Every summary covered all motifs and connected them well. The short summaries showed little text-specific influence and they were relatively stable over the four sessions. All summaries except the first contained an above-average number of supporting facts.

Relative to the amount he had learned, George's summaries contained an average amount of information, 19% across the four summaries. His average summary contained 58% of the core events he learned, 22% of the learned noncore events, 14% of learned core supporting facts, and 6% of learned noncore supporting facts. Thus, unlike Dave, our other subject with historical knowledge, George was a core event summarizer who used important previously learned details to identify the events.

In contrast to his learning pattern, George's summaries contained mainly initial supporting facts (average = 18) rather than noninitial supporting facts (average = 1). So, for George there was a sharp difference between learning, which was characterized by continuing acquisition of new information, and summarizing, which was characterized by the continuing inclusion of previously learned material.

Reasoning Profile

George's reasoning was quite complex and reflective of substantial knowledge. He consistently gave complex responses from the beginning. For counterfactuals, confrontationals, and value judgments, he provided more reasons than any other subject. He also had a high distance score for the counterfactual questions. In addition, he challenged the assumption of many of the counterfactuals. Indeed, he challenged more counterfactual questions than anyone else. He knew enough to question, for example, the possibility of the Panamanian revolution failing when it was supported by the United States. As a result of this questioning, he gave more outcome-preserved options than the other students.

George's second reasoning characteristic, his use of knowledge, was unique among the subjects. His responses were laced with knowledge beyond the texts (historical analogies, facts, and current events). In some cases, this included an attempt at historical framing. For example, in discussing likely U.S. action in the case of an unsuccessful Panamanian revolution, he referred to "their style at the time of the whole gunboat diplomacy thing." George also included analogies (e.g., "If the U.S. tried to intervene and lost, it would be like Vietnam"). Other responses reflected political and historical assumptions rather than specific knowledge. When asked if the U.S.–Panamanian negotiations would have been different if Bunau-Varilla had not been the sole Panamanian negotiator, all other students agreed that the American representative would have signed a treaty that granted fewer concessions to the United States. George, however, said the outcome would have remained the same because the United States wanted certain rights and would have forced the newly independent, weaker nation to yield to U.S. demands.

George, like Mitch and Robbie, was a legalist. If an action was legal, he evaluated it as fair. However, unlike Robbie, he occasionally noted that even legal events can be ethically questionable. In other cases, he seemed to think that questionable actions on one side determined if the other party's behavior was justified. For example, George said Panama was "just leeching off the American canal to begin with" to justify his belief that the United States was fair to Panama.

George showed some text influence, although somewhat less than most other students, in response to the questions about the Panamanian revolution. After reading Congressman X, who argued that Panamanians rebelled because they wanted a canal, George apparently agreed, responding that a revolution would not have occurred if Colombia had ratified the Hay–Herran Treaty.

We think that one reason George showed less text influence was that he was very aware that the texts were written to persuade their audience. He was very conscious of Congressman X's bias and noted that the text was not objective on several occasions. He did surprise us when he commented "I liked [Professor Y's] article a lot better than the others." He did not favor the more pro-American text of Congressman X because "[Y] was a little more detailed. It gave me more of an insight to some of the people involved. The other article [X's text] made Bunau-Varilla sound like a real saint. I think he probably would've sold his mother to get that treaty."

In summary, George had significant history knowledge and interest in current events. A political conservative, he expressed primarily moderate opinions, but stood out among the subjects in his strong conservative opinions concerning the fate of the Panama Canal Zone. His learning was superior by every measure, and appeared to be strongly cumulative as well as rapid. He learned new facts at every opportunity and integrated them with initially learned facts. His summaries were distinctive in their stable use of the initial facts of the story. His reasoning was characterized by its complexity and use of knowledge, and he took a legalist perspective on fairness.

CONCLUSIONS

Examining the students as individual learners and reasoners provides a view convergent with the conclusions based on group patterns and also makes visible the considerable variation that arises.

Learning

We see that individual learners show a common pattern in several aspects: (a) a strong increase in learning following the second assignment; (b) uniformly strong learning of a central motif in the story, the *Panamanian Revolution*; and (c) uniform sensitivity to the distinction between core events and noncore events. All subjects learned more about the core events than the noncore events, and differentially included these event categories in their summaries.

In other respects, individual differences rather than commonalities are visible:

1. Students varied in their final level of learning and in their rate of learning. Although all students produced large learning gains after their second assignment, some went on to achieve considerably higher levels (George, Dave, Eileen), whereas others gained less subsequently. Mitch's event learning came to a stop after the second session when he had learned almost all the events, whereas his

supporting fact learning continued to improve. Jen had trouble gaining new supporting facts (i.e., facts that were not laid out in the initial text), and even her learning of events remained incomplete. Robbie learned comparatively little from the first text, then learned most of the events that he would eventually learn after the second text. Like Jen, his learning was incomplete.

2. Students varied in their attention to dates and names. Eileen and especially George excelled in this respect and all other students, by comparison, failed to learn names of treaties and various relevant dates. Interestingly, Eileen and George were quite different in other respects, George having higher knowledge and an avowed interest in history. The other higher knowledge student, Dave, showed no learning of dates and names. Eileen's learning of dates may reflect a learning "style," a habitual attitude toward text learning that leads her to attend closely to text detail, whereas George's date and name learning are an intrinsic part of his attempts to understand history.

3. Students varied in their approach to summarizing. Some were quite vague, omitting factual content. Mitch showed the worst case of hyperabstraction, but Jen also tended toward this approach. Others made use of facts in summaries, notably Eileen, George, and Dave. Only some of these differences can be attributed to differential learning, because the percentage of information contained in the summaries, controlled for amount learned, produced the same pattern of individual differences. The use of facts in summaries was a learner characteristic. The students who learned the most supporting facts also used a higher percentage of facts they had learned in their summaries. Mitch remained an exception. He chose, despite some fact learning, not to use facts in his summaries.

There are many other less pronounced differences that might be examined; their interpretation would be difficult. Our goal is to highlight those that are most visible and most likely to be stable. We do not necessarily take individual text learning styles as stable characteristics of students.

Linking learning to student characteristics is interesting but difficult. Some of our learning differences, but not all, stem from relevant knowledge, and that would hardly be news. But we do not know the extent to which knowledge itself made George the best learner of the group. His knowledge can be thought of as a marker for motivation to learn in this domain. Furthermore, among other students, one of the best learners, Eileen, did not have much knowledge. Social-political attitudes appeared to be irrelevant to learning within this group of students. Our best learner was a conservative with mostly moderate opinions, whereas one of our next best learners was a political-social liberal.

Reasoning

There were differences in reasoning along at least three dimensions that we examined. First, there were differences in complexity indicated by several different measures. Dave, George, and Mitch were high in complexity; Eileen, Robbie, and Jen were low in complexity. To some extent, students who showed more complex reasoning were those who had learned more, and thus had more information with which to display complex reasoning. However, this coupling of learning with complexity must be qualified. Eileen was a better learner than Dave on all measures but Dave's reasoning was more complex. Factors beyond learning contribute to complexity. A certain amount of learning, we suggest, is critical for displaying complex reasoning; thus we would not envision any additional complexity from someone like Robbie. Dave's higher complexity, a willingness to consider larger parts of the story in responding, is something one might not have expected based on his average learning. But average learning, in our case, is really quite a bit of learning. The students learned a lot about the story, and their ability to do more or less with that learning is partly a matter of some additional factor—an approach to our tasks, a disposition regarding questions without "right answers," or other individual difference factors.

Second, there were differences in stability and text influence on reasoning. All students allowed what they read to influence their responses to reasoning probes, including questions about fairness. But Eileen and Dave were influenced more than Jen; and Robbie, Mitch, and George were quite stable in their opinions over different texts. It is interesting that the degree of influence was not related to amount of learning in any obvious way; the one who learned most, George, and the one who learned least, Robbie, were both text-resistant. The students showing the most influence were among the best learners. We suggest the more general relationship here is that more learning leads to more text influence in reasoning, even in questions of value, provided the learning is specifically informative for the questions being asked. George is an understandable exception: He appeared to adopt a critical attitude toward the texts; he also appeared to take some pride in his own abilities and knowledge, adding to his text resistance. Our hunch is that it is more typical, under conditions of low knowledge, to allow information presented in texts to affect reasoning on questions for which it is relevant.

Third, part of the difference we observed about students' reasoning on fairness issues—fairness to Panama and Colombia; did the United States do the right thing?—could be attributed to differences in the way students thought about fairness in these contexts. Students from a relatively homogenous background, as these were, can be expected to have a common ethical value to apply to everyday issues of fairness. In international relations, however, the idea of fairness can be interpreted in legalistic, financial, national sovereignty, and other perspectives. Three students—George, Mitch, Robbie—took a strictly legalistic approach to fairness; Jen and Dave took a noninterventionist approach, one that placed value on a nation's right to be free of outside interference. (Their differences have obvious parallels in discussions of basic foreign policy that center on ethics, "realpolitik," etc.) These differences are partly predictable from the attitudes students expressed in our opinion survey and background questioning: Dave, the liberal skeptic of U.S.

foreign policy, valued the right of a small nation to be free from intervention; George, the conservative, valued U.S. national interests that could be pursued strongly within legal limits. Thus, the political-social attitudes that were irrelevant for learning were relevant for value-based reasoning about what was learned.

Part II

The Return Controversy

Chapter 7

Learning and Reasoning About the 1977 Treaties Controversy

To this point, we have focused on the Acquisition Story, how students learned and reasoned about the events following the 1848 Gold Rush through the 1903 treaty between Panama and the United States. In this chapter, we turn to more recent history of the Panama Canal, the 1977 treaties between the United States and Panama that provided for the return of the Canal Zone to Panama in 1999. The two treaties, the Panama Canal Treaty and the Neutrality Treaty, are closely related; we refer to them simply as the 1977 treaties.

The Return Controversy occupied center stage in American politics for much of 1977, the beginning of the Carter administration. The treaties were the product of years of discussions between the governments of the two nations. President Carter, elected in 1976, and President Torrijos of Panama signed the treaties in September 1977. President Carter made their ratification by the Senate a key goal of his first year in office. Opposition to the treaties was strong, however. The argument that the Canal was essentially and rightfully a strategic and economic part of the United States and should not be given away had a strong appeal and assured an intense political debate on the treaties. The texts by Congressman X and Professor Y were part of this discussion, although we have no evidence that either book was a major part of the public debate.

Of course, this history, although recent, was scarcely known to our students, who were young children at the time. This debate, emotionally compelling in 1977, was for them an academic exercise in the learning of recent history from texts.

The learning and reasoning questions we asked in Part 2 were similar to those we asked about the Acquisition Story. There was a shift in emphasis, however. The authors of the two main texts were addressing the 1977 treaties, arguing either for their ratification by the U.S. Congress (Professor Y) or against ratification (Congressman X). Accordingly, we focused on how students would handle the arguments of the two texts. This includes what they learned from the texts and how they reasoned about the Return Controversy. In reasoning, we examined in particular the stability of students' opinions. Because they were given texts with opposing views on the treaties, we could observe the extent to which they noticed and were influenced by such text differences. Finally, we hoped to examine individual differences, especially the extent to which such differences were consistent with those we had observed in Part 1.

METHODS

The Texts

The students read three texts for Part 2. The first text was comparable to the first text used in Part 1: A short (601 word), neutral text read in the lab, written by the authors based on the history of the Panama Canal and U.S.–Panama relations between 1903 and 1977. Its purpose was to give the students a brief introduction to the Canal itself, the Canal Zone, and the continuing friction between the United States and Panama over the Canal. For the two key texts with persuasive intent, the students read excerpts from both Congressman X and Professor Y in the same order as they had in Part 1.

Congressman X's Text.   The pro-U.S., anti-return text written by Congressman X was 38 pages long, intermixing the 1970s events and earlier history. The author argued that returning the Canal Zone to Panama and relinquishing control of the Canal were strongly against U.S. interests and, accordingly, that the treaties should not be approved. Congressman X, in making this argument, at no point acknowledged arguments on the other side of the controversy. His text can be fairly characterized as a very one-sided polemic against ratification of the 1977 treaties. It contained strong antitreaty quotations and evoked vivid images. Judging by our students' responses, his prose was effective in holding readers' attention and apparently persuasive on the question at hand.

The text served its purpose in swaying the opinions of our students. As Dave said "In terms of facts [X] used, I think he supported himself a hell of a lot better than [Y] did. If I were sitting on the fence, I'd be more swayed by [X] than by [Y]. I felt that [X] backed up his points better. I also think the tone of [X] played a lot into it."

Nearly one third of X's text was quotes, many from former military sources. This excerpt is illustrative of his prose:

> The late author and commentator, Elmer Davis, once wrote that America "will remain the land of the free only so long as it is the home of the brave." The bottom-line cost of surrender in Panama would be the United States' humiliating retreat in the face of blustering threats from the corrupt dictator of a backward banana republic. In such a case, even the construction of a new, two-ocean fleet would not be enough to restore our credibility in the eyes of the world, and our dignity and self-respect in the eyes of our own citizens.

In another passage, X argues for the military value of the canal:

> [Retired Admiral McCain] concluded his testimony by a stern warning that "The loss of sovereign control over the Canal Zone would result in transforming the Caribbean and the Gulf of Mexico into Red Lakes."

To be clear, Congressman X also made use of evidence in making his argument, as in the following passage on Panama's wealth:

> [Panama] is the wealthiest country in Central America and one of the wealthiest in all Latin America. Much of this wealth is derived, directly or indirectly, from the efficient American running of the Canal. At least one-third of Panama's foreign exchange is drawn from the Canal Zone. The zone is also responsible for twenty percent of Panamanian jobs, while operation of the canal contributes an estimated 14 percent to the Panamanian gross national product.

Professor Y's Text.   The excerpt from Professor Y's book was 47 pages long. The text included considerable material on Canal negotiations that occurred in the 1970s, and it provided detail on individuals in the story. The text, as in Y's text on the Acquisition Story, contained specific data, names, and numbers. Thus Y's text, as one would expect of a scholarly text, was informative; however, it lacked the urgency of X's text. Some passages provided process information:

> Snyder [a member of Congress] amended a State Department appropriation bill so no funds could be used for "negotiating the surrender or relinquishment of any U.S. rights" in the Zone. Without committee hearings or significant debate, it passed 246–164 on June 26, 1975.

Other passages contained evaluative and partly argumentative content, but always more muted than X's, as the following passage indicates:

> Given previous Panamanian demands, the exposed North American position in the Zone, and limitations imposed on Washington's power by the Third Cold War, the treaty drafts represented a United States diplomatic triumph.

One of the rare passages with some emotional appeal is Professor Y's concluding sentences:

> The real opportunity … is to [construct] policies that preserve republican virtues precisely by renouncing imperial practices. Panama presents one such opportunity. After three-quarters of a century, it is past time to close the chapter of North American colonialism on the Isthmus.

In addition to being more informative, Professor Y provided a more balanced presentation of the issues than did Congressman X. For example, he acknowledged criticisms of the Torrijos government, criticisms used by treaty opponents to argue that the Canal would be returned to a corrupt and unstable government in Panama.

Although Professor Y weighed the balance of factors in favor of treaty ratification, his balanced and low-key style may have been less persuasive for our students, compared with the text of Congressman X. When asked what Y's opinion of the 1977 treaties was, George noted Professor Y's tendency to present characters and their opinions, rather than his own: "I think he is basically, 'why not the treaties?' He gave several reasons for why not the treaties. He didn't go harping on any particular reason, just presented the facts. He talked about reasons for the Senators' opposition and why the American public felt the way they did. So I think he presented both sides. So he gave reasoning and it wasn't exactly his reasoning but more of a perspective of other people put together as far as why shouldn't we have a treaty for the canal." This is a fair summary of Professor Y's persuasive style, a discussion of different perspectives provided by figures in the debate.

The Procedures

Part 2 of the study, the Return Controversy, centered on events occurring after the signing of the 1903 treaty with Panama and was carried out during the last part of Meeting 5 and Meetings 6 through 8. Students had completed their learning and reasoning about the Acquisition Story prior to the Part 2 assignments.

At the end of Meeting 5 students were asked to read the short, neutral text to learn about what happened in Panama after the signing of the treaty in 1903. The students were told the text was a brief overview of the history of the Canal between 1903 and 1977 and that we would ask them some comprehension questions when they completed the reading. The purpose of this text was to give the students some background information before they started learning about the Return Controversy. Meetings 6 and 7 covered the Return Controversy assignments. At each meeting, the procedures were similar to those in Part 1.

The students wrote 24-line and 8-line summaries after reading both texts. The instructions for these summaries, however, were not directed at a causal model of the events, as they were in Part 1. Instead, students were told to "summarize the text." This reflects a change of focus in the texts. In Part 1, the two authors told a common story, providing the events and characters for a single situation model. In Part 2, each author argued for a particular interpretation of the events in the 1970s, using information not common to the two texts. Thus, one goal in the essays of Part 2 was to examine whether students understood each author's intent and believed it to be important enough to influence the structure of a short summary.

The students were asked four comprehension questions and any necessary probes, similar in form to those in Part 1. The questions tapped information available from both texts, although in different forms and in different levels of detail:

1. Outline the importance of the Panama Canal to the United States in the late 1970s.
    (p) How much was it used?
    (p) What about its strategic importance?

2. What role did General Omar Torrijos have in treaty negotiations?
   (p) How did he affect the start of negotiations?
   (p) From a U.S. standpoint, what positive/negative contributions did he make to the talks?
3. After the treaty negotiations in 1977, two treaties were signed, the Panama Canal Treaty and the Neutrality Treaty. What were the terms of each treaty and who signed them?
   (p) What did Panama want and receive from the Panama Canal Treaty?
   (p) How would the Canal be governed?
4. What are the arguments the author gives in favor of the two treaties? Against the two treaties?

The reasoning questions were also modeled after those of Part 1. The 13 reasoning questions included two counterfactuals, five value judgments, one confrontational, four source evaluations, and one metaknowledge question. Examples of each are given here:

Counterfactual: What would have happened if General Omar Torrijos was not the leader of Panama?

Value Judgment: Were the treaties fair to Panama?

Confrontational: Why did the United States negotiate with General Torrijos if he had connections with known drug dealers and had a questionable human rights record?

Source Evaluation: Do you think the author has an opinion about how President Carter and General Torrijos handled the negotiations? If so, what is that opinion?

Metaknowledge: What else would you like to know that was not given in the text?

LEARNING RESULTS

Scoring

Because the texts were different in length, emphasis, and even information, students' responses were not scored against a common template, but rather in reference to specific text-based schemes, which covered several overlapping events. For each text, we constructed a scheme representing its account of each event and all of its associated supporting facts. Although we modeled these schemes after the causal models of Part 1, we collapsed the distinction between events and supporting facts, in favor of a count of total points. For example, the following statement from Jen's summary includes two events and two supporting facts: "One particular antitreaty sentiment was stated by Ronald Reagan, who at the time wanted the party nomination for President. He felt that the U.S. owned the Canal and the Canal Zone just as the U.S. owns Alaska and Texas." The two events were (a) Reagan was a candidate for President at the time and (b) he argued that the U.S.'s sovereignty over Panama was as unquestionable as its sovereignty over Alaska. The two supporting facts (from the first clause) were the name "Ronald Reagan" (cf. "someone") and the correct attribution of his antitreaty sentiment. One point was given for each correct mention of an event or supporting fact. Thus Jen received 4 points for her statement.

As in Part 1, we calculated learning scores by including any correct information provided by the students in their long and short summaries, or in answer to the comprehension or reasoning questions. We then categorized the event/supporting facts points into the 11 motifs shown in Table 7.1. Not every motif was covered by both authors, and the extent of their coverage (the number of points) varied for motifs that were covered by both. The chapters provided from Congressman X's text included no material on three of the motifs: *Panama Opposition to Treaties*, *U.S. Support for Treaties*, and *Ratification of Treaties*. Three motifs were also absent from the chapters selected from Professor Y's text: *Building Canal*, *Panama Information*, *U.S.–Panama Relations (1914–1964)*.

What the Students Learned

Overall, students earned an average of 67 points after reading a text. Our most complete learner (George) recalled an average of 90 points and our least complete learner (Robbie) recalled an average of 48 points. The other students were intermediate, with averages of 60 (Mitch), 63 (Jen), 71 (Eileen), and 72 (Dave). Students made very few factual mistakes (averaging one error per text). Most errors concerned a treaty detail (e.g., a specific date or provision of a treaty). Robbie made the most errors (5 across the two texts) and Jen made the fewest (no errors across the two texts). Confusions were even more rare. Only Robbie showed any real confusion, making two after reading Congressman X.

Table 7.1 shows the distribution, across motifs, of events/supporting facts learned by subjects from each text. It provides a comparison of what students learned from each text, and, indirectly, a comparison of the emphasis of the two texts.

Congressman X. On average, after reading Congressman X, students recalled or summarized 65 events/supporting facts, ranging from 86 points (Dave) to 47 (Robbie). Most of what was learned from X's antitreaty text was part of the *1977 Treaties* motif (24%) and, as we would expect, the *U.S. Opposition to Treaties* motif (32%). These two motifs accounted for 56% of the total information learned. The only other motif learned well was information about *Torrijos*. This appears to reflect X's negative focus on Torrijos, as well as our questions about him. Only one subject, George, used much background information and this was primarily in his summary.

The information that the students learned about the 1977 treaties typically included the persons who signed them, the major rights granted to both countries,

TABLE 7.1
Distribution of Student Learning Across Motifs

	Congressman X		Professor Y	
	Mean (%)	S.D.	Mean (%)	S.D.
Building Canal	.2	.5	0	0
Canal Statistics	6.7	3.2	.9	1.5
Panama Information	6.1	4.5	.3	.4
Torrijos	12.2	7.2	6.2	4.4
U.S.–Panama Relations (1914–1964)	7.4	7.8	.7	1.8
Canal Renegotiations (1970s)	5.4	3.3	26.1	7.0
1977 Treaties	24.0	5.4	20.8	6.3
U.S. Opposition to Treaties	31.6	11.9	11.7	5.8
Panama Opposition to Treaties	.3	.8	5.2	3.7
U.S. Support for Treaties	.5	.9	18.6	5.0
Ratification of Treaties	0	0	5.9	5.3
Background	5.4	9.3	3.4	4.7

Note. Data are percentages of total points earned that fell into each motif. Mean percentages do not equal 100 because of rounding.

when the terms would take effect, and some of the financial data. Some students also learned the terms of the agreements elaborated by the author in his arguments against the treaty. For example, they learned that Panama could detain ships based on health and sanitation restrictions because Congressman X argued that this provision could be used to stop U.S. access to the Canal. The only other aspect of the agreement that students learned well was a minor one, not elaborated by either author: the number of U.S. and Panamanian representatives running the Canal Commission. It is not clear why this fact was so salient.

For the arguments against the treaties, students learned about six of the eight arguments used by Congressman X. Best learned were the author's arguments concerning (a) economic need for a U.S.-owned canal, (b) military need for a canal, (c) world perception that the United States would be weak for giving in to Panama, and (d) Panama's ability to bar U.S. ships from the Canal because of health restrictions. The three students who read Professor Y first also recalled a couple of his arguments following X's text.

Professor Y.   On average, students recalled 70 events/supporting facts after reading Professor Y, ranging from George's 101 points to Robbie's 48 points. The motifs that students learned the most about after reading this protreaty text were the *Canal Renegotiations (1970s)* (26%), the *1977 Treaties* (21%), and *U.S. Support for Treaties* (19%). These three motifs, two of which were not well represented in Congressman X's text, accounted for 66% of the total information learned. The treaty information learned was the same as that learned after Congressman X's text.

After reading Y, students recalled about the same number of author arguments (six) as after reading Congressman X. However, unlike their responses after X, students' recall of arguments reflected the fact that Professor Y presented information that could be used on both sides of the controversy. Four protreaty arguments and two antitreaty arguments were recalled or summarized. Three protreaty arguments were the best learned: (1) Larger ships could not use the Canal (limiting its economic value). (2) U.S.–Panamanian relations would benefit from a new treaty. (3) The United States did not own the Canal Zone in the same way it owned Alaska. After this text, the three students who read Congressman X first also recalled a couple of his arguments following Y's text.

In summary, the students learned a considerable amount about the Return Controversy, with only rare errors and confusions. Their learning was influenced by the texts, and they demonstrated learning of an author's arguments. Thus, after Congressman X, students learned most about U.S. opposition to the treaties and after Professor Y, they learned more about U.S. support for the 1977 treaties. In the next section, we examine what students selected as the central information from the texts, as indicated by their summaries.

SUMMARY RESULTS

In contrast to Part 1, where we were interested in students' ability to write brief summaries of the situation, we now report observations on the students' longer and more informative 24-line summaries. The amount of information subjects included in their summaries was about the same after each text, about 19 points or 28% of what they learned. The summaries, however, were very different for the two texts. We show the summaries written following both texts in Appendix F to illustrate how students expressed the information and arguments to which they had been exposed.

Congressman X.   Three students (Eileen, Dave, and Mitch) wrote summaries reflecting their view that X's text is about an argument. Their first sentences are statements of the controversy, followed with antitreaty claims and then arguments to support their claims. Eileen and Dave referred to specific evidence that the author used (e.g., "statements by military officials," "economic trends and statistics," "One Panamanian official is quoted from a speech.").

The other three students failed to mention the argumentative nature of X's text in their long summaries. In fact, Jen and Robbie had difficulty writing a connected summary of the events described in the text. Instead, their summaries resembled lists of events. As Jen wrote "[X] explains first...," "Then he goes on to describe...," "[X] discusses...," "He describes...." Robbie, in his first sentence, noted the apparent lack of structure to the article: "The article [X] wrote actually seemed like several articles put together." Like Jen, he merely listed the events: "It spoke a lot of...," "It spoke of his family...," "It spoke of the 1936 treaty...," "Then it spoke about U.S. thinking of giving up the Canal." Neither student mentioned that Congressman X's text was predominately an argument. Jen may have simply been unaware of the argumentative nature of X's text. (She was the only student not to notice the obvious bias of Congressman X when asked later to compare the neutrality of the two authors, responding "I think [X] was more neutral.") George, who read X first, was the other subject whose summary failed to reflect the argumentative character of X's text. His summary is a remarkably detailed temporal description of the events from the 1903 treaty through the 1977 treaties. It views the text as about the signing of treaties, rather than an argument for not turning the Canal over to Panama. We think this merely reflected his summarizing strategy, which we saw also in Part 1, rather than a misapprehension of the argument structure. George may have seen his task as giving an accurate event-based account of the story.

Professor Y. The long summaries following Professor Y's text had a different character, less reflective of argument and more reflective of historical context. All summaries began with an overview statement that placed events in context: For example, Eileen began her summary "[Y]'s text discussed the problems preceding the signing of the 1977 Panama Canal Treaty in light of a third cold war." Dave began, "[Y]'s second article describes events concerning the Panama Canal from the 1903 treaty up to modern times." His summary placed particular emphasis on the development of anti-American sentiments in Panama and on the political and diplomatic activities in the U.S. during attempts to revise the 1903 treaty. Most summaries then discussed the negotiations, referring to many of the distinct characters involved (e.g., Carter, Reagan, Congress, the American people, and Torrijos).

Unlike the summaries after Congressman X, the summaries after Professor Y did not state directly that there was controversy in the story. Instead, the students noted that the participants had different views and goals. For example, Robbie wrote, "This whole deal also made politicians which were running for office very alert of [sic] what U.S. citizens wanted. The politicians wanted to figure out negotiations so they could be elected. Reagan was doing this well. I remember Kissinger wanted to almost tell Panama tough luck, that the canal is ours. A lot of people disagreed. Carter wanted negotiations but with U.S. control indefinitely. Reagan looked at the Panama Canal as Alaska or Texas, that we owned it."

In summary, students wrote summaries that reflected specific text information and rhetorical goals, in contrast to the situation summaries that were produced for the Acquisition Story. There were interesting individual differences, however, especially in whether students made the argumentative character of Congressman X's text a part of their summaries. In the next section, we discuss the texts' effect on the students' comprehension and reasoning answers.

REASONING RESULTS

Our analysis of reasoning about the Return Controversy focuses on the students' sensitivity to a text's perspective and their ability to corroborate facts from the different texts.

Text Perspective

Did Students Notice the Bias of the Texts?

Although both Professor Y and Congressman X wrote persuasive texts, they differed in their objectivity, with that of Congressman X much more subjective and one sided. Two students commented on the bias of Congressman X before we explicitly asked. Mitch, in his summary, wrote "[X], who believed that the U.S. was sovereign over the land of Panama, wrote this in order to sway the public into taking an anti-treaty stance." In answer to a later comprehension question, Mitch commented, "[X] comes out with things like its against God's will. He's just out and out against the treaties." George also offered, "This is obviously a man who doesn't like the idea of signing away the Canal."

As in Part 1, one of the reasoning questions asked students to comment on their perspective of the author's bias (*Did the author present a neutral coverage of the events? If not, what do you think the author's attitude was?*). Five of the six students stated quite clearly that Congressman X's text was not neutral. In answer to the question, these students either stated "No...," that it was "biased ...," or that it "tried but failed" to be neutral. Eileen's comment on X's bias provided the clearest case of bias detection: "No, not at all. He had a definite opinion. He went through the information to pick out facts to support his opinion, which was that the treaties were not good. Also some of the language he used. He talked about Communism and Marxism, red lakes." Jen was the only subject to be less than clear in noting this bias. She answered the question by saying, "[X] was presenting an American view. I don't think Panamanians would like it. Definitely an American view of what happened. Definitely following the title [Surrender in Panama]." Jen was the only student to believe that Congressman X's text was less biased than Professor Y's text.

Consistent with a general perception that Professor Y's text was less biased, no student raised an issue of bias prior to our asking about it, and everyone except Jen judged Y's text to be less biased than X's. When asked whether Professor Y's text was neutral, most students leaned in that direction but only two gave simple YES responses. Others were more hedged, suggesting the text was partly neutral but perceiving that Y did express a viewpoint on the treaties. Eileen said, "I think he had a little bit of an attitude that we should get out of the Panama Canal. Change our foreign policy a little bit. But I think he tried to provide a neutral coverage of what went on in the U.S." Dave answered, "Yes, pretty much, for the most part neutral. He editorializes a bit in the very last section of the article. I think he also sermonizes a bit on Carter's handling of the affair. He really portrays Carter as a bit of a bumbler.... Overall, he's leaning towards the treaties. He felt the treaties were a good idea and the U.S. getting out of Central America was a good idea." Mitch commented on the complexity of neutrality, saying, "When you write something like that, there's only so much neutrality you can show. He showed both sides of the argument but in the end he gave his opinion. I think he was showing the protreaty opinion." Jen, who saw no bias in X's text saw at least a viewpoint in Professor Y, commenting that "he was pro-signing of the treaties. I think his attitude came through."

Thus, students generally recognized the one-sided nature of one of the texts (Congressman X) and most could correctly assess the viewpoint of the more balanced text (Professor Y). Given that they noticed the bias, were the students affected by it?

Were Students Affected by the Bias in the Texts?

A text's bias can affect the reader's attitudes toward the characters, events, and actions covered in the text, and these attitudes, in turn, can affect a student's interpretation of a story. We wanted to see whether our students were influenced by the two persuasive texts. One type of reasoning question, value judgments, seems especially able to tap both student attitudes and their representation of the story. We attended, in particular, to the consistency, or lack of it, in the students' responses as they read more texts. Responses to the four value judgments were placed on the same 5-point scale introduced in chapter 5. Opinions were either positive or negative and could be either definite or hedged. The unequivocal answers were either YES or NO responses, the less definite answers were either YES, BUT or NO, BUT replies. NEUTRAL positions were those that took no real stand on the issue. We report the assessment of these responses, making note also of those relatively rare occasions when subjects used background knowledge or information they had learned from the Acquisition Story.

Were the Treaties Fair to Panama? U.S. fairness to Panama is an essential part of the relations between the two countries since 1903. As in the Acquisition Story, the United States dealt from a position of strength, a strength differential that caused obvious problems for the Panamanians. President Carter's Latin American policy aimed to change the decades of imbalance in favor of a more equitable relationship. As a result, the treaties offered Panama a substantial amount of money, a transfer of U.S. land and businesses in the Zone to Panamanian ownership, and immediate inclusion in the operation of the Canal. However, full ownership would not come to Panama until December 31, 1999, more than 20 years in the future. Although the Panamanians would be included in governing the Canal, the nine-member commission running the Canal would have a U.S. majority and the four Panamanians had to be confirmed by the United States. The final, and to the Panamanians, most onerous, condition was that the United States maintained the right to keep the Canal open, with force if necessary, after the Canal became fully Panamanian.

Students were in agreement: The treaties were considered fair to Panama. Only one student (Eileen) thought otherwise, and that was only after reading Professor Y. Her concern was that the prolonged U.S. presence in the Canal Zone would be problematic for Panama.

The texts were quite influential on the students' answers. After reading Congressman X, everyone agreed that the treaties were fair to Panama; Dave and George believed that the treaties were "overly fair" (i.e., too generous to Panama). This view reflects X's treatment of the financial parts of the treaties, which, he argued, would cost the United States millions of dollars in addition to the indignity of giving up the Canal. Indeed, all the students except Mitch noted the cost of the treaties to justify their opinion that the treaties were fair to Panama. Eileen was the only student to qualify her statement after X's text, noting that the Panamanians did not get control immediately.

Professor Y's text, in addition to leading to Eileen's change in opinion about fairness, also influenced other students to qualify their endorsement of fairness. After reading Y's text, George and Mitch both gave a qualified YES, acknowledging that Panamanians might have believed the treaties were unfair to them. Congressman X's text did not promote such thoughts.

There is evidence that three students (Eileen, Mitch, and George) were influenced by the authors' perspective. Jen and Robbie, however, were not at all influenced by the texts; Dave showed a text influence only in his justification of his opinion. After Professor Y he thought the United States was fair because it was the Panamanians' land, but after Congressman X, he thought the United States was excessively fair because the United States gave Panama generous concessions.

Were the Treaties Fair to the United States?

As already noted, the Carter administration, wanting Panama to find the treaties fair, offered more attractive terms than the United States had been willing to give in the past. Some provisions of the Panama Canal Treaty were interpreted by some Americans as unfair to the United States: the $10 million annuity, another $10 million a year if profits allowed, restrictions on U.S. ownership of businesses in the Zone, preferential hiring of Panamanian personnel. Some groups and individuals, Congressman X among them, believed that the entire idea of transferring control of the Canal to Panama was unfair to the United States.

There was less agreement in answer to this question because the students were more influenced by the particular text they read. George completely changed his opinion from believing the treaties were not fair to the United States after Congressman X to believing they were fair after Professor Y. His reasoning was that the Canal would become more of a problem over time and the treaty provided adequate assurance that the United States could maintain use and protection of the Canal.

The responses after students read Congressman X were variable. In general, however, students leaned toward believing the treaties were unfair after reading X and no student believed wholeheartedly that the treaties were fair to the United States. Three students (Eileen, Robbie, and George), consistent with the author's central rhetorical goal, claimed that the treaties were unfair to the United States.

The others were either noncommittal (Jen) or thought they were only partially fair to the United States (Mitch and Dave). No student, after reading X, believed the treaties were fair without qualification.

Contrary to their opinions after Congressman X, not one of the students thought that the treaties were unfair to the United States after reading Professor Y; four students believed they were simply fair. Eileen and Robbie were the only students to respond with a more mixed opinion. Robbie's answer is typical of a mixed response to these value probes: "My feelings say no, they weren't fair because we gave them so much money. We made a treaty a long time ago and it was ours. But then I know for the best interest of the country and world peace it was good to have a treaty like this. We signed it so fair's fair. It was kind of smart for us because it made us have a good rapport with South America. Made other nations see we weren't jerks. But there's still part of me that says that's a lot of money we were giving them and giving them the canal. We weren't buying it from them, we were paying them to take it."

As in the previous question, the text influenced the students. In fact, all the students modified their opinion, at least slightly, following the second text and these changes were always consistent with the author's perspective. That is, for the students who read Professor Y first, their belief moved towards the idea that the treaties were unfair to the United States after reading Congressman X. Students who read X first moved towards believing that the treaties were fair to the United States after reading Professor Y.

Should the United States Turn the Canal Over to Panama in 1999?

This question is the heart of the 1977 treaties and the ensuing debate. Treaty supporters argued that the United States had an ethical responsibility to erase the stigma of the 1903 treaty and the 75 subsequent years of paternalistic treatment of Panama. They argued that the Canal is useful but no longer necessary, an antique that threatened to become an expensive burden. Part of this argument was that the Canal's military value had diminished because it could not accommodate U.S. aircraft carriers or nuclear submarines. Those opposed to the treaties appealed to patriotism and nationalism, and warned that the treaties jeopardized the nation's military and economic security. Further, they argued that the United States would irreparably damage its reputation as a world power by giving in to a "banana republic."

Students were in relative agreement: The United States is obligated to return the Canal to Panama because of the treaties. Only two students (Jen and Robbie) concluded otherwise, in both cases after reading Congressman X's text. Robbie thought that the Canal was still too important to give up and Jen thought the United States should renegotiate a new deal with Panama. Students, after both texts, generally favored return of the Canal only with hedges. Only 5 of the 12 responses were unqualified YES answers. The others answers fell into the "neutral" or YES,

BUT categories. Nevertheless, the strong consensus was that the United States should turn the Panama Canal over to Panama at the turn of the century.[21]

The texts were quite influential. Congressman X produced considerable variability in the responses, ranging from Mitch's simple YES to Jen's and Robbie's simple NO. Eileen, Dave, and George all argued that the United States should probably turn the Canal over because of the signed treaties but each included a qualifier. Eileen believed, "unless we build another canal I don't think we should turn it over." Dave's comment was that the United States should "keep a wary eye on it and be ready to move down there at a moment's notice," and George said "However, if we manage to conveniently find another problem and rush in there like we did in 1989 in 1999, then no we shouldn't give the Canal to the Panamanians." Thus, Congressman X's text produced, in some students, an attitude of resistance toward returning the Canal.

Professor Y's text, in contrast, resulted in general agreement about what should be done. After reading Y's text, all students agreed that the United States should turn the Canal over and only two students (Eileen and Dave) gave hedged remarks (i.e., YES, BUT). Mitch said, "We have to. We signed a treaty. I think we should have negotiated this a long time ago. At World War II the significance of the canal declined. The U.S. traditionally drags its feet. We should've done this in 1964 after the riots. They could've had it when Nixon was in office. They thought of it as a colony. It could've been handled a lot better. I think we should've signed them a long time ago. It separated their country. If we had something running down the Mississippi River, we'd be up in arms."

Further evidence for text influence, despite general agreement on this question, comes from the fact that two students (Jen and Robbie) completely changed their opinion following their second text. In general, Professor Y's text yielded general agreement in favor of compliance with the treaties, whereas Congressman X's text led to some resistance. Finally, many of the responses followed a difficult, hedge-filled path to a conclusion.

The texts sometimes led students to reevaluate their original opinions in light of new information and arguments. An example of apparently painful reevaluation came from Dave, who initially favored the treaties but, after reading Congressman X, became confused and uncertain. He debated with himself during the course of an 888 word response which we present here in its entirety to illustrate the kind of complexity students sometimes dealt with, trading off values on different sides of

---

[21]Unlike responses evaluating the fairness of the treaties, responses to the treaty itself referred to outside knowledge, especially contemporary events. Eileen and Jen mentioned Noriega, who had recently been captured by the United States. Jen also mentioned then-President Bush. Dave acknowledged that the world situation has changed since the treaties were signed: "Now with what's happening in the world.... When this was written, things were different." George referred to America's 1989 Panama invasion, SALT, and treaties with Eastern Europe.

the question. Some of what Dave learned from Part 1 made its way into his thinking, and this is shown in italics:

> ...I didn't think you'd ask me something like that! I can't dance around on this. Given the treaties, "no". The more I think about it, "no, I don't think we should." This is really weird because when I came into this I thought "yes, we should." It's their country, it's their land, we should give it back. The key phrase is "in light of the agreed upon '77 treaties." Now that I know a lot more about the treaties, I don't think that there's enough control remaining for the U.S. for us to comfortably give the Canal away. I would be more comfortable with relinquishing control if 1) we had a bit more administrative control of the Canal. It is still an American majority (on the Canal Commission) and the Panamanians are chosen by America. But the fundamental objective I'd like to see would be that military bases would be established along the Canal route and be kept staffed. There'd be a constant military presence so if there were problems, we'd be there to stop it if necessary rather than having to bring them in from the mainland or nearby military bases. I also think something needs to be done with the political and labor end of it. In that the Panamanian nationalists shouldn't be permitted the right to strike or close the Canal. Not without the right to bring in replacements to keep the Canal open. If those stipulations were met, I could be a lot more agreeable to turn the Canal over. And, in fact I still believe that it's not right of the U.S. to consider part of a foreign nation as part of its own turf, like another state. In a lot of ways that's how it was treated. I think U.S. control should be maintained. U.S. should have a stronger hand in it than what it looks like we'll have come the turn of the century. *But, by the same token, I don't think that it should be under as complete control as it was in say 1903 right after the original treaty was signed.*
>
> (We then asked "Would Panama agree to that?") I doubt it. I think Panamanians' attitude is "what do you want?" You agreed to the treaty, your Senate ratified it and now you're coming back down the line and saying we've changed our mind, we want to modify it. We bargained in good faith and that's the way it's going to be. In which case that puts the U.S. between a rock and a hard place. Either they let the treaties go through and keep their fingers crossed that nothing does happen or they say we've changed our mind and we're going to show you we changed our mind by taking it back by force. What I think may happen will be that come the turn of the century the U.S. will keep a close eye on how the Canal is being managed and if it looks like things are shifting so that U.S. use will be excluded, we may go in, heavy handed or subtly, and regain an influence in the Canal, and, when we're established that way, renegotiate the treaties. Maybe Panamanians will even see that. Because maybe the Canal will slip out of Panamanian control. Panamanians can't run it as efficiently, as well as U.S. Also, maybe if they refuse to negotiate, U.S. may come in with a much heavier hand. There's the big loophole of saying that U.S. has to keep the Canal open. By renegotiating the treaties, it would put us in a more favorable light with the rest of the world. Sure, we have the right to go down and use military force to keep the Canal open but I think world opinion would be—there goes the imperialistic U.S. again, kicking the shit out of anybody who disagrees with them at the slightest provocation. I think it would be better if we had more of a military presence down there at all times. It would make it seem less like an invasion [if the U.S. needed to

use force to reopen the Canal]. In other words, we had an interest there, we had military there already. We're coming in to keep the peace rather than an invasion from the mainland coming in to take control.

(We finally asked Dave to get "back to the bottom line: If no renegotiations go through, should we turn over the Panama Canal in 1999?") At this point I'd say "yes." OK, contradiction! You've got me in a corner. We have to. We signed treaties. We agreed to it, what else are we going to do. We can go back against our word but that's really going to...Anybody won't sign a treaty with U.S. Oh, there goes the two-faced U.S. again. The guts of me says no. This was a bad treaty, we shouldn't relinquish control. The more pragmatic side, the more diplomatic side of me says we made our bed, now we have to sleep in it. We should hand control of the Canal over and hope for the best. At the same time, keep a wary eye on it and be ready to move down there at a moment's notice. I kind of suspect that's what may be necessary after all. Now with what's happening in the world... When this was written things were different. This guy [X] almost has a McCarthyistic bend to him. But now with what's apparently happening to communism, there's no saying what will actually happen in the Third World with communism.

What Do You Think of General Omar Torrijos? Opinions of major characters can color a student's view of the entire story. Like the parallel question in Part 1 asking the students' opinions of Bunau-Varilla, this question probed their view of a controversial and important negotiator for Panama. Torrijos, as leader of Panama, was a major player in the 1977 drama. He was seen by some as a villain who blackmailed the United States into signing new treaties by threatening to blow up the Canal locks; by others, he was seen as a patient diplomat who endured the 1976 elections in the United States, bitter denunciations as a traitor at home, and lurid insults about himself and his country from U.S. politicians debating the treaties. Torrijos was accused by the State Department as having questionable ties to drug traffickers. Amnesty International questioned his human rights record. In his favor, Professor Y noted that he peacefully quelled unruly students at the U.S. embassy and made many compromises when the U.S. negotiators rejected his initial proposals.

Students were in less agreement about what they thought of Torrijos. Eileen always thought positively of Torrijos; she argued that "he was an effective leader in Panama." Jen, in contrast, always thought negatively of him. She commented that he was "a maniacal, selfish dictator who wanted power." The other students' judgments were dependent on the text. As expected, Congressman X's text yielded more negative opinions than Professor Y's. In addition, four of the six students rated Torrijos more positively after reading Y than after reading X. Robbie and Dave were most affected by the texts; both changed opinions dramatically. After reading Professor Y, Robbie concluded with "I think he was a good guy" but after X's text he finished his opinion of Torrijos with "I think he was a slime." (Robbie was aware of his opinion shift, noting that he had totally reversed his opinion of Torrijos based on Congressman X.) Dave, after reading Professor Y, had a rather positive impression of Torrijos, stating, "I think he was a very effective leader. I kind of get a feeling of respect for him but kind of begrudging because I think he was a harsh leader also. I think he was good for Panama, pretty much." This somewhat positive impression turned quite negative after Congressman X saying "I think [X]'s assessment of him is essentially correct. I think he's a heavy handed dictator. He's looking to prop up his own military regime. He probably does have communist ties."

As in the previous question, some students included some knowledge in their answers to this question. Dave compared Torrijos directly to an important figure from the Acquisition Story ("I kind of see him in a similar light as Bunau-Varilla.") and Jen made a similar, but more general comparison ("I think he followed in the footsteps of Panamanian political history since 1903."). George compared Torrijos to a current political figure, saying, "I'm sure he was as big an oppressor, if not more than Manuel Noriega. He had just as much a hand in the drug trafficking as Noriega did...."

In summary, the value judgments were affected, sometimes rather dramatically, by the authors. Even when the students' opinions weren't altered by a text, their reasons for those opinions were swayed by Congressman X and Professor Y. Beyond this question of single author influence is the extent to which students compared the two texts, a question taken up in the next section.

Corroboration: Comparing Across Texts

Because the two authors emphasized different kinds of information as part of their opposing arguments on the Return Controversy, the texts presented parts of the story quite differently. As Wineburg (1991) noted, historians compare the alternative versions of a story as they read, using a corroboration heuristic. Would our students, who read multiple texts covering the same story, explicitly note differences between the texts? Would they want more information to clear up controversies the different authors' interpretations might create?

The Importance of the Canal in the 1970s

The first comprehension question asked students about the importance of the Panama Canal to the United States in the late 1970s. We expected different responses after the two texts, because they expressed different views on the importance of the Canal. Congressman X provided evidence to support his argument that the United States, as well as many other countries, relied heavily on the Canal. Professor Y provided evidence for arguments that U.S. use of the Panama Canal had diminished in the 1970s.

Interestingly, four students (Dave, Jen, Mitch, and Robbie) mentioned that the two authors differed in their evaluation of the Canal's worth. Jen, in answer to the question after Professor Y, said "I think the last thing in [X] I read said that without the Canal we wouldn't have been able to fight some wars. In Vietnam, we wouldn't have been able to get the ships there fast enough. But I think it said in [Y]—it quoted one naval officer that not having it wouldn't have hurt us in the Vietnam War because we have now built up a bicoastal naval fleet." Mitch also referred to a contradiction between the two: "[Congressman X] would say that the U.S. still needed it. Used it a lot. [X] said 60%–70% of GNP. Whereas the other writer said it wasn't used almost at all."

The results suggest that students were trying to construct an accumulated understanding of what they had read, at least when they had to face questions about their understanding. Part of this process was comparing what the two authors wrote about the Canal's importance.

Noticing Holes in the Story

Another indication that students were comparing the content of the two texts comes from two reasoning questions that asked them to evaluate the completeness of the material they read so far. The first question asked students *Do you believe the author presented enough of the facts to paint a complete picture?* On most of the occasions the response was YES. However, there were two notable exceptions. Mitch noticed that one text was not complete by comparing it to information that the other author mentioned. "[Congressman X] left a lot out that he could have put in. He claimed one time that the Panamanians received 70% of wages, 70% of the wages were given to Panamanian people but he left out completely the fact that all the 8 highest wage scales are all American. You're talking thousands of people making 70% and maybe 20 people making the other 30%. [X] left out information so he would seem more just."

Another response, at least for the two students who were the least effective learners, was that there were *too* many details in Professor Y's text. Robbie joked that his text added "More than enough to paint a complete picture. It was so complete it got blurry!" Jen, in comparing the two authors' texts, complained that she "found [Y's text] hard to read because of the names. How many people voted for it, against it. That threw me. I think that was difficult. Some of it lost me on the U.S.–Latin American relations. I don't know that much about U.S.–Latin American relations so I found it really hard to read."

A second reasoning question we asked was *What else would you like to know that was not given in the text?* This question aims at the extent to which students monitored their learning for knowledge gaps. Students were more satisfied with Professor Y's text (Dave, Jen, Robbie, and George wanted nothing more) than with Congressman X's text (only Jen wanted nothing more). However, students did find holes in both the stories. Students expressed interest in filling knowledge gaps of two types: *story information* and *controversy information.* Some students (Eileen, Mitch, and Robbie) wanted more information about events either prior or subsequent to those covered by an author, indicating an interest in getting the whole story. Robbie, for example, wanted to know how it all turned out in the end: "It said that Carter signed the treaties. Now that has to go through Senate, right? Did it go through? ("Yes," he was informed.) So it was ratified? (Again, "yes.") So it's going to happen. That's kind of scary."

Other students (Eileen, Dave, Mitch, and George) wanted another view on the controversy. Eileen wanted to know "how much support [Torrijos] had from Panamanian citizens and how Panamanians felt about the canal treaties. [Professor Y] talked a lot about U.S. public opinion being divided but he didn't say anything about the Panamanians being divided or what they wanted or debate going on in that country"; George wanted to "see [the] other side's reasons why we should give the canal to the Panamanians."

All six students at some point compared information across the texts. Students, when given multiple texts to read about the same events, attempted to check for consistency and compare the information in the texts. Considering that our assignments were separated by an average of 6 days, this appears to be an encouraging indicator of students' potential for representing such information over time.

Sourcing

Students clearly paid attention to sources, as indicated by results presented so far. Sourcing, however, goes beyond attention to the text itself. In second order sourcing, the student considers sources the authors themselves cited for their information and arguments. Although it was a strictly optional part of the students' task, all students demonstrated some of this second order sourcing, from two or three references to as many as eight or nine across the two texts.

Congressman X's text included substantial quoted material, which provided many of his facts and arguments. Students often used this quoted information in their comprehension responses and their summaries, but only rarely included such external references in response to reasoning probes. That students did not avoid quotations as sources of information is of some interest. It is counter to the impression that students often exclude material that can be viewed as "external" to a narrowly defined "main part."[22]

Students, however, were usually vague and incomplete in their reference to cited material. Dave's comment was typical: "[Congressman X] quoted someone as saying..." Students tended to recall that some piece of information was attributed to a specific source, but they were unable to cite the source specifically. Thus, references took various imprecise forms: "quoted some naval officers that said..."; "One Panamanian official is quoted from a speech ..."; "There were numerous quotes from generals and stuff that said...." On occasion, however, more specific

---

[22]Although we know of no evidence that college students avoid extended quotes in reading, many do avoid graphs and footnotes. In a study of history learning, Britt, Marron, Foltz, Perfetti, and Rouet (1994) found that many subjects claimed that they ignored footnotes. Students also honor a distinction between "required" and "optional" assignments, even in our study: Dave was the only student to read the "optional" treaties.

sources were cited as when Eileen recalled that X "quoted Davis, a Latin American historian...."

In summary, we find only superficial attention to sources cited by the authors. Although even uninformed students might ask, in effect, "Who are these people being quoted?", they seldom did. No one suggested that the qualifications of cited sources should be questioned. Thus, there is a contrast, at least to some extent, in the generally accurate perception of an author's perspective (and some awareness of discrepancies between the texts) and the lack of a critical attitude toward the sources cited by the author.

INDIVIDUAL SUMMARIES

We turn now to the students as individuals. Chapter 6 provided the basic descriptions of the students and their variability in learning and reasoning about the Acquisition Story. We examine here the kind of variability present in how students learned and reasoned about the Return Controversy and the consistencies with what we observed for the Acquisition Story.

Eileen

Eileen learned an average amount from both texts, slightly more from Professor Y (79 points) than from Congressman X (63 points). Her learning was general across all motifs, and her responses reflected little background information. She was typical in earning most of her learning points after Congressman X from the *1977 Treaties* motif (16 points) and *U.S. Opposition to Treaties* motif (28 points), whereas most of her points from Professor Y came from the *Canal Renegotiations (1970s)* motif (26 points) and the *U.S. Support for Treaties* motif (15 points). Like all students, Eileen learned something from both the *U.S. Support for Treaties* motif and the *U.S. Opposition to Treaties* motif from Professor Y, although, like many students, she mentioned more information supporting the treaties.

Three patterns of Eileen's learning and reasoning that emerged in Part 1 reemerged in Part 2. First, Eileen again was "text driven." She noticed and commented on specific aspects of the text. Eileen recalled one picturesque image of Torrijos from X: "The text compared him to Al Capone." Also more than once she explicitly referred to one of the authors, saying, "I think the author brought up a good point..." Eileen rarely answered questions using information not given by the two texts. Information from Part 1 or general history knowledge was never part of her comprehension answers and only twice could be seen in her reasoning responses. Her focus on details from a text also reflected her text-driven approach. In Part 2, in contrast to Part 1, she learned treaty and character names but not dates. We think this is partly a reflection of the difference between the two parts of the Canal story. Because the Acquisition Story covered approximately 50 years of history, it was important to learn dates. In the Return Controversy, the time span was much shorter; dates were less critical in keeping the story straight than were character names. Eileen was better than all other subjects at treaty names, referring to three of the five treaties covered in the two texts by name after each reading. She also paid particular attention to character names after Professor Y's text, mentioning 9 of the 16 characters by name.

Second, Eileen again wrote long summaries (272 and 304 words compared to the average of 217) that included quite representative material. She correctly summarized the fact that Congressman X's text centered around the controversial decision to turn the Panama Canal over to Panamanian control. Her summary of arguments in Professor Y's text reflected his attempt to put the Return Controversy into a context (i.e., the third cold war) and to use this context to interpret the event and actions taken by the many characters in negotiations and debates occurring in the 1970s.

Third, she was still reluctant to give her own opinions, instead citing opinions of the author or other people. For example, when talking about the Panama Canal's importance, she said "The author felt it was politically important" and "A lot of people that…were against signing the treaty felt that it was strategically important." After reading Congressman X's text, she was careful to attribute rather than assimilate opinions: "some Americans…" and "according to the author." After both texts, Eileen continued to avoid opinions on the grounds that information was not sufficient: "I didn't get enough information to decide if…"; "I don't know…;" "It's so hard to say because…."

Dave

Dave learned more than anyone from Congressman X's text (86 points), but only an average amount from Professor Y's text (57 points). Like the other two good learners (Eileen and George), he learned the most from the last text he read. His learning was general across motifs; he used little background information in his answers. Most of his learning points after Congressman X came from the *1977 Treaties* motif (15 points) and the *U.S. Opposition to Treaties* motif (34 points). His learning from Professor Y was widely distributed across the motifs covering the controversial topics: 13 points from *Canal Renegotiations (1970s)*, 14 points from *1977 Treaties*, 10 points from *U.S. Opposition to Treaties*, and 12 points from *U.S. Support for Treaties*. After Professor Y's text, Dave cited more information supporting the treaties (16 points) than opposing the treaties (10 points).

Dave referred to more of the authors' arguments than the other students. Across the reasoning and comprehension questions, he gave 16 arguments (compared to an average of 12.8 arguments). Also, his use of arguments was more balanced than the others; he gave arguments both for and against the treaties after each text. Following X's text, 8 of his 10 arguments were for the treaties. Following Y's text, half of his six arguments were for the treaties. Overall, Dave reported 11 arguments that supported the opinion of the author he had just read and 5 opposed to that position.

Some patterns of Dave's learning and reasoning that emerged in Part 1 were repeated here in the Return Controversy. First, as before, he avoided details, generally omitting treaty names, and dates. (He produced one treaty name during his discussion of the Acquisition Story and, in Part 2, he again mentioned only one of the five treaties discussed in the two texts.) Dave focused more on the political aspects of the story—the negotiations and the deal making.

Second, Dave again became more engaged than most students by the reasoning questions and the discussions these generated. He usually gave longer answers than average and, in a few instances, he gave multiple possibilities and argued both sides: "It would depend. One of two things I see there is…. Or it would be…."

Third, generally Dave's responses could be classified as skeptically liberal. In both the Acquisition Story and the Return Controversy, he sometimes questioned U.S. motives and he used examples of dubious U.S. actions to support his assertion that U.S. policy and politicians sometimes were motivated by selfishness or greed. However, he seemed to be the most affected by Congressman X's pro-American arguments, although often only reluctantly. His long, wavering answer to the question of whether the United States should transfer Panama Canal ownership to Panama is one example of his hesitant agreement with Congressman X. Dave noted that "[X] gives an air of urgency that was totally lacking from [Professor Y]'s text". The lack of urgency weakened Y's arguments for Dave and made it harder for him to support his initial beliefs. At one point he said, "I guess what I'd really like to read now would be something that's as persuasive as [X] but with the viewpoint of [Y]."

Jen

Jen learned an average amount from both texts, 65 points from Professor Y's text and 61 points from Congressman X's text. Jen recalled less than all other students about negotiations after both texts. Most of her learning points after Congressman X came from the *1977 Treaties* motif (13 points) and the *U.S. Opposition to Treaties* motif (25 points). After reading Professor Y, Jen, like most of the other students, gave answers that contained a substantial amount of information about the two 1977 treaties (17 points) and support for those treaties in the United States (11 points). However, in contrast to many of the others, she also learned a lot about U.S. opposition to the treaties. In fact, she was the only student to have learned from Y as much about the *U.S. Opposition to Treaties* motif (11 points) as the *U.S. Support for Treaties* motif (12 points).

Jen gave shorter responses to our reasoning questions than some of the other students. She sometimes added outside information from either her knowledge of the world or from what she learned in Part 1. In one instance, she mentioned the 1903 treaties: "I think the U.S. was still feeling the reverberations from dealing with a Frenchman in 1903." For another question, Jen used knowledge from outside the text by comparing Torrijos to other dictators: "When I hear the name, I get the impression of Marcos and Noriega." However, asked who Marcos is, she said "You know, dictator of, of that country, had the wife with the shoes." Jen also mentioned Marcos later, when justifying why the United States should not have negotiated with Torrijos: "I think the U.S. should've set a good example. I think after him was the Marcoses and other dictators...."

Jen did not show clear patterns of learning and reasoning across the two parts of the study. One consistent pattern, however, was her avoidance of details. In Part 1, she failed to learn dates and, at her best, gave only half the treaty names. In Part 2, Jen produced the lowest number of character names (only 4 of 16) and she mentioned only one of the five treaties by name.

Mitch

Mitch's learning was average, with 67 points after Professor Y and 52 after Congressman X. Mitch was the only student to learn less from the second text than the first text. His motif learning was very typical, showing some learning from all the motifs covered in the texts. Like other students, most of his learning points after Congressman X came from the *1977 Treaties* motif (17 points) and the *U.S. Opposition to Treaties* motif (15 points). After reading Professor Y, he earned most of his points in the *Canal Renegotiations (1970s)* motif (19 points) and the *1977 Treaties* motif (19 points). Compared with other students, Mitch had the largest difference between the amount he learned after Professor Y in support of the 1977 treaties and in opposition to them (12 vs. 2 points).

Mitch mentioned fewer arguments than any other student (9 compared to an average of 12.8 arguments). His arguments were also the least balanced, reflecting mainly the author's position; across the two texts, 8 of Mitch's arguments supported the author's position and only 1 was against. However, Mitch's reasoning responses usually were more complete than most other students. In some cases, he provided more than one justification in a response; he usually elaborated his opinion responses.

Only one pattern of Mitch's learning and reasoning that emerged in Part 1 reemerged in Part 2. He again wrote short summaries (119 and 134 words compared to average of 217) with little specific information. As in Part 1, his summaries were not representative of the information he had learned.

There was also one noticeable difference between his learning of the Acquisition Story and his learning of the Return Controversy. In Part 1, his learning of details—names and dates, especially—was rather weak. After the final reading in Part 2, however, Mitch included a larger than average number of character names (half of the 16 possible).

Robbie

Robbie showed less learning than most students, 48 points after Congressman X and 47 points after Professor Y. Interestingly, he used slightly more background information than everyone except George. He was the most selective learner. He learned nothing about 25% of the motifs in each text and the only motif that he learned much about concerned General Torrijos. Oddly, after reading Congressman X's text, he put less emphasis than anyone else on U.S. opposition to the treaties, which was the main thrust of X's text. (Only 44% of his points were earned in this motif, whereas the group averaged 64.5%.) Instead, most of his learning after Congressman X came from the *1977 Treaties* motif (13 points) and the *Torrijos* motif (11 points). Most of his points earned after Professor Y were in the *Canal Renegotiations (1970s)* motif (13 points) and the *U.S. Support for Treaties* motif (13 points). Also atypical was that Robbie, after reading Professor Y, mentioned more information opposing the treaties than supporting the treaties (12 vs. 2 points), despite the fact that Y's text more strongly favored the treaties.

Robbie's Part 2 learning and reasoning performance showed patterns similar to those in Part 1. First, his learning was relatively weak. He learned less than most of the students and he again failed to master any motif. Vivid images, rather than precise details, highlighted his learning. In one case, the image of Panama being filled with lawless individuals that was presented in the Acquisition Story of Professor Y stayed with Robbie. For one learning response, he said, "Panama is full of hoodlums and the dregs of society." This assertion, we infer, was derived from Professor Y's Part 1 characterization of early Panama, inhabited by "the rootless, lawless, transient who obeyed no authority." There is certainly no description of Panama's inhabitants (other than Torrijos) in Part 2's texts. This image surfaces also in a reasoning question when Robbie described Torrijos, he said, "I think he was a drug user, a drug trafficker, dirty scoundrel but that's all that seemed like was down in Panama anyway."

Second, Robbie was willing to answer anything, but he was limited by his lack of relevant knowledge. Instead, he relied on the texts for all of his information. On occasion, this led to contradictions, as in his opinion reversal concerning Torrijos, who Robbie saw as "a good guy" after Professor Y but as "a slime" after Congressman X. Second, and probably as a result of his lack of knowledge, Robbie was a naive reasoner. For example, he listed three reasons why the United States should not turn the Canal over to Panama: The United States still needs it, Panama doesn't like the United States, and Panama may "be jerks" by preventing U.S. access to the Canal. When asked whether his answer meant that the United States should break the treaty, Robbie responded, "I would discuss the treaty. Maybe not break it, maybe both of us can run it, maybe we can share." He made this comment following the last reading, and we were surprised how little understanding he seemed to have for the long, arduous negotiations described by both authors.

George

George showed a high level of learning, earning 79 points following Congressman X and a very high 101 points following Professor Y, his second text. His motif learning was typical after X's text, concentrated in the *1977 Treaties* (16 points) and the *U.S. Opposition to Treaties* motifs (17 points). Less typically, he also learned a substantial amount about the *U.S.–Panama Relations (1914–1964)* motif. Also less typically, George included information from Part 1 in his summary. Following Professor Y's text, he learned most about the *U.S. Support for Treaties* motif (32 points), but, like most students, he also learned about the *U.S. Opposition to Treaties* motif.

George's learning and reasoning responses reflected his background knowledge and his conservative political viewpoints. He was strongly opposed to the treaties. Showing a remarkable (although unverifiable) memory of childhood, he recalled, "I wasn't happy with it in '77 and I'm not happy with it now. (An experimenter asked "How old were you in 1977?") 10, 10 years old. I mean, it was a big issue. It was on the news talking about it. I remember seeing right after they signed it, them lowering the American flag and putting up the Panamanian flag in the zone. The reasons I felt at the time were that the Americans built and spent their money on the canal, why shouldn't we be allowed to keep it? The Panamanians didn't want the treaty in the first place, they should have never signed. Now, that's looking at it from a 10-year-old's point of view. Basically, that type of opinion is still held. I wasn't looking at it in military reasons in that point in time but there are a lot of other reasons."

This attitude toward the treaty is also reflected in George's hope for a reversal of the treaty implementation: "I have a feeling [Panama is] planning on reneging on that treaty. If this should occur, if there's a reason for them to have to, I hope they do, then the United States can renege on their half of the treaty and take the whole thing back again." He seemed to have little respect for Panama: "A country like Panama just breeds the type of people like Torrijos and Noriega to take power."

However, George also occasionally expressed more subtle judgments, as in his response to why the United States negotiated with Torrijos: "I think largely, and this is just my opinion, that's the type of person Carter was. He wasn't a man given to any type of hostility or warfare. That's one thing I do respect about Carter is the fact that his intentions were honest and peaceful. The contribution he had in solving the Middle East crisis with Israel and Egypt is an indication of that....I don't believe he ever lied to the country. One of the reasons why Torrijos managed to get that treaty pushed through was because of the nature of Carter. He took total advantage of the kind of man that Carter was."

Three patterns of George's learning and reasoning that emerged in Part 1 also appeared in his Part 2 answers. First, his summaries were information packed. His summary contained more information than average after both texts, more than any student after Congressman X (38 points compared with an average of 21), and 30 points compared with the average of 18 after Professor Y. Second, he attended to details. After both assignments, he cited more dates than the others, 9 of the 13 dates after Congressman X and 7 after Professor Y. Across the two texts he mentioned 12 of the 13 dates at least once. He also noted the character names unusually well, 11 of the 16 important characters involved in the story across the two texts.

Third, George included more history and current events knowledge than the other students. George compared Torrijos to Noriega: "I'm sure he was as big an oppressor, if not more, than Manuel Noriega. He had just as much a hand in the drug trafficking as Noriega did." The 1989 U.S. invasion of Panama also was used in his response to the question of whether the United States should turn the Canal over to Panama in 1999: "If we manage to conveniently find another problem and rush in there like we did in 1989 in 1999, then…we can stage some kind of crisis down there…. The Americans have done it before and are quite capable of doing it again."

SUMMARY AND CONCLUSIONS

Students, having learned about the Panama Canal Acquisition Story, participated in a second learning phase, in which they read arguments about the 1977 U.S.–Panama treaties from additional excerpts of two of the texts they read in Part 1. Congressman X's text argued strongly, and without discussion of counterarguments, against ratification of the treaties that would return control of the Canal to Panama in 1999. Professor Y, in a more balanced and more factual account, argued in favor of ratifying the 1977 treaties. In procedures parallel to those of Part 1, students responded to comprehension and reasoning questions and wrote summaries following each text.

The two texts emphasized different parts (motifs) of the history of the Return Controversy, and students typically learned different things from the two texts. They learned mainly about the treaties themselves and U.S. opposition to the texts from Congressman X and more about the history of negotiations and reasons to favor the treaty, in addition to the treaty itself, from Professor Y.

Differences between the two texts were reflected in other ways. In summarizing Congressman X's text, some students acknowledged the argumentative structure of the text, in fact making the controversy about the return the central part of the story. Summaries following Professor Y placed events in a fuller historical context and did not highlight the controversies about the return. Differences in the bias of the two texts showed several effects. First, although Professor Y's text argued for ratification of the 1977 treaties, he presented arguments on both sides, and students used his supporting arguments as well as his opposing arguments in their reasoning. Second, students spontaneously noted the bias in X's text, and all except one student perceived it as more biased than Y's text.

As we also observed in the Acquisition Story, student reasoning on value questions was influenced by the texts. For example, some, but not all, students were more likely to conclude that the new treaties were fair to the United States after Y's text than after X's text. Students' opinions on whether the United States should actually return the Canal as stipulated also showed some text influence. Thus, although perhaps not as strongly as in Part 1, instability characterized students' opinions about controversial issues. Texts had a significant influence on most students in one or more question.

Equally important, if less dramatic, was evidence that students attempted to develop a consistent accumulative learning across texts. They tended to notice important text differences, for example, in the relative importance the two texts placed on the economic and strategic value of the Canal. And they detected gaps in the texts. That the students had to consider two texts and one issue may have brought such gaps to attention. Students, although sometimes noting discrepancies between the two texts (as well as differences in the authors' opinions), showed little spontaneous questioning of the authors' sources.

We observed individual differences in learning and reasoning that were largely consistent with students' performance on the Acquisition Story. The students who learned best in Part 1 also learned best in Part 2. The student who learned the least in Part 1 also learned the least in Part 2. Styles of learning also showed some consistency. For example, Eileen and George again attended to details, and Dave and Jen again did not. However, one student, Mitch moved from ignoring to attending to details. Students varied also in their responsiveness to text influence. However, differences in responsiveness were not a simple matter of resistance to text bias by sophisticated students; one of our best learners, Dave, was highly responsive to text influence and one of our poorest learners, Robbie, was the least responsive. A general implication of the pattern of results is that this responsiveness to text arguments is a straightforward consequence of acquiring information from the text. Only students more sophisticated or more knowledgeable can be expected to discount text arguments as a result of sourcing.

Chapter 8

Reasoning About a Hypothetical Scenario

As a final exercise in history-related reasoning, we provided our students with a scenario, a situation created by the authors. In this scenario, the government of Panama falls to a military coup, which in turn is the object of rebel military action. The perceived threat to stability and thus to the Canal causes some in the United States to argue for delaying indefinitely the final implementation of the 1977 treaties (i.e., the withdrawal of American forces), in effect failing to honor the commitment to convert absolute control of the Canal Zone to Panama. A "Postponement Bill" to this effect is introduced in the Senate. The key question before our subjects was this: *Given this scenario, how would you recommend that your senators vote on the Postponement Bill?*

In addition, we asked subjects for their opinions about the 1977 treaties. In both the scenario and the questions about the 1977 treaties, we were interested in certain aspects of the subjects' reasoning. Would students' reasoning reflect what they had learned? Would it reflect opinions they had formed about the wisdom of the 1977 treaties, which had been the central issue in their last assignments? More generally, would reasoning be dominated by general knowledge and pragmatic reasoning schemas (Holland, Holyoak, Nisbett, & Thagard, 1986) that anyone might be expected to use in these situations or would there be some influence of learning a bit of relevant history? Our assumption is that relevant learning attenuates the dominant roles played by general knowledge and pragmatic reasoning schemas. In our case, learning about the Panama Canal could be expected to provide a context for reasoning about a relevant scenario, just as learning about the Acquisition Story provided a context for reasoning about the Return Controversy (chapter 7).

In reasoning about the scenario, several sources of information could be used. Subjects could use the information in the scenario to reason about the hypothetical events. Also, we assume that most students have a supply of schematic knowledge concerning *military dictatorships*, *guerrilla warfare*, *Latin American instability*, *Yankee Imperialism*, including some "scripts" (Schank & Abelson, 1977) about how popular uprisings play out. These schemata and scripts could serve students in reasoning about situations. In addition, learning about the Acquisition Story and the Return Controversy should allow subjects to replace schemata and stereotypes with contextualizing knowledge. Subjects might make historical references and show some influence of texts. Or, more generally, they might use knowledge about the history of the Canal to provide a context for the interpretation of the scenario. To assess these possibilities, we can examine differences in reasoning between the subjects who had learned about the Canal and a group of control subjects who had not.

THE PROCEDURES

Nine students, our six learning subjects and three controls who had not participated in the history learning phase of the study, participated in the eighth session. Brief descriptions of the control subjects follow:

Control 1, Suzanne, was a senior majoring in economics. Her Panama knowledge was higher than average, perhaps because she had a class in American history and one in Latin American history. She demonstrated a solid basic knowledge about the Canal, its history, and the 1977 treaties, but lacked detailed information.

Control 2, Sean, was a psychology major. His Panama knowledge was average for the subjects and controls. Although he knew general information about the Canal, he knew practically none of its history and only provided vague answers about the 1977 treaties.

Control 3, Emily, was a senior in the nursing school. She had very little knowledge about the Canal, its history, or the 1977 treaties.

Students first summarized what they knew about the 1977 treaties. (The learning subjects had learned about the treaties during Part 2 of the study. The control subjects read a brief text covering the treaties after their first session.) We assumed correctly that subjects would remember the most important parts of the treaties. We tested their knowledge for the following key treaty provisions: All operations and ownership of the Canal would become Panama's; the effective date was Dec. 31, 1999; the United States had to pay Panama; the Canal would stay neutral and open to all countries. All nine students indicated a satisfactory knowledge of the key terms of the treaties. Next, the students were asked three questions concerning their attitudes toward the 1977 treaties. The remainder of Session 8 was devoted to the scenario. Students read the scenario of hypothetical events in Panama leading to the introduction of the Postponement Bill in the U.S. Senate, and then summarized it. Finally, they were asked a series of questions based on the scenario. We first report their attitudes toward the treaties and then their responses to the questions.

ATTITUDES TOWARD THE TREATIES

There were three important questions concerning subjects' attitudes toward the 1977 treaties: whether students favored the 1977 treaties, whether they believed the

United States should fulfill the terms of the treaties, and whether there were any circumstances under which they thought the United States should not honor the treaties. Responses to these questions are summarized in the following paragraphs.

Should the United States Have Negotiated and Signed New Treaties with Panama?

All students except one supported the 1977 treaties, four without serious reservations (Eileen, Jen, Mitch, George) and one subject (Dave) with a hedge. Dave supported the treaty but wanted to assure that the United States would "have some degree of control." Only Robbie said NO to the idea of negotiating and signing new treaties in 1977. Thus, contrary to the central thesis of Congressman X, who in other ways showed much influence on students' reasoning, all except one student indicated some degree of approval with the 1977 treaties, in accordance with Professor Y's arguments.[23]

In justifying their opinions on the 1977 treaties, students most frequently cited *economic* and *ethical* considerations. Text influences were clear. In the *economic* category, two students echoed the two-part argument of Professor Y: The United States needed to be on good terms with Latin America for economic gain, and the treaties provided a means to be on good terms. A second "economic" justification came from Robbie, who in justifying his response against the U.S. signing of the treaties, claimed that the treaties would cost the United States too much.

An *ethical* justification used by two students can be summarized as follows: "It is America's responsibility because it's the right thing to do." Robbie, again, had a different kind of ethical justification, that the United States should not have negotiated with Torrijos because of his drug ties.

We see use of the Canal's history in students' responses. George gave a detailed account of the 1903–1977 history that included this: "We have been (negotiating) since the Canal was built. In 1921 we had to give money to Colombia and raise the annuity from $250,000 to $430,000...and Ike raised it up to $1.93 million or something to that extent. And in 1964–1967, 1974 Richard Nixon had Kissinger negotiating with them. So 1977 was just the final situation...." This detailed reference to history is consistent with George's superior learning of the Canal story and his better than average history knowledge. Mitch also made reference to this earlier history but his comment was less specific. He said "we vaguely promised that the Panamanians would eventually get control. We never set a particular date. After each president got into office, after the '30s, after we had it for a while, the Panamanians became unruly and demanded a set date...." Less detailed use of what they had learned came from other subjects, including Robbie, whose arguments

---

[23]It is possible that students were more persuaded by Congressman X in forming their opinions about the United States role in the history of the Canal than by his fundamental thesis concerning ownership of the Canal. However, it is also possible that subjects were more likely to agree with an actual decision taken by their government than with an argument that had already failed to carry the day.

that Torrijos or his family were involved in drug trafficking and the idea that turning over the Canal was "making us look bad" echoed observations of Congressman X. The hedge offered by Dave in his support of the treaty also reflected an argument made by X about the risk of differing interpretations of the treaty provisions.

The control subjects also agreed with the 1977 treaties, but their reasoning was more impoverished. Their responses were shorter, and they depended more on generalized schemata. Two students justified the treaty on vague ethical grounds. For example, Suzanne said, "...because the land belonged to Panama in the first place..." and Sean commented, "It's their country..." The third subject, Emily, appeared to use a practical justification when she stated, "I think there was a definite problem with the future of the Canal..."

This pattern is one we see generally in comparing learning subjects with control subjects. Students who have not learned the relevant history have recourse only to general ethical and practical reasons to justify their opinions. This is important in suggesting the ways that historical learning can influence reasoning. It provides not so much specific historical events to use in reasoning as a historical perspective that frames basically ahistorical ethical, economic, and pragmatic reasoning.

Given That We Signed the Treaties, Should We Follow Through with the Terms of the Treaties?

Four of the six learning subjects gave unqualified YES answers to this question, and two (Dave, Robbie) gave hedged (YES, BUT) responses, essentially a hope that the treaties would be modified. Robbie came close to a negative response: "I guess we have to. My personal opinion would be no...." Here Robbie expresses the conflict between a sense of legal obligation and his own attitude against the treaties.

This legal obligation was indeed the dominant justification given by subjects. All six subjects said, in essence, that now that the treaties are signed, the United States is obligated to follow through on them. Two students (Eileen, Jen) showed a more elaborate legal justification, agreeing that the United States should follow through with its treaty obligation, but seek legal justifications for possible noncompliance. Eileen said, "It seems we should follow through. [But] if there were serious problems, if the Canal would be closed, refusing to let us through...." Jen said, "Terms of the treaty say we can't intervene but I think it's how you look at it. If we say we intervened because we wanted to intervene then it's against the treaty. But if we intervene because the Canal is in danger then it goes along with what the treaty says."

The three control subjects agreed that the United States should follow through on its treaty obligations, but again provided simpler justifications than the learning subjects. One subject (Sean) gave a legal justification, and another (Emily) provided a pragmatic justification in which legal obligation was implied but not central: "Yes, because if we don't, our credibility would be lousy." The third control subject, Suzanne, provided a more naive response: "It was a good idea in the first place. Wouldn't be very nice (to renege on the treaty) I suppose." This expression of a treaty obligation, perhaps seen as not much stronger than an agreement between neighbors, stands in contrast to the richer treaty-based justifications of some (but not all) learning subjects.

This question about honoring the treaties was essentially asked in Part 2 of the study in a slightly different form: "Should we turn the Canal over to Panama in 1999?" As we reported in chapter 7, students answered this question affirmatively in 11 of 12 opportunities, with one subject responding YES after reading Professor Y and NO after reading Congressman X. Thus students were consistent over time in their affirmation of U.S. treaty obligations, and in their primarily legal justifications for this opinion.

Interestingly, the two students who provided hedges had also not given completely affirmative answers in Part 2 after reading Congressman X. One of these was Robbie, who responded NO in Part 2 after reading Congressman X. Robbie believed that the United States should not return the Canal but also believed that the treaties are an obligation. The other student who hedged on treaty obligations (Dave), earlier had great difficulty answering the treaties obligation question after reading Congressman X. Dave (see chapter 7) struggled through more than 800 words trying to formulate a satisfying answer.

Are There Any Circumstances Under Which the United States Should Not Honor the Treaties?

All subjects envisioned some circumstance that would justify the United States reneging on the treaties. There were three kinds of circumstances: if Panama first violated its treaty obligations (4 students, 2 learning and 2 control), if Panama neglected the Canal (2 students, 1 learning and 1 control), or if there were a war in Panama (2 learning students). One subject, Jen, constructed a circumstance with knowledge about U.S.–Panama relations: "I think Noriega may have a vendetta to pay back the U.S....If Noriega did something so drastic that we couldn't feasibly turn it over...."

In summary, we conclude that both learners and control subjects held a primarily legal attitude toward the U.S. 1977 treaty obligations. Four of the six learning students had supported the treaties at the end of Part 2. Now, even subjects with reservations about the wisdom of the 1977 treaties indicated that the United States should fulfill its treaty obligations. The three control subjects, who did not experience the learning phase of the study, were unanimous in their support of the 1977 treaties and in their belief that they should be honored. Nevertheless, none of the subjects, learning or control, were absolutists on the matter of treaty obligations. All readily imagined circumstances that would justify reneging on the treaty.

THE SCENARIO

The scenario provided a situation that shared features with these imagined circumstances: Instability and an armed rebellion inside Panama. The question was how the students would respond to the prospects of treaty noncompliance raised by the scenario. The complete scenario is as follows:

In October 1992, the last of the U.S. invasion force leaves Panama. The current government is in control. One year later, the current government retains power by a narrow margin. The economy of the country, which has steadily declined since 1990 despite increases in United States aid, worsens during 1994 and 1995. The unemployment rate reaches 31% in the summer of 1995. There are daily reports of strikes and general disorder. The crime rate has soared.

As a result of unrest, in September 1995, control of the government is seized in a military coup by the head of the army, General Jorge Castillero. The new government proclaims its intention to have friendly relations with the U.S. No Panamanian troops move toward the Canal. Inside Panama, strong opposition is voiced against the coup. "La Pressa", the major independent newspaper of Panama City proclaims it "a dark day for democracy". However the coup has wide support among the army. In October, the new Panama Government announces that the change of government was necessary to restore order to the country and to revive its economy. The job will take 5 years and free elections will be held in February 2000. The U.S. and all Latin American governments recognize the new government of Castillero.

In December 1995, in commemoration of the 50th anniversary of the end of WWII and in recognition of five years of democracy and stability throughout Europe, a treaty ending NATO and the Warsaw Pact is signed in Switzerland.

In May 1996, word of lightly armed guerrilla units, opposed to the military dictatorship, reaches Washington. Six months later, the guerrilla units make a surprise attack on Panamanian Army maneuvers in a small eastern village. Casualties are reported on both sides. In January 1997, Intelligence reports say guerrilla units have increased in number. A report of the Panama Field Commander for the Eastern Region estimates no more than 900, while the CIA report estimates guerrilla strength at around 2,500. Both reports say the rebels have Cuban-made automatic weapons and grenade launchers.

In November 1997, increased search and destroy missions by the army fail to defeat the rebels. They continue to extend their activities using attacks on small army groups and sabotage. A power plant about 100 miles west of the Canal is blown up and a Panamanian colonel is assassinated near the former Canal Zone.

As a result, the U.S. President announces 1000 additional American troops are on their way to Panama to increase security around the Canal. Senator Jesse Helms, in a speech on the Senate Floor, calls for the nullification of the Panama Canal Treaty of 1977. He cites the growing strength of the rebels and says that the security of the Panama Canal clearly cannot be guaranteed by the government. Other Senators argue that American military presence in the canal is in effect until December 31, 1999 and that it is too early to take any such action against the terms of the treaty.

In 1998, the Panama Canal Commission boasts that its employees, now 92% Panamanian, have reached a high productivity level and returned a profit for the first time since 1982 without raising tolls. However the first six months of 1998 are marked with increasingly vocal opposition to the Panama government. After Panamanian troops shoot and kill 41 civilians during a sweep for rebels, opposition leaders protest the government's human rights violations and claim increasing support for their cause. A demonstration in Panama City against the government draws about 5000 people and is forcibly broken up. Demonstrations in the capital continue. In one incident, shots are exchanged and dozens are wounded. At least 23 are killed and 200 are arrested.

In January 1999, the Panamanian Government, citing increased rebel success and their use of Cuban training and weapons, asks for U.S. assistance in halting Cuban shipments to the rebels. Senator Helms, appearing on Night Line, renews his call for nullification.

In March 1999, a bill is introduced into Congress to postpone American troop withdrawal from the Canal indefinitely, or "until such time that the President verifies that the security of the Canal Zone and the safety of Americans living in Panama can be guaranteed." The rebel leaders announce that they will lay down their arms if free elections are held immediately. The government responds by saying the election for February, 2000 will be held as scheduled, but not before. The fighting escalates. In April, two off-duty American soldiers stationed in Panama are shot and killed while shopping in Panama City.

In October, after 7 weeks of debate, the Senate prepares to vote on the "Postponement Bill". International observers in Panama to supervise the campaign process report strong support for the opposition party and are optimistic about a fair and democratic election in February because they find no evidence of intimidation or bribery in the rural provinces.

The scenario established a plausible situation for subjects to consider. What kinds of arguments would they make on the question of the Postponement Bill? For our purposes, there are several possibilities to consider: Arguments can appeal pragmatically to the situation described in the scenario and the student's beliefs about the consequences of the proposed action. And arguments can appeal to legal obligations, to ethical values, and to historical events. Of course, one expects a mix of these arguments generally, rather than the exclusive use of only one.

Situation-Based Arguments

Arguments can appeal to the situation itself, supplemented by the subjects' beliefs about the consequences of postponement. For example, one might argue that withdrawing the remaining U.S. troops would jeopardize the operation of the Canal, disrupting international commerce, or leading to some other negative outcome. One might argue against the same concern from the opposite premise: The operation of the Canal by Panama, according to the scenario, has been successful despite the crisis, and there's no reason to believe that would change. As a final example, one might argue against the Postponement Bill not because it violates a treaty commitment, but on the grounds that it would cause resentment against the United

States in Panama and perhaps throughout Latin America. What's interesting about situation-based arguments is that they rely mainly on the student's beliefs about how things work out in such situations, coupled with the student's values concerning the outcomes. These beliefs are informed by actual knowledge as well as stereotyped beliefs (about military dictatorships, populist rebellions, Latin American instability, etc.).

Legal (Treaty-Based) Arguments

One response to the Postponement Bill is to point to the binding nature of treaties and to the terms of the U.S.–Panama treaties. Such an argument would lead to a recommendation against the Postponement Bill.

Ethical Principles Arguments

One might argue, perhaps but not necessarily reciting the sanctity of treaties, that ethical considerations require the United States to complete its withdrawal from Panama. Other ethical arguments might work in the opposite direction: Abandoning the citizens of Panama or the Canal to the continuing dangers of both dictatorship and instability would be unethical.

Historical Arguments

In support of situation-based, legal, or ethical arguments, one might argue that the history of U.S.–Panamanian relations suggests a vote either for or against the Postponement Bill. Because historical arguments were more detailed arguments within the other three categories, they overlapped instead of being a separate category. The students, having been exposed to texts that deal both with the acquisition of the Canal Zone by the United States and with the 1977 treaties, might see these histories as relevant. For example, one might have come to believe that Panama had been victimized in the Acquisition Story, and that fairness requires honoring the treaties that ended the "victimization." Contrastingly, one might have come to believe not only that the U.S. acquisition of the Canal came about by proper and just means, but that the 1977 treaties mistakenly abandoned legitimate U.S. interest for the sake of a misguided repair of history. (This was essentially Congressman X's argument against the 1977 treaties.) Other forms of historical argument would be more general and dependent on analogic reasoning, making reference to historical events (e.g., the consequence of abandonment of other treaties). Such arguments would, of course, depend on specific historical knowledge that we would not expect our subjects to have.

With these categories of arguments in mind, we examine how our subjects dealt with questions prompted by the scenario.

How Would You Recommend That Your Senator Vote on the Postponement Bill? Why?

Our subjects were strongly in favor of the Postponement Bill. Only one of our nine subjects, Eileen, a learning subject, indicated a recommendation against it. All other students were in favor of the bill, in essence, favoring reneging on the treaties. This attitude is consistent with the opinion, voiced by subjects prior to the scenario, that there were circumstances under which they would favor noncompliance by the United States. In explaining their opinions, students provided justifications that were primarily "ethical" (3 subjects) and "situation-based" (3 subjects), the latter essentially pragmatic extrapolations of likely consequences from the scenario. No historical justifications were used.

Ethical Justifications.   Three students, two learning subjects and one control subject, argued that keeping U.S. troops in Panama would help Panama. Jen, a learning subject, said, "they'd be helping Panama by postponing the pullout." Dave, also a learning subject, said, "I'd want to see the U.S. postpone giving the Canal away until after the February 2000 elections." The ethical basis for this justification lies in Dave's belief that U.S. troops would be there to ensure fair elections. The control subject, Emily, said, "seems like we want to work with the government of Panama."

Situation-Based Justifications.   The common theme to situation-based justifications is the idea that the Canal should not be turned over to a country in chaos, which is the rationale the scenario attributes to proponents of the Postponement Bill. Two learning subjects (Mitch, Robbie) asserted that Panama is unstable and provided examples from the scenario in support of this assertion. Suzanne, a control subject, showed less use of scenario information and was less sure of her recommendation. She said, "I guess it would be right to postpone it until the government is stable. I guess, depending upon the results of the election. It wouldn't be until February 2000, 2 months after. No one would know if the government was a hostile government."

Legal Justifications.   One learning subject, George, gave a "legal" justification. He observed that the 1977 treaties allow the United States to protect the Canal if it is in danger, and he believed that the Canal was threatened. Accordingly, postponing troop withdrawal is legally allowed by the treaties.

Other Justifications.   Eileen, the only student to recommend against the Postponement Bill, provided no justification: "Against it. They should pull the troops out." The final subject, a control (Sean), said, "It sounds like there are a lot of military things going on. I think the U.S. should stay down there until things settled down." This could be considered either an appeal to pragmatic self-interest (situation-based) or an appeal to ethical values (protecting people), but does not unambiguously fit into a single category.

Role of the Elections.   Three students, two learning subjects (Dave and George) and one control subject (Suzanne), tied their recommendation for the Postponement Bill to the February 2000 elections. Their reasoning illustrates that an apparently important part of the situation can be used in very different ways. (In fact, the justifications of these subjects fell into three different categories, as described earlier.) Dave, who was both more politically aware and more liberal than most students, assumed the postponement would be a temporary action that would encourage democracy because the American troops in Panama would act as election monitors. George, a legal justifier, used the elections in a different way—to argue that postponement would have only short term effects: "...if free elections are held in February 2000, then the Americans will only be there for another 2 months...4 or 5 months, tops." The third student, Suzanne, added a practical constraint on the role of the elections, suggesting postponement until the government is stable, "depending on the results of the election."

Prior Attitudes and the Scenario Judgments

Students' recommendations and justifications on the Postponement Bill were generally related to their attitudes toward the 1977 treaties, as assessed before the scenario. The scenario functioned as an application of their previously formed attitudes on the 1977 treaties. There are two different components to this application: students' attitude toward the 1977 treaties and their attitude toward noncompliance with the treaties. The only subject against the treaties (Robbie), readily recommended noncompliance (postponement). A second student (Dave), who was painfully ambivalent about the treaties, also readily recommended noncompliance in the scenario. Three of the four learning subjects who favored the 1977 treaties also recommended noncompliance in the scenario. For these students, what they thought in advance about possible circumstances of noncompliance predicted their recommendations.

Eileen's attitude and her recommendation were consistent in the belief that the United States should honor the 1977 treaties, and with her support of the treaties themselves. Her earlier attitude was that a failure by Panama to honor the treaties would be the only circumstance that would justify noncompliance by the United States. The scenario gave her no strong reason for concern on this point, so her recommendation was against postponement.

Dave had said that he would favor breaking the 1977 treaties under circumstances of civil war in Panama. The scenario establishes military actions that approach civil war and Dave referred to this in his summary of the scenario.

Jen was the only subject, prior to the scenario, not to provide a specific circumstance that would lead to noncompliance, instead answering that question in terms of real-world possibilities. Her summary listed a number of things that have occurred to make Panama less stable.

Mitch, prior to the scenario, said that "radical change in Panama" would be a reason to ignore the treaties. He favored postponement because "it's obvious that there's unrest, that there's no stability. It's typical Panama...."

Robbie, prior to the scenario, provided a narrow range of circumstances for U.S. noncompliance. "No, we signed it, we have to go by it. Except maybe if they would attack the U.S. for any reason. ...I think we could disregard the treaty if there was a war. That would be the only circumstance." After the scenario, however, Robbie recommended postponement quite strongly: "I'd vote yes to nullify the treaty because obviously Panama can't control their own government, let alone have control of the Canal." The scenario seems to have altered Robbie's view on compliance by providing circumstances that were beyond what he considered. Robbie was personally opposed to the 1977 treaties, and this appears to have made it easier to advocate postponement.

George, prior to the scenario, allowed noncompliance if Panama first failed to honor the treaties. Because he strongly believed that postponement at this point was not a violation of the treaties, his prior attitude and his postponement justification were consistent. Postponement was needed because Panama was so unstable that the operation of the Canal is threatened.

The three control subjects all favored postponement and all had foreseen circumstances, prior to the scenario, that would justify noncompliance by the United States. There were not strong connections, however, for any of these students. Emily's response to the circumstances question was "if they renege on their promises, close down the Canal or something," whereas she favored postponement because of the problems in Panama. Similarly, Sean favored postponement "...until things settled down," but his circumstances for reneging were actions by Panama directly against the United States or Panamanian neglect of the Canal, neither of which are part of the scenario. Finally, Suzanne, prior to the scenario, would abrogate the treaties "only if Panama did something against the treaties...," whereas she favored postponement "...until the government is stable..." .

In summary, there are links between responses to the scenario and prior attitudes toward the treaties themselves as well as attitudes toward treaty compliance. All students saw circumstances that would justify noncompliance with the 1977 treaties, and all except one subject judged the scenario to have established circumstances consistent with postponement. This student was quite consistent in believing that the treaties should be honored and in not recommending the Postponement Bill. Overall, the learning subjects seemed to have closer links between the circumstances they believed would justify not honoring the treaties and their reasons for supporting the Postponement Bill. It is also clear, however, that even learning subjects' responses to the scenario were not completely predictable from their earlier attitudes toward noncompliance. Most students

TABLE 8.1
Number of Arguments in Each Category

	Situation	Legal	Text	Opinion	Unclassified
Learning	30	6	3	2	9
Control	23	1	0	0	0

favored the 1977 treaties and suggested noncompliance only in limited circumstances. By providing specific circumstances not identical to ones that subjects could imagine in the abstract, the scenario moved students toward noncompliance.

Arguments For and Against Postponement

We next asked students to list, in writing, arguments for and against the proposition contained in the Postponement Bill: "The U.S. should postpone the withdrawal of the troops indefinitely."

Students generated more arguments that agreed with their position than with the position they opposed.[24] The only student who would vote against the Postponement Bill, Eileen, was also the only student to give more arguments against than for postponement. Overall there were 74 arguments generated, 45 for postponement and 29 against.

Arguments were dominated by reference to the specific situation, rather than legal, ethical or historical considerations. Table 8.1 indicates the number of arguments classifiable into each of our major categories.

As shown in Table 8.1, most arguments relied primarily on the "facts" of the situation described in the scenario. Among control subjects, situation-based arguments accounted for all except one argument. Furthermore, only 7 of their 23 situation-based arguments went beyond listing a simple fact. Learning subjects showed more diversity, with occasional legal arguments and references to texts they had read.

Subjects were asked to select their three best arguments on each side and elaborate them. Our analysis of arguments is restricted here to those arguments, which are shown in Table 8.2. This table also contains history-based arguments that were included as explanations for the other reasoning categories.

Although all students produced three arguments supporting postponement, only Eileen, Dave, Mitch, and Robbie, four learning subjects, could give three arguments against postponement, therefore there were only 48 expanded arguments.

Situation-Based Arguments. All situation-based arguments make explicit and substantial use of information from the scenario or from similar

---

[24]This ability to generate more arguments on the side one favors has also been observed by Voss, Schooler, Kennet, Wolfe, and Silfies (1990).

situations that occur in the real world. The student typically augments this information with inferences based on beliefs about the world, well-known scripts about military coups, popular rebellion, security forces, supervised elections in Third World countries, etc. Thus, in some cases, the student can be said to use situation + script in making an argument. We refer more simply to situation-based arguments, however. Situation-based arguments included the large majority of arguments, 73% of learning subjects' arguments and 87% of control subjects' arguments.

Learning subjects Eileen and Dave both gave good examples of arguments that draw on the situation. Eileen argued, "The Canal could very well close during a fight between Castillero and opposition leaders." Dave argued, "Continued troop presence may serve to further guerrilla activity, possibly with U.S. troops as targets." In both cases, there is some contribution of scripted belief (e.g., the action likely to be taken by guerrillas). The three controls relied very heavily on this type of situation-based argument. For instance, Emily argued, "The Canal's security can't be secured by the government right now because they are so busy trying to keep their own country under control."

Other situation-based arguments showed a stronger influence of scripted beliefs and knowledge. One rather sophisticated example came from Dave who mentioned the "possibility of troops acting beyond their jurisdiction, possibly opening fire on innocent Panamanians, provoking international outrage against the U.S."

George provided an especially elaborate example of the use of scripted knowledge: "There are a lot of rebels. They're Cuban trained and Cuban backed which means they're using Russian weapons. And if they are Cuban trained, they're probably going to be very good at jungle warfare. If the rebels get a good foothold on the country, it could very well become Communist…." The scenario contributed much less to this argument than did George's beliefs about the world.

Legal Arguments. Legal arguments relied on treaty provisions. Such arguments were made by five out of the six learning subjects and one of the three control subjects. The legal arguments of the control subject were much shorter than the learners' arguments.

All except one of the legal arguments were against postponement. These arguments were of two types: Four students said that a postponement would violate the 1977 treaties and one, Eileen, argued that the 1977 treaties would allow the U.S. to re-enter the Canal Zone if necessary, so there was no reason to postpone

TABLE 8.2
Categories of Students' Best Arguments

	Situation	Legal	Text	Opinion	History*
Learning	24	5	3	1	3
Control	13	2	0	0	0

*History overlaps with the other categories.

implementation of the treaty. Mitch illustrated the view that postponement violates the treaties: "The U.S. is bound by the 1977 treaties. We can do all the arguments we want, we signed the treaties. We can't get out of the treaties unless we renegotiate with Panama."

Whereas all four learning subjects who used a legal argument against postponement made elaborate arguments that referred to treaties, control subjects gave shorter responses containing less specifically about the treaties. The more complete of the two control arguments was: "We're going against the treaty that we signed."

The learning subject George, in contrast to all other subjects, used a legal argument to argue in favor of postponement. He reasoned that because the treaties allow for U.S. intervention if the Canal is threatened, postponing troop withdrawal is not violating the treaty. He believed the scenario situation constituted a threat to the Canal. "The treaty provides that American troops can intervene if the safety of the Canal is threatened. In this case it is. You have a colonel that was killed by the Zone so there is obviously rebel activity by the Zone. American soldiers were killed which means the rebels will have no problem doing that. And they'd have no problem rolling into the Zone and causing damage to the Canal if they saw fit...."

Text-Based Historical Arguments. Text-based arguments were rare, only three and all made by learning subjects. Eileen argued, "Once we left the Zone, it might be tougher to reenter," an argument made by Congressman X's text. Eileen's arguments against postponement include one she appears to have learned from Professor Y: "The Canal is a vital part of the Panamanian economy and it would be in their best advantage to keep it open."

Robbie also gave a text argument used by Congressman X against the 1977 treaties. Congressman X cited a passage in one of the treaties that gives Panama the right to detain ships to check for sanitary violations, arguing that Panama could use this provision against all U.S. ships to hold up military and commercial vessels. Robbie appeared to have the warning of Congressman X in mind when he argued that "[Panama] could be real jerks to the U.S. because in that treaty it says they could stop us and check our whole ship if they want to at any time."

Historical Arguments. We did not explicitly encourage students to use historical arguments and few arguments fell into this category. Only one student, George, made a clear historical analogy while arguing about the Postponement Bill. In his only argument against postponement, he said "The Panamanians might uprise [*sic*] and attack the Zone anyway. And this may not be all of them. The rebels and the people could have a unification against the Americans—have a common goal to fight against. The same thing happened with the communists and the nationalist Chinese in World War II when the Japanese invaded. They actually had a common goal to try to get rid of the Japanese. This could very well happen here."

Robbie tried, with limited success, to tie some history into an argument against postponement: "Americans are getting killed because of the revolution in Panama.

I think that's dumb because if they're having a revolution down there, it's sort of like a Vietnam deal...." He also said, "When we made this treaty, we gave them millions of dollars. Obviously that hasn't worked, they've still gone through 60 rulers in 70 years."

Opinions. Opinions masquerading as arguments were actually very rare, and the only two clear instances came from students who asserted their opinions that the United States is not responsible for Panama.

Eileen said that the "U.S. should let the Panamanians fight their own civil war." To get this opinion, any opinion, from the text-driven Eileen was interesting. This may be the only occasion on which she volunteered an opinion. Robbie gave this "let 'em fight their own war" opinion as one of his initial arguments but he didn't choose it as one of his expanded arguments: "We've been taking care of them for long enough."

Argument Themes

Another way to shed light on the students' arguments is to examine their underlying "themes." Most arguments favoring postponement were built on the need for stability in Panama. These arguments included explicit references to a threat to the Canal, political instability, or general references to unrest and problems in Panama. The control subjects' arguments expressed the stability theme almost exclusively (89% of the arguments). Arguments of learning subjects also expressed the stability theme (56% of the arguments), but their arguments expressed a wider range of concerns.

Simple stability arguments were similar across learning and control subjects. For example, learning subject Mitch said, "Violent conditions are present. It would be easy for either group to sabotage the Canal." And control subject Suzanne said, "Just a lot of unrest in the country. Because the Canal is so important that it should be governed by a stable government." However, more complete stability arguments were expressed only by learning subjects. For example, Jen commented, "The Canal needs to remain open. A lot of Central American countries depend on the Canal. It's their lifeline for trade. I think the Canal needs to be open in time of fighting. If U.S. pulls out, we're leaving the little Panamanian army to defend it against the rebels. There's no guarantee the Canal will stay open and operate correctly. I think the rebels blew up something 100 miles from the Canal. There's nothing to stop them from getting closer unless the U.S. army stays." Jen's learning about the Canal shows in this argument, and it contrasts with the simpler stability arguments that control subjects made.

Other themes expressed by the learning subjects in favor of postponement included the ideas that pulling troops out would be detrimental to the United States and that Panama might violate the treaties without a U.S. presence. An example of this is George's comment, "Well, American lives are at stake in the Zone." Dave voiced the concern that Panama may ignore the treaties, saying, "The guerrillas could gain control and agree not to recognize the treaty."

Themes expressed in the arguments against postponement were also more varied for the learning subjects. One third of their arguments expressed concern with problems the United States would face if the troops failed to pull out. One example is Dave's comment that "with U.S. troops remaining in the area, they would be used as targets [of guerrilla activity]."

The treaty violation argument can also be considered a theme, especially in the context of the ethical argument that it's not right to break a treaty. Jen said, "I don't think the treaty should be broken." A third theme seen in arguments against postponement is that there is no direct threat to the Canal. For instance, Mitch said, "Although there has been violence in the country, there's no visible or mentioned threat to the Canal...."

Like their arguments for postponement, control subjects' arguments against postponement expressed primarily one theme: Four of six arguments expressed the idea that Panama seems to be doing all right on its own. Sean noted that the scenario "says in 1998 with 92% Panamanians they had a profit without raising tolls so it sounds like they're doing all right by themselves."

Counter Arguments

The task of listing arguments on both sides sometimes forced the students to make arguments that directly countered their own position or provided facts that weakened their earlier argument. The learning subjects gave 15 arguments against their position on the Postponement Bill. Seven of those arguments can be seen as rebuttals to their arguments supporting their position about postponement. In the case of the controls, there were only six arguments given against postponement but four of those can be used as rebuttals against arguments for postponement.

There appear to be two varieties of argument-counterargument pairs. In one type, an argument *against* a student's belief does not share common ground with an argument *for* that belief. For example, a student might list the threat of instability as an argument for postponement and the success of the Panamanian Canal operation as an argument against postponement. A lack of explicit common ground thus avoids a contradiction.[25] The second type of argument pair brings each argument of the pair into common ground by referring to a single proposition. For example, a student might list instability as an argument *for* postponement and also as an argument *against* postponement. Under conditions of real uncertainty, this common grounding is useful. The arguments share a concern about a single

---

[25]It is of course possible to bring an argument that instability jeopardizes Canal operations into common ground with an argument that the Canal operations are effective. However, without some elaboration, the two arguments refer to two different propositions, one having to do with stability and the other having to do with effectiveness.

dimension and contrast on the outcome along that dimension (e.g., "Will Panama be more stable with troops present or with troops withdrawn?").

Learning and control students appear to have differed in their argument-counterargument types. The learning subjects often gave *for* and *against* arguments with common ground, or a single proposition. Control subjects tended to give "for" and "against" arguments that had different propositions.

An example of common ground is whether there is a direct threat to the Canal. Mitch used this proposition in two of his arguments. First, he supported postponement because the United States will have "very little power to stop any direct threat to the Canal." Then he argued against postponement by saying, "there is no visible or mentioned threat to the Canal."

A second example of a one-proposition argument pair is the effect of U.S. troops. Dave argued that U.S. "troops could be used to insure free and fair elections..." but he worried that those troops could become guerrilla targets or that they would "...act beyond their jurisdiction...and provoke an international outcry." Eileen, the only student who was against postponing troop withdrawal, argued that the U.S. troops might face fighting from both the Panamanian rebels and the Panamanian government. But one of her arguments for postponement was that "the U.S. presence might be a stabilizer." George gave a similar but more complex argument. When arguing in favor of postponement, he said the U.S. military had the right to be in Panama because the treaties allow the U.S. to protect the Canal if it is in danger, and he believed "in this case it is." However, he also worried, "The rebels and the people could have a unification against the Americans—have a common goal to fight against...."

The greater use of common ground arguments by the learning subjects may reflect their reasoning experience on other Panama Canal issues. They may have been more tuned to complexity, or may have become adept at focusing on issues that had two sides. In any event, their arguments can be judged somewhat more sophisticated in this respect. The controls, more naive reasoners on these issues, less often gave counterarguments that challenged their own preferred position.

Student Responses to Others' Arguments

Subjects, in addition to generating their own arguments, were asked to evaluate arguments that we provided. First, they were presented with a list of 9 arguments that opposed their own recommendation on the Postponement Bill. Subjects were asked to indicate their agreement or disagreement with each of the 9 arguments and to offer a rebuttal to any argument with which they disagreed. Later, subjects were given the alternative set of 9 arguments that agreed with their own position on the Postponement Bill, and again asked to rebut any with which they disagreed. The lists of arguments are included in Table 8.3 and Table 8.4, which also indicate which students agreed and disagreed with each argument.

Subjects agreed more with arguments on their side of the Postponement Bill, as one would expect. Indeed all subjects conformed to this expectation, except for one

TABLE 8.3

Arguments For the Postponement Bill and Number of Students Who Agreed and Disagreed

1. *Treaties are negotiated and signed when it is in the best interest of the countries involved. It is not in the best interest of the United States, or for that matter the world, to withdraw U.S. troops from Panama. Therefore, the United States can legitimately ignore the part of the Neutrality Treaty allowing only Panama's military in Panama.*

   3 Agree   Dave, Jen, Sean
   6 Disagree   Eileen, Mitch, Robbie, George, Emily, Suzanne

   Why students disagreed: Four students disagreed with the claim that the United States can legitimately ignore the treaty. Two (Eileen and George) argued that the United States would actually be upholding the treaty on the grounds that it allows such action if the Canal is in danger.

2. *Panama has a long history of unstable, undemocratic governments led by men like Torrijos and Noriega. The current government of Castillero is also a dictatorship. Because the government is so unstable and changes so frequently, it would not be able to effectively run the Canal.*

   4 Agree   Robbie, Emily, Sean, Suzanne
   5 Disagree   Eileen, Dave, Jen, Mitch, George

   Why students disagreed: Four of the five claimed the type of government does not have any bearing on whether or not the Canal is efficiently run.

3. *The present leader is a dictator who gained power through a military coup. He claims free elections will take place but after the United States leaves Panama, there is no guarantee he will honor his promise to hold elections in February.*

   7 Agree   Dave, Jen, Mitch, Robbie, Emily, Sean, Suzanne
   2 Disagree   Eileen, George

   Why students disagreed: Whether or not elections are held is not a problem for the United States to solve.

4. *After the Panama Canal Treaty ends, the United States has no control over who operates the canal. The current Advisor of the Panama Canal Commission was approved by the United States. Once the United States has no say about members of the PCC board, corruption and bribery could become widespread. Despite a profit in 1998, the operation of the Canal still has Americans involved and all Panamanian workers were trained by the United States. The United States has no guarantee that the next generation of workers will be adequately trained.*

   5 Agree   Eileen, Dave, Jen, Robbie, Suzanne
   4 Disagree   Mitch, George, Emily, Sean

   Why students disagreed: Three students disagreed with the premise of the argument that Panamanian workers would be incapable.

5. *There is nothing in the treaties that allows the United States to return to Panama if the Canal is threatened. The military should stay in Panama as a deterrent to violence not be forced to restore order when needed.*

   6 Agree   Eileen, Dave, Jen, Mitch, Sean, Suzanne
   3 Disagree   Robbie, George, Emily

(Continued)

TABLE 8.3 *(Continued)*

Why students disagreed: Not a strong enough factor to negate treaty. Robbie believed that if the United States wanted to maintain troops, it should renegotiate the treaties. The others said that leaving troops would violate the treaties.

6. *The Canal is still a necessary passageway for U.S. warships. The Navy needs to travel safely through the Canal at their will. Once the Panama Canal Treaty ends and there is no U.S. military in Panama, the warships could be attacked, or Panama could legally prevent U.S. passage at any time, leaving the United States no recourse.*

   4 Agree   Eileen, Dave, Robbie, Emily
   5 Disagree   Jen, Mitch, George, Sean, Suzanne

Why students disagreed: George and the two controls (Sean and Emily) claimed the treaties provide recourse for the United States. The learning subjects Jen and Mitch, using knowledge of the Return Controversy, argued that the Canal is helpful but no longer necessary for U.S. warships.

7. *By removing U.S. troops and jeopardizing the security and efficiency of the Canal, the United States faces world-wide embarrassment for its inability to safeguard international trade.*

   4 Agree   Dave, Jen, Mitch, Sean
   5 Disagree   Eileen, Robbie, George, Emily, Suzanne

Why students disagreed: Three thought that embarrassment was a "stupid" reason for violating the treaties. George argued that troop withdrawal would not necessarily lead to inefficiency and Eileen believed that the United States would not be faulted if Canal operations failed.

8. *The United States has spent the last 90 years making concessions to Panamanians for a treaty that was ratified by the Panamanian people in 1903. The United States has given Panama millions of dollars in fees and aid, provided training and turned over control of the Canal. The United States should at least be able to protect its investment.*

   9 Agree   Eileen, Dave, Jen, Mitch, Robbie, George, Emily, Sean, Suzanne
   0 Disagree

9. *Without the presence of U.S. military, American citizens are defenseless against the Panamanian mobs. Already two American soldiers were killed in Panama City. Faced with the threat of violence, the Americans still involved with the Canal will have to leave the area.*

   7 Agree   Dave, Jen, Mitch, Robbie, George, Emily, Sean
   2 Disagree   Eileen, Suzanne

Why students disagreed: Eileen suggested that violence results from military presence. Suzanne objected to an argument that seemed to put a higher value on U.S. lives compared with others' lives.

---

control subject (Emily), who agreed with five of the nine arguments in favor of postponement but seven of the nine arguments against postponement, despite being in favor of postponement herself. The remaining seven subjects favoring postponement agreed with between zero and four arguments (*Mean* = 2.6) against postponement and disagreed with between five and nine (*Mean* = 6.4) arguments. Eileen, the subject recommending against postponement, agreed with seven of the

TABLE 8.4

Arguments Against the Postponement Bill and Number of Students Who Agreed and Disagreed and Their Congruence Scores

---

1. *According to the Neutrality Treaty, the United States must remove all its military personnel by Dec. 31, 1999. If we postpone the withdrawl of U.S. troops beyond that date and time it is a clear violation of the treaty.*

    4 Agree   Eileen, Jen, Robbie, Emily
    5 Disagree   Dave, Mitch, George, Sean, Suzanne

Why students disagreed: Four of the five acknowledged the validity of the argument, but claimed that other factors take precedence, especially threats to the Canal's security that hadn't been foreseen.

2. *When the treaties were negotiated in the 1970s, the United States was fully aware of the risk of political instability, because Panama had a history of instability, including military coups. Nothing in the treaty requires either political stability nor a democratic government in Panama. The United States acknowledged the risk of instability in agreeing to the treaty.*

    5 Agree   Eileen, Dave, Jen, Mitch, Emily
    4 Disagree   Robbie, George, Sean, Suzanne

Why students disagreed: Only one actually disputed the argument that the United States acknowledged the risk of Panamanian instability by signing the 1977 treaties. Other subjects argued that other factors warranted priority.

3. *General Castillero has remained the leader for 5 years and free elections are scheduled in February and the international observers believe free elections are possible. Thus the risk of continued instability is not as high as it appears.*

    3 Agree   Dave, Jen, Suzanne
    6 Disagree   Eileen, Mitch, Robbie, George, Emily, Sean

Why students disagreed: All six disputed part of the argument, either that "the risk of continued instability is not as high as it appears;" or the argument that free elections will decrease instability. Eileen, although the argument supports her position, did not think elections were a sufficient reason to postpone troop withdrawal.

4. *The Canal has never been directly threatened, and has remained open throughout the transition period, and during Panama's operation has even returned a profit. Thus the threat to the Canal is exaggerated by proponents of the Postponement Bill.*

    3 Agree   Eileen, Emily, Suzanne
    6 Disagree   Dave, Jen, Mitch, Robbie, George, Sean

Why students disagreed: Four of the learning students rejected the premise, believing the Canal was threatened. Sean conceded the correctness of the argument but countered that the Canal may be threatened in the future.

5. *If the situation deteriorates to the point that the maintenance and operation of the Canal is seriously threatened so that neutral passage is impossible, the United States could send troops down.*

    6 Agree   Eileen, Jen, Robbie, Emily, Sean, Suzanne
    3 Disagree   Dave, Mitch, George

Why students disagreed: They argued that it's not sensible to remove troops and then have to send them back. This would miss the deterrent value of leaving them. Dave mentioned Congressman X's claim about it being easier to defend a position than to retake it.

TABLE 8.4 (*Continued*)

6. *The strategic importance of the Canal has greatly decreased since the threat of war with the Soviet Union and other Warsaw Pact countries is minor.*

   0 Agree
   9 Disagree   Eileen, Dave, Jen, Mitch, Robbie, George, Emily, Sean, Suzanne

Why students disagreed: The rebuttals fell into two categories. Five students (three learning subjects) disputed the argument that the Canal was strategically less important. Four students (also three learning subjects) conceded the Canal's strategic importance may be diminished but is still important for other reasons. Three students used an argument that would fall into the "historical" category used in Table 8.2.

7. *Failing to remove the troops as required by the treaty will be interpreted internationally as a clear violation of international law. The U.S. relations with other countries, especially Latin American countries, most of whom objected to the December 1989 invasion of Panama, will suffer further damage.*

   5 Agree   Eileen, Robbie, Emily, Sean, Suzanne
   4 Disagree   Dave, Jen, Mitch, George

Why students disagreed: This argument appears similar to #1 in arguing that postponing troop withdrawal violates the 1977 treaties. Despite the similarities, three students gave opposite agreement responses to the two arguments. The counterarguments were widely variable.

8. *Over the years, going back to when the United States first acquired the canal zone, U.S. policy toward the Panama region has essentially ignored the legitimate aspiration of the people of Panama and the neighboring area. The treaty is an attempt to set things right. To fail to honor it would be yet another blow against fairness.*

   2 Agree   Eileen, Emily
   7 Disagree   Dave, Jen, Mitch, Robbie, George, Sean, Suzanne

Why students disagreed: Three learning students (Jen, Robbie, and George) rejected the premise, countering (and using knowledge from the story) that the United States has not ignored Panama's aspirations. The other two learning students recognized the fairness argument, but objected to its use as "a little heavy-handed" (Dave) or as irrelevant because the aspirations of Panama's citizens are unclear here (Mitch).

9. *There are very few U.S. civilians still in the Canal zone and the threat to them is minimal. However, if the U.S. troops stay, American civilians as well as troops are more likely to be targets of violence.*

   4 Agree   Eileen, Dave, Mitch, Emily
   5 Disagree   Jen, Robbie, George, Sean, Suzanne

Why students disagreed: The three learning subjects (Jen, Robbie, and George) rejected the argument that the threat to Americans is minimal and they pointed to an event in the scenario as proof. The controls focused their disagreement on the presence of U.S. troops.

Congruence Scores

Eileen	Dave	Jen	Mitch	Robbie	George	Emily	Sean	Suzanne
12	14	12	12	12	11	7	14	10

nine antipostponement arguments and four of the nine propostponement arguments.

For each student, the sum of agreements with arguments supporting that subject's position and disagreements with arguments against the subject's position is an indicator of argument *congruence*. All subjects, again with the exception of Emily, showed high congruence ranging from 10 to 14 (maximum = 18). Notice that there are two ways to be congruent: agreeing with arguments that support and disagreeing with arguments that oppose a subject's position. Of the six learning subjects, three (Eileen, Dave, and Jen) were "agreers," showing more agreement with supporting arguments than disagreement with opposing arguments. Two learning subjects, George and Mitch, however, were "arguers" more often disagreeing with opposing arguments than agreeing with supporting arguments.

George especially was an "arguer." Although he was for postponement, only two of the nine propostponement arguments appealed to him. And he rejected all nine of the opposing arguments. One can characterize George as having his own ideas about this issue. He disagreed with the basic assumption that the Postponement Bill threatens to violate the 1977 treaties. In seven of the nine reasons he gave for disagreeing, he claimed that leaving troops in Panama is not a violation of the treaties because the treaties allow for a U.S. presence if the Canal is endangered. He argued that the Canal is threatened, so there is no treaty violation.

The reasons subjects gave for disagreeing with arguments reflected some shared perceptions on the scenario and generally converged with what subjects said in their own arguments. Learning subjects used information they had learned in this task as well as the others. An especially clear example is seen in Argument 5 *against* the Postponement Bill (see Table 8.4). All control subjects accepted this argument that the United States could go ahead with troop withdrawal as planned because it could always send troops later if necessary. They accepted this despite their own recommendation in favor of postponement. By contrast, three of the five learning subjects favoring postponement argued against it, taking the position that it is harder to send troops to trouble than to leave them in the first place, an argument made by Congressman X. This joins several other instances where we can see the effect of learning on reasoning about the scenario. Tables 8.3 and 8.4 contain a brief summary of why students disagreed with each argument.

SUMMARY AND CONCLUSIONS

The effects of history learning on reasoning can extend beyond actual historical situations to modeling the future. Such "modeling" requires students to envision situations for which what they have learned provides a context. Accordingly, hypothetical scenarios appear to provide a means of evaluating historical reasoning of students. Their value in this respect may be similar to what we have observed in counterfactual reasoning (chapter 5), where students were able to provide outcome-altered views when asked to consider the consequences of a counterfactual. In both cases, students envision, or model, a counterfactual world by applying their knowledge of actual history along with their general knowledge and pragmatic reasoning schemes.

In this context, we examined students' attitudes toward the 1977 Panama–U.S. treaties and their responses to a scenario that could encourage U.S. noncompliance with the final implementation of the treaties. Subjects, both those who had learned Panama Canal history and those who had not, believed that the 1977 treaties, once signed, should be honored. Two of the learning subjects, but none of the control subjects, however, were either opposed to or had reservations about the 1977 treaties. All students envisioned circumstances that would permit noncompliance, however, and all except one responded to the scenario by favoring the Postponement Bill, which would put the United States in noncompliance with the 1977 treaties. Students' arguments on this issue were most frequently *situation-based*, with some additional *legal* and *text-based* arguments by learning subjects. A theme of the threat of instability underlay most arguments for postponement. The students also evaluated arguments of others, showing a slight preference for arguments that agreed with their own positions and they used a variety of situation-based information to rebut counterarguments.

Throughout the analyses, we found indications that students who had participated in learning performed differently from students who had not. They tended generally to provide more specific information and more elaborated arguments, and occasionally used information from the texts they had read. Indeed, we can see the scenario as having been an opportunity for students to apply what they had learned, although usually in an indirect way. It was not, after all, a scenario that modeled a condition of "near-transfer." Providing students a scenario in which a new Panama–U.S. treaty might be negotiated, for example, might have produced more direct applications of learning. Our scenario was full of familiar situational information that could be filtered through relevant knowledge schemata, stereotypes, and scripted beliefs. And students' reasoning about the scenario was dominated by these situation-plus-script approaches. But it was the learning subjects who were able to supplement this basic approach with information that had been learned. Not only did they occasionally refer to information they had learned, they demonstrated richer reasoning. Their responses were more elaborate, more likely to contain text and historical references, and their arguments and counterarguments in closer contact with each other. Students who had not learned much about the Panama Canal were very good at evoking generalized reasoning schemes, based on legal and ethical considerations, for example. Students who had learned about the Canal did this also, but their use of these generalized schemes were richer in connection to specific elements such as treaties.

The scenario also added to the individual differences observed elsewhere in the study. One of our high knowledge students, George, proved to be "argumentative" as well as quick to learn. George showed an internally consistent logic in dealing with the scenario, and this consistency led him to reject even arguments on his side of the controversy. Our single holdout against the Postponement Bill, Eileen, showed another kind of consistency. Always reserved in her opinions and speculations, the scenario forced her to deal with things beyond what she had learned from texts. She dealt with them consistently, and with thoughtfulness, if still with her usual reserve.

Chapter 9

Conclusions and Implications

In considering the implications of the study we have already described, we now highlight its important results and discuss their implications. In the final chapter, we extend the discussion to broader questions of history learning and instruction.

LEARNING ABOUT THE PANAMA CANAL

We posed for this study some general questions about learning and understanding history. We examine in this section what we seem to have learned about these questions from a handful of college students who took our minicourse on the history of the Panama Canal.

What Does It Mean To Learn History?

History learning is a case of learning. It shares general principles of learning with all other instances of intellectual learning, especially those involving texts. Our study was, in effect, a case study of learning from texts. Is there anything special about learning history?

One of our major claims is that learning history is learning a story. It shares with story learning several key elements: First there are characters, both individual (President Roosevelt, Philippe Bunau-Varilla) and collective characters (Panama, Colombia, the Senate), with motivated actions in connection with goals and obstacles to those goals. Second, these actions collect into events that are related through webs of causal–temporal connections. As the characters and their actions are the ingredients of a story (Mandler & Johnson, 1977; Stein & Glenn, 1979), so the causal–temporal connections are the cohesive fabric of the story (Trabasso, 1989; Trabasso & van den Broek, 1985; van den Broek, 1989b).

In the case of history, we have proposed a basic cognitive representation hypothesis: that history stories are represented as *causal–temporal* event chains. Individual characters remain important ingredients, but it is the events and their connections that are the core of the representation. Our study of history learning was not designed to provide detailed evidence for this hypothesis. But the results of the study nevertheless provide some evidence.

If causal–temporal representations are acquired by learners, then a casual–temporal model of the historical events should be visible in some aspect of learning. And it was. As we reported in chapter 4, student learning was captured by a distinction between events and supporting facts, as well as a secondary distinction between "core" events and details versus peripheral (noncore) events and details. Students learned the events of the story very rapidly and relatively completely. Furthermore, we found that subjects wrote summaries that picked out the event level over the detail level, just as one would expect if our hypothesis is correct and if our analysis had correctly identified the event level. We take the time course of learning events and facts, and, especially, the event-dominated summaries, as evidence that learners acquired a representation something along the lines that we modeled in our causal–temporal event template.

A third source of evidence for the validity of the causal–temporal model comes from counterfactual reasoning. When we asked students to assume that some event had not occurred and asked for their speculations about what would have happened, they more often than not speculated that some outcome on the causal chain would have been altered. At least for the events we probed, this suggests that subjects' understanding of the story made use of casual links about events. Altering events causally linked to other events altered outcomes. Our subjects' responses also provided information about the type of causal link. In effect, when subjects suggested an unaltered outcome, they were indicating that the altered event was not a necessary cause. If removing an event on a causal chain doesn't alter an outcome for a subject, then the event is not necessary *in the context of other events*.

We must reemphasize an important observation about the learning of events. They are not learned as abstractions, free of supporting facts. On the contrary, we found that students learned supporting details, facts that connect to events, at the earliest opportunity. The story is learned as events plus supporting facts from the beginning. But the privilege of events in the mental representation of the story is seen at the same time in their earlier mastery and, especially, in their role in summaries.

As we observed in chapter 1, we certainly do not imply that learning a causal event structure is all there is to learning history. We do conclude, however, that it is an important part. Students learn history as stories. We can even more strongly suggest that the essential cognition of historical events, whether learned through "living" history or reading about it, is the construction of event models of the kind we have described. For education, the good news is the implication that history-as-story ought to be quite learnable. It makes use of the kind of mental structures that are used daily in understanding stories and in social situations. We return to what is left out in the history-as-story analysis in chapter 10.

Real Learning Over Time

Learning, including school-based learning, is often an event stretched out over time and instructional events, in contrast to the brief times available for learning experiments. Of course, there have been long-term learning studies, and even in history there is an example of observations of student learning over an entire school year (Leinhardt, 1993, 1994; Leinhardt, Stainton, Virji, & Odoroff, 1994).[26] Our learning situation was intermediate between an uncontrolled year-long observation of a classroom and a controlled but brief learning experiment. Our minicourse, extending over eight sessions and about 6 weeks, provided a distinctive glimpse of learning, one available from neither shorter, more controlled nor longer, less controlled studies.

One clear conclusion is deceptively simple: Learning actually occurs over time with instruction. What is most important here may be the complementary triangulated characteristics of learning that we observed: rapid, gradual, and incomplete. Student learning of the basic Panama Canal Acquisition Story was rapid and event driven. To demonstrate learning of about 75% of the events of the story, students needed only a few minutes with a text containing approximately 1,700 words. This result validates the value of ordinary learning studies that occupy an hour or so of a subject's time. Learning in an hour is in no obvious way qualitatively different from learning in a month. It is just an hour's worth of learning.

What is missing in short experimental studies of learning, and highly visible in our extended study, is the opportunity for increased learning. Students learned more on each opportunity, especially acquiring more details in support of the basic story that they learned relatively quickly. Obviously, this is what ordinary learning is really about: an extended opportunity to acquire information from multiple sources. Our study provided a clear window on the gradual acquisition of the story and its complexities. And, although it is more difficult to point to in specific results, there is an additional kind of learning, an ability to reason about the events of the story. Superficial reasoning is possible with only minimal information. We believe that the ability of our students to reason about the questions we put to them improved with their learning.

Although there is evidence for this conclusion scattered throughout the preceding chapters, perhaps the clearest evidence comes in the last session of Part 2, where we are able to compare control subjects with our learning subjects. Over several opportunities for comparison, we observed that subjects who had learned

---

[26]Leinhardt and her collaborators studied an entire high school history classroom over a school year. Their study, rich in close observation of interactions between teacher and students, shows a particular kind of growth, or learning, in the knowledge shared by class members and teacher over months of classroom discussion.

reasoned differently from subjects who had not learned. They used knowledge, elaborated their reasons, and generally showed a more sophisticated approach to reasoning about issues. We think this connection between reasoning and learning is one of the most important observations to come from our study. And it depends on extended learning, not a brief exposure to a single text.

Our study exposed not only the gradualness of learning, but also its incompleteness. Students learned a lot about the Canal Acquisition Story, indeed virtually all the events of the story. But they were still learning supporting facts, especially details that, by our definition, were peripheral to the core of the story. The fact is that learning would have shown further gains with additional reading. And it is possible that supporting facts that were still being learned, noncore or core, would have been important in some part of the event structure. An important point to keep in mind is that what is peripheral or central is a matter of story perspective. For some related story about the history of the Panama Canal, an event we considered peripheral would become central. For example, the internal events in Colombia, which were a peripheral part of the Acquisition Story, would have been more central to a story about Colombia's decision to reject the Canal treaty.

What we do not know for sure is the extent to which the learning of facts is dependent on their connection to central events (Omanson, 1982). To some extent, such a connection must be important, at least if attention to central events is guiding learning. What is important for the learner is to acquire the details that make the story a story rather than a diagram. We have noted our preference against considering the event chain as the "heart" of a history story. It is the events plus the supporting facts together that comprise the heart of the story.

Multiple Texts

Of course, it was not just multiple learning trials that helped our students, it was multiple texts. We believe that learning from more than one text facilitates learning, as well as reasoning. Certainly, the weaker argument that reasoning is different for multiple texts seems correct. In our case, the very existence of controversy depended on different texts providing either different emphasis or opposing arguments. For neither reasoning nor learning, however, can we point to clear evidence for the value of multiple texts. Our study was not designed to test such a difference, so our argument is based less on data than on plausibility.

Consider the case of learning from a single text: The reader reads the text, and then rereads it a week later. Then again a week later, and so on, in a schedule corresponding to our minicourse, but without the multiple texts. What should happen? Well, learning should become very good, as it did in our study. If we ask the same questions each time, as we did in our study, the subject in fact can become quite selective in rereading the text, examining especially, or perhaps only, the pages that contain answers to the questions we are asking. Perhaps such learning would actually be superior to what we observed—provided there are no surprise questions that require reading a different part of the text.

But consider an alternative account. In reading a single text repeatedly, a student can come to know it rather well, and can use it to answer questions selectively. But there are costs. First, attention is bound to wane with repeated readings of the same text. The student, at least the student who is a skilled reader, cannot shake the impression that this text is exactly the same as what he or she has read before. Second, for a given proposition, or piece of information, every encounter has the same packaging: the same syntax, the same context, indeed exactly the context that reflects the author's view of the information's role in the story. Suppose the reader's representation of this information, and hence his or her access to the information, depends on this packaging. Will this information be available when the reader is required to access it by a different path?

Consider the key treaty between Colombia and the United States, the Hay–Herran Treaty. Information about this treaty could be expressed in the following sentence: "The U.S. and Colombia negotiated the terms of a treaty, the Hay–Herran Treaty, by which the U.S. would pay Colombia for the right to control a canal through Panama." If the student is repeatedly asked to name the treaty between the United States and Colombia, he or she will eventually, with multiple readings and some motivation, learn the treaty name. But suppose the student is asked, "Who represented the United States in signing the treaty with Colombia?" or some other phrasing that reflects an alternative access (i.e., alternative to the "name-of treaty" connection). Will the student do as well? Perhaps the student would do better if she or he had also read a text that referred to "Secretary Hay" or some other phrase, that, without providing more information about the treaty name enriches the context, and hence the access, for the name of the treaty.

The fact that our example has made use of a "minor" fact, a treaty name, should not be taken to limit the generality we think applies to the value of multiple text learning. The advantages of multiple texts may increase for information that is essential to interpretation and argument. For example, if one text uses statistical information in service of an argument, a second text can refer to the same information in a critical context as part of a counterargument. A reader's representation of this information is potentially enriched by its embedding in these two contexts.

We suggest that a value of multiple texts is to provide students with a more flexible representation of the information contained in the texts. This flexibility pays off in an increased variety of circumstances under which the information can be accessed. Domain experts certainly show this characteristic of being text-independent. We know of no direct evidence for this hypothesis, but we think it describes part of what happens when students get to read several texts on the same topic, rather than just one.[27] Thus, there are, by our account, two virtues of multiple

---

[27]We have carried out studies in search of such evidence, but without convincing results. One question is how different texts have to have both properties that we suggest. For attention differences, minor syntactic and stylistic variation might be enough. But very different contexts might be needed to observe the flexibility advantage.

texts: better learning through increased attention caused by novelty and increased access to information caused by more flexible representations.

Some final observations about multiple text learning concerns summaries. First, students generally wrote good representative summaries that (in Part 1) centered on core events and some supporting facts. More interesting is that their summaries tended to be summaries of the situation rather than of the text. Other assessments (e.g., questions about texts), showed students also had text-specific information. Thus, multiple texts contribute their shared information to a learner's situation representation and their distinctive information to a learner's text-specific representation. We return to this point in the final chapter.

Individual Differences

In learning, individual differences are usually ignored, or, occasionally, elevated to enduring personal traits or "learning styles." Our approach has been to expose individual differences in a direct way, as an intrinsic component of overall learning trends. Our students could be said to represent a homogenous group of college students at a particular university. Nevertheless, as learners, they varied in background, educational focus, knowledge of history, and political attitudes. These individual characteristics had some effect on the patterns of learning we observed. The student with the highest knowledge of history used his knowledge in detail and in many different circumstances. Our student with the lowest general knowledge, also the youngest, showed the lowest level of learning and the most naive reasoning. Differences between these two subjects were visible in nearly every circumstance of learning and reasoning. Had we done a typical group study with a focus on central tendencies only, these two subjects would have been merely noisy data points.

Also interesting are differences in what students learned. All students learned the Acquisition Story well, and that means they learned the same story. Individual differences do not lie in different students learning "different stories," but rather in their learning some parts better than others. The idea that each individual "constructs" his or her own meaning is not something that applies to this study.[28]

Let us consider, by comparing three students, some of the individual differences in how students approached the learning task and in what they learned. Eileen was a close-to-the-text learner. Unlike most students, she reviewed the assignments before coming into the interview. She was a motivated, conscientious learner. What

---

[28]Of course, the deconstructionist thesis that meaning comes only to individuals in specific historical and cultural circumstances and is not in a text, is not an empirical claim. We can say that for our relatively homogenous group of individuals, there was an acquisition of a common story, one that was also in the texts they read.

was special about her learning was her mastery of treaties and dates. This mastery was not a special gift, but the result of her close reading: She spent more time in reading sections of the text that described treaties. But this does not mean that her understanding of the "bigger picture" was sacrificed. Indeed, she showed superior understanding of the relationships among the countries involved. Studying treaty terms helped her master essential relations as well as dates and names. But Eileen demonstrated that to be text-based in learning is not to be overly text-influenced in constructing the main story. Her summaries were extractions of the heart of the story across the texts, showing little influence from the most recently read text.

Dave provides some contrast with Eileen. First, he had more history knowledge than she did. More dramatic was his "knowledge-driven" approach, as opposed to Eileen's text-based style. (We put "knowledge" in quotes because none of our subjects had enough relevant knowledge to make this a successful strategy. Dave did not know much about the history of the Panama Canal.) Where Eileen was good on treaty dates, and names, Dave was not. He appeared to ignore them over time, perhaps thinking they were not important. He differed from Eileen in another interesting way. His summaries reflected a less balanced event representation, emphasizing the U.S.–Panama treaties at the expense of other events. His summaries were also more influenced by the most recent text than were Eileen's. Dave not only changed his opinions about things, he was less successful at separating the common story (as told in summaries) from his attempts to sort out interpretations.

Contrasting with the text-driven Eileen and the knowledge-driven, but changeable Dave was Robbie. Young and innocent of significant knowledge, Robbie entered the learning situation with conceptual confusions. (He was only average in reading skill, whereas the other students were above average relative to college norms.) Words like *imperialism* and *apartheid* were just beyond his grasp, and, of more direct consequence, his concept of *revolution*, important in understanding events in the Panama Canal story, was confused. Robbie was undeveloped talent, showing a high score on the analytic section of a GRE that was perhaps reflective of potential for analytic reasoning. Along with his low knowledge came an appropriate lack of opinions on most social-political issues. Robbie's learning was slow and gradual, reaching a lower final level than that of other students. This largely reflected less learning of new details with subsequent learning. Robbie, in essence, learned those details that were presented initially and then repeated in subsequent texts as well as most students. But his lower knowledge and perhaps his more casual study habits slowed his progress in learning new information. He spent little reading time on treaty information and learned little about specific names and dates of treaties. His summaries, like Eileen's, were good extractions of the common story across texts. He too distinguished between the basic story and the way the text told the story.

This sampling of individual differences suggests systematic comprehensible patterns in which learning is related to prior knowledge, study habits, and "styles" that reflect the student's mix of text-based and knowledge-based representations. These differences, we hope, lack any sense of mystery. The student who spent time reading about treaty names and dates learned more about these things than the student who did not. The student who had more knowledge learned more rapidly and more completely than the student who did not. And had we chosen readers of different reading skill, rather than basically the same reading skill, that difference also would have associated with learning differences.

Not every difference, however, is easily explained or even especially interesting. The fact that what subjects learned best varied is an example. Eileen learned more about the French part of the story than other students and Dave learned less about the French and more about the U.S.–Panama treaty than other students. Such differences are at least partly reflective of normal variation; they are statistically inevitable. The attention of students across sections of texts is completely uncontrolled, for example. But these differences might also be interpreted in terms of students' interests or study habits. Maybe Eileen was planning a trip to France. Whether one should find it interesting that this student or that student learned more about the problems facing de Lesseps or the acquiescence of the British to U.S. diplomatic initiatives in Central America is a matter of taste. In our view, the standard to apply is how individual variation coheres to some more general issue. Compared with other individual differences, these differences are not coherent in any discernable way within the framework of our major questions. They are just differences.

REASONING ABOUT THE CANAL ISSUES

The reasoning component of our study aimed at general questions about how students would reason about a historical topic. The controversies of the Canal story allowed value judgments to be formed readily, and value-based reasoning was a major focus of our reasoning probes. At the same time, the psychological remoteness of the Panama story for our students made it likely that their reasoning would reflect much more than preconceived attitudes. We were especially interested in questions concerning the relationship between learning and reasoning: Does learning affect reasoning in any specific way? How are students influenced by the particular texts they have read? Is there any evidence for students acquiring a historical context (as a result of learning) for their reasoning?

Effects of Learning on Reasoning

In some nontrivial way, reasoning must depend on knowledge. Reasoning research is indeed full of examples in which subjects' knowledge supports reasoning, although not examples in which learning and reasoning are observed together over an extended time.[29] To some extent, our interest in this question reflects a rationalist hope shared by educators generally: Although students may not reason very well in a variety of circumstances, learning leads to better reasoning.

Our students showed clear evidence of linking their reasoning, including reasoning about issues with value components, to what they had learned. No student failed to demonstrate knowledge acquired from learning in their responses to at least some questions. Of course, some questions may more directly suggest that students use knowledge, as when they were asked their opinion of Bunau-Varilla. Because this is someone they had just learned about, it would be difficult to respond without referring to what had been learned. But other questions, especially questions of fairness, could be addressed by references mainly to general ethical or legal standards. Nevertheless, students who had learned something used what they had learned in evaluating fairness. They also demonstrated what they had learned when they responded to counterfactual questions. Indeed, having to think about *What would have happened if...* provides considerable pressure for knowledge, both specific knowledge from the story and other pragmatic knowledge and beliefs about the world. Students with some knowledge of historical contexts (especially George) showed use of this knowledge in creating plausible counterfactual stories. Not only did students use what they learned in reasoning, the more they learned the more complex their reasoning became, in general. Students' responses explored more options and produced more hedges as they learned more.

Responses to counterfactual questions, as well as value questions, often showed this increase in complexity: For example, *What would have happened if the Panamanian revolution had not been successful?* If a student sees the revolution's success as a necessary cause for a U.S. canal in Panama, the response might be that there would have been no canal under the conditions of this counterfactual. However, this superficial line of reasoning might give way to a second line of reasoning, which places greater weight on U.S. determination: The United States would have gone back to Colombia and renegotiated the Hay–Herran Treaty. One student (Mitch), in fact took this line of reasoning after the second text, but by the end of the assignments had added complexity to his reasoning in the form of multiple options: The United States would have renegotiated with Colombia, but it is possible that Colombia would have been unwilling to allow a U.S. canal in Panama (especially after the United States had interfered with the revolution); in that case the United States would turn to Nicaragua. (Interestingly, the Nicaragua option had been available to the student from the beginning.) This and other examples illustrate that as students learned more, their reasoning sometimes reflected an increased accessibility of the information they were learning.

---

[29]Some examples come from the use of knowledge in formal reasoning (e.g., Johnson-Laird, Lagrenzi, & Sonino Lagrenzi, 1972), and others come from knowledge use in informal reasoning (Cheng & Holyoak, 1985). Our approach differed from these studies in establishing conditions in which substantial learning would occur.

Reasoning Stability and the Influence of Texts

One of the most interesting results was the clear pattern of instability shown in student reasoning. Learning is accumulative, with new information assimilated with old information. Reasoning, at least when it is linked to learning, can show a pattern of discontinuity. Opinions changed, occasionally reversing, more often shifting noticeably by the addition or deletion of hedges. All students showed some degree of instability in their responses to reasoning probes.

The tentativeness demonstrated by our subjects contrasts with the image of the fixed-belief system, impervious to information and change. Certainly, preconceptions and misconceptions of the kind found in other reasoning situations (McCloskey, Caramazza, & Green, 1980) are not relevant here. In the absence of strong preconceptions our students were free to learn about the story and use what they learned to reason. Subjects did, of course, have relevant beliefs and relevant knowledge to serve both learning and reasoning. (And some of the subjects had confused concepts, e.g., Robbie's confusion about "revolution," that sometimes led to problems in sorting out key parts of the story.) But learning, we suggest, largely supplanted the role that preconceived ideas might have otherwise played. An entering stance, either pro–U.S. or skeptical about its international behavior, unless it is a fiercely held belief, is not enough to fix a value-opinion about the U.S. role in the Panama story. Students were learning from texts, and what the texts had to say was useful to students' attempts to deal with complex issues about the Panama story.

The texts' influences indeed were readily detectable at least some of the time. Other times the influence of specific texts was more subtle and even delayed. Subjects' movements in their opinions usually, although not always, followed the direction of the text most recently read. Congressman X's arguments, in both the Acquisition Story and the Return Controversy took some students with him. But they also moved in the opposite direction, with Professor Y, on other occasions. And, as we emphasized in chapter 5, text influence was not one of mimicking opinions. Subjects used not just the opinions of the authors, but the reasons (and facts) the authors cited in making their arguments.

The information-induced shifts in reasoning are especially visible in a few situations in which opinions following Professor Y shifted in the direction advocated by Congressman X. As we have emphasized, both the degree of advocacy and the amount of information was unequal in these two texts. The two texts were indeed on opposite sides of the question of the 1977 treaties question. But X's degree of opposition exceeded Y's degree of support. And more important, we think, Y provided more relevant information throughout, both in the Acquisition Story and the Return Controversy. This we assume is a general and meaningful association: Authors who are the most ardent in espousing their cause are the most selective in their presentation of facts. Authors who have studied the topic more thoroughly and choose to expose the reader to a fuller range of their own information (i.e., scholars), are likely to be less ardent.[30]

In these observations is the core of a suggestion about the relationships between learning and reasoning. They are not very different in a situation that allows learning to take place. Where uninformed reasoning is merely an elaboration of preconceived and impoverished ideas, informed reasoning is the application of learning. The instability of reasoning should come as no surprise. Following study of multiple sources that share some information while diverging on other information and interpretations, changing one's mind is a natural consequence. Informed reasoning should be unstable, reflective of information that changes, and dependent on interpretation of the information in the context of a set of values, beliefs, and so on. These key features are lacking when people hold strong beliefs about emotionally charged topics. In these cases, information may be acquired selectively and opinions, once formed, held firmly.[31]

One conclusion from our argument, mundane enough perhaps, is simply that learning works. Learning from texts, especially learning from more than one text, produces cognitive change that is used in a variety of circumstances, whether a student is asked specifically about factual details or about his or her view of the fairness of it all. Obviously, entering attitudes are important. But except in the extremes, not the decisive factor.

Our final point about text influence concerns students' perceptions of the author. Text influences, as we have emphasized, are complex and not mere mimicries of authors' opinions. Equally important, students acquire some idea of the authors' rhetorical goals. Most of our students could see the difference between the texts of X and Y, especially that one text was more "biased" than the other. There were exceptions, and at least one student who showed evidence of specific text influence did not seem to be aware of its bias.

We do not think it is inevitable that college students take full notice of the rhetorical goals of authors they read. It is likely that many students, given a single text, will conflate a representation of the situation and a representation of the text. And why not? Stories and the texts that tell them are typically inseparable. To the limited extent that people have experience with stories told in different texts, it is usually a matter of mere packaging of authorless texts (e.g., some children's stories). Experiences with the same story being told in slightly different ways

---

[30]Of course there is a genre difference here. Scholars write with rhetorical goals, text forms, and styles that are different from those of political advocates. It is the curse of honest scholarship that the fruits of research can be used against the scholar's own conclusions.

[31]Studies from social psychology indicate persuasive messages are less effective for issues that subjects consider more important (e.g., Rhine & Severance, 1970) and for which they have greater "ego-involvement" (see, e.g., studies reviewed in Eagly & Chaiken, 1993). Moreover, attitudes toward political topics appear to be more stable over time for people reporting strong convictions (Abelson, 1988).

appear to be more limited. But these experiences must be important in making the separation of situation from text salient to a reader. We think this is another important value of multiple texts. They not only promote better learning of the basic story, they increase the learner's ability to form distinct representations of text and situation.

Individual Differences in Reasoning

As in learning, there were individual differences in reasoning. We illustrate them with the same three subjects we discussed in the learning section—Eileen, Dave, and Robbie.

There was a continuity of style in our students' approach to reasoning probes. Eileen, whom we described as text driven in her learning style, was also text driven in her reasoning. Her close-to-the-text style was most clearly indicated in her refusal to answer most of our questions at the beginning. Only when she was sure she had read some relevant information was she willing to venture an opinion. On this point she contrasted dramatically with Dave and other subjects, who seemed to express opinions more readily and, often with no more information than Eileen.

Eileen's attention to detail, prominent in her learning, showed itself in her reasoning also. Most interesting was her tendency, when asked about the texts, to fault the authors for not providing enough information. Eileen showed a close monitoring of her comprehension of the story, enabled perhaps by her goal of acquiring details. Eileen, like most subjects, showed instability in her reasoning responses and was influenced by texts. For example, reading Professor Y shifted the attitude she had expressed on the legality of U.S. troops in Panama during the Panamanian uprising against Colombia.

Dave was different in several ways. As we have seen, he was less text-driven than belief-driven in his learning. Although this carried over to his reasoning, there was an interesting difference. Although Dave might have been expected to maintain a stance based on prior opinion, he was in fact the student most affected by the texts he read. His responses to reasoning probes were a continuing state of change, depending on what he had read. It is not that he completely reversed his opinions, although he did occasionally. He shifted in the direction of the author, adding or deleting hedges. Most clearly, Dave was a student who allowed the text to influence his own biases. He did have higher than average history knowledge and was more attuned to news and current events as well. He was opinionated about a variety of issues, unlike both Eileen and Robbie. One might have expected a stronger hold on beliefs, once formed. Instead we found our most malleable subject. But his change did not come easily. More than any other student, Dave seemed to suffer in reasoning about the issues, especially the ethical issues, raised by the Canal story. He gave evidence of sympathy toward Panama and skepticism toward the U.S. action that he reluctantly abandoned in the face of Congressman X's arguments.

Robbie was different from Dave and Eileen in several ways. As with his slower learning, some of these differences can be attributed to his low general knowledge, and his avoidance of news and information. Although he showed a lack of opinions on most of the attitude questions we asked prior to the study, he tended to develop opinions quickly for the Canal story. Eileen was sparing in her opinions and moderately unstable; Dave was opinionated yet quite unstable; Robbie was unopinionated in general, but developed opinions through learning and tended to stick with them. To be sure, he showed instability, as did all students. But he sometimes stuck to opinions after reading texts that influenced other subjects. We are not sure how to explain Robbie, and indeed it's not completely clear how to describe his pattern of learning. We don't conclude that he reasoned from an unchangeable stance, because he did change some. Nor was how he reasoned uninformed by learning, because there was evidence that his reasoning was enriched by what he had learned. What is clear is that Robbie was influenced by Congressman X's text. Other students were also, but he was the only student to prefer X's text to Y's text. The reason is not ideology but comprehensibility. We knew that Professor Y's text was a bit more sophisticated than Congressman X's text. But Robbie brought this home clearly in his observation that he was able to get more out of X's text.

What we conclude from these subjects' differences is that the differences in reasoning were a matter of degree. All students used some of what they learned in their reasoning. All students showed some malleability in their reasoning. And all students reflected text arguments in their reasoning. We do not wish to minimize the potential for profound differences in reasoning styles, because our study was not designed to discover such differences. Within the limits of what we can observe here, individual differences in this kind of reasoning are closely linked to individual differences in learning and, to a modest extent, to prior knowledge and beliefs. We think a closer analysis of what students had learned would lead to the conclusion that learning accounts for much of what variation there is in reasoning. Indeed, our evidence clearly demonstrates a highly general effect of learning on reasoning, one quantifiable in the effects of learning on complexity of responses, and observable in a variety of text influences on students' arguments.

DOES LEARNING HISTORY MATTER FOR THE INTERPRETATION OF CONTROVERSY?

The title of this section suggests a question much bigger than we can address. But there are observations to make about a more modest question: Did what students learned about the acquisition of the Panama Canal by the United States influence what they thought about the 1977 treaties returning the Canal to Panama? In learning terms, this is a case of "far transfer." One could argue there were only tenuous connections between the two Panama stories. We might agree, but we would also point to two important facts. First, it was clear that Panamanians, and at least some U.S. citizens, believed there was a connection. Panamanian resentment over U.S.–Panamanian relations was an important element in the Return Story, indeed throughout the entire period since 1903. Second, the authors the students read made this link. Congressman X especially made it clear that the purpose of his text was to rally opinion against the 1977 treaties. Part of that effort explicitly involved giving readers ample reason to conclude that the Acquisition Story, including the 1903 treaty between Panama and the United States, was one for which the United States should feel no shame. If the author held this connection, what about the students?

The Acquisition Story did seem to affect students' reasoning about the 1977 treaties in several ways, but overall the influence was modest and subtle. One kind of influence was analogy between figures in the two stories, especially Omar Torrijos, who was seen as similar to Bunau-Varilla by one student and similar to another student's perception of the typical 20th century Panamanian leader. (The first comparison was offered by the historically minded Dave, whereas the second was offered by Jen, our least-effort student.) Torrijos was also compared with the more recent General Noriega (by our other subject with history knowledge, George). This kind of analogy is based on specific imagery of a character, and appears to play a role in interpretation. In evoking the Noriega imagery, George was placing the 1977 treaty negotiations in a negative light. In evoking the Bunau-Varilla comparison, Dave was tapping a more complex, if less vivid analogy, involving a perception of self-interest and self-promotion. When a story introduces interesting individuals in central roles, students interpret their character in terms of familiar figures. The default analogy is a stereotype—of a Latin American military dictator in this case. History provides specific characters in place of these stereotypes.

At best, however, this use of history is quite superficial. Citing a specific figure does little more than citing a stereotype, in the absence of some differentiation or elaboration. Moreover, it makes no reference to situations and events and more complex causal factors.

A more important role that earlier history might play in the interpretation of recent history is to provide a context for interpretation. Knowing something about a relevant history story can situate a new event or a controversy in the context of this earlier history. There is no doubt that in learning about the Acquisition Story, our students developed a historical context in which to judge the 1977 events. They were prepared to understand, at least partly, Panama's historic interest in regaining control of the Canal Zone; they understood the historical interest of the United States in a canal and the circumstances by which the United States obtained the Canal Zone; they understood something of the economic component of the Canal. We see the effect of this context in their familiarity with the characters, the motivations, and the controversy surrounding the 1977 treaties. The controversy itself would have been difficult to understand without at least some historical context. Indeed this is the assumption of both authors of the two major texts about the Return Controversy that our students read.

Beyond this contextualizing use of previously learned history, specific use of history was less common in our students. One clear possibility for influence was the students' attitude toward U.S. fairness to Panama. If students came to believe that the United States had been unfair to Panama in the Acquisition Story, would they not be more inclined to support a treaty by which the United States returned the canal to Panama? Or, consistent with the approach of Congressman X, if students were persuaded that the United States had been quite fair to Panama, then would they think the treaties to return the Canal were a mistake?[32] Evidence for this linkage was difficult to obtain for two reasons. First, subjects were very unstable in arriving at an original judgment on the fairness issue. Second, all except one student indicated support for the 1977 treaties.

Nevertheless, we can see some linkage using students' final opinion on fairness-to-Panama from Part 1: Eileen thought the United States had been unfair to Panama in 1903 and later supported the 1977 treaties returning the Canal Zone to Panama. (Jen was another subject who showed this same "fairness compensation" effect.) Robbie showed the contrasting pattern, concluding that the United States was fair to Panama in 1903, later rejecting the 1977 treaties, and supporting the hypothetical postponement of U.S. troop withdrawal. Dave showed a more complex linkage. In Part 1, he finally concluded that the United States had treated Panama fairly in 1903 and later showed a highly qualified acceptance of the 1977 treaties. Although Dave was satisfied about the fairness of actions in 1903, he entered his study of the Return Controversy inclined to think that "it's their country; it's their land; we should give it back." Instead he found the arguments made by Congressman X to be persuasive, and shifted towards a skeptical attitude toward the 1977 treaties.

We saw the effect of prior learning as well when students reasoned about a hypothetical scenario connected to recent events. One might make a case for specific linkage: Eileen, who had shown a consistent fairness linkage, showed consistency in believing the U.S. troops should withdraw as required by the 1977 treaties; Robbie showed an equally consistent contrasting pattern favoring U.S. Canal interests. However, the important effect of prior learning on scenario reasoning was not on specific conclusions, but on the contexts of reasoning. Students reasoned in a more elaborated way about the scenario, compared with students who had not learned. Although their reasoning was dominated by information from the situation, they supplemented information learned from the story, and embedded this information in richer, more elaborate reasoning.

---

[32]Of course this logic of compensating for the crimes of one's fathers is not compelling. According to a perhaps apocryphal story, Ronald Reagan, as governor of California and candidate for President, is supposed to have said that the Canal was ours and should not be returned because we had "stole it fair and square."

In summary, we conclude that there is some effect of learning about relevant history on reasoning about recent (and even hypothetical) events. The main effect is that this learning provides a context for both further learning and reasoning. Reasoning that involves value components can affect later reasoning for which these values might be seen as relevant. But these values are not likely to dominate a student's view of a new situation in which a fuller range of considerations are seen as relevant. The events of a new story are interpreted by reference to relevant information of all kinds. Having a historical context in which to embed these events makes a difference. This context does not tell students how to reason about the new story, but it does provide a framework for understanding parts of it.

SUMMARY

The observations from our study support several conclusions. First, the assumption that history learning consists partly in the learning of causal–temporal event structures was confirmed. The story is acquired over time, with rapid learning of events and related facts, and gradual additional learning.

Second, this learning has an effect on student reasoning. Students who participated in the leaning study showed both more use of knowledge and more elaborated reasoning than subjects who had not participated in the learning study. Furthermore, their own reasoning became more complex as they learned more.

Third, we suggest that an important factor to both the quality of learning and the quality of reasoning was the use of multiple texts. Although the study was not designed to establish this conclusion, it appears that both learning and reasoning were affected by the requirement of learning from more than one text. More clearly, reasoning was directly affected by what students had read, with many instances of altered views and modified arguments as a result of the most recently read text. The instability of responses over texts with opposing viewpoints was, indeed, one of the most intriguing results. These text influences appeared to result from the information and arguments provided by the texts; although students were aware of bias in the texts, few subjects (perhaps Eileen and George) showed evidence of discounting an author's arguments because of bias.

Fourth, there is some evidence that students take into account earlier relevant history in considering controversy in a more recent history. The influence of earlier history on later history was seen primarily in the contextualizing of the more recent events, and not in specific historical arguments.

Finally, individual differences are prominent in both learning and reasoning, but they are largely limited to components that reflect students' control of learning (e.g., to attend or not to attend to details), and their background knowledge. The pattern of learning, in terms of the basic story acquisition, was similar for all students. Students did vary, as well, in the extent to which their reasoning was influenced by the texts.

Chapter 10

Beyond Story Learning

Learning the story is the foundational component of learning history. There is more than the story to consider, however. In this final chapter we turn to some of the additional components of history learning, especially components that we have studied in related research.

TEXT REPRESENTATIONS

One question has to do with text learning. As a problem of cognitive psychology, learning history through texts is a problem in text comprehension and text representation. Models of text representation have been advanced with substantial empirical support. Models that distinguish between the linguistic representation of the text and the situation described in the text seem to be necessary (van Dijk & Kintsch, 1983). And models must and do accommodate the facts of limited capacity processing and the role of the reader's knowledge, in addition to basic language processing operations applied to the words and sentences of a text (Kintsch, 1988). Other models emphasize the structure of stories (Stein & Glenn, 1979) and the structure of causal event chains (Trabasso & van den Broek, 1985) in establishing coherent representations of texts. Our study of history learning has led us to suggest that some complications to these views of text representation are in order.

The problem can be illustrated by an ambiguity created by an earlier contribution to the study of reading by the first author. Perfetti (1985) described the reader's *text model*, illustrating the idea with concepts and event nodes intended to refer to a situation described by the text, rather than to the text itself. But the term *text model* actually suggests a model of the text itself, creating an ambiguity resolved by a distinction between texts and situation models (van Dijk & Kintsch, 1983). But the ambiguity gets compounded: Is a model of the text a model of the text's semantic propositional content (the *text base*), a model of the text's rhetorical stance, its constituent sections, or something else? If it is a text more cited than read, the reader's representation of the text is likely to be very impoverished, perhaps containing a topic and an argument or two.

The study of multiple texts forces the issue of text models to be considered. Our students learned not from one, but from four texts, all on the same topic. Imagine an ideal reader/learner who masters all four texts. Will the learner have a single situation model and four distinct text models? A less ideal reader would surely have trouble maintaining accurate representations of all four texts, and some conflation and confusion would be expected. But in principle, multiple text representations could co-exist in the mind of the reader along with one or more separable situation models. Notice that this does not answer the question of what is in the model. Each text model could be more or less complete along a number of different dimensions (propositional content, affective tone, argument types, author's credentials, etc.).

Along with J.–F. Rouet, we have approached a small piece of this text model problem, the representation of the reader's model of the arguments of texts.[33] Our proposal is that readers, under some circumstances, develop models of text arguments at two different levels. The connections between texts and situations constitute the *global representation*, and representations of arguments within texts constitute a *local representation*.

Information from every text may be included in this representation. In terms of texts used in our study, a reader may represent X's arguments about the U.S. intervention in the Panamanian revolution, Y's arguments about the U.S. intervention, and a model of the intervention situation. The last of these three is a model of a situation, and ordinarily would be part of a situation model. Thus, the global level of argument-level representation must connect text arguments to situation models. Within the argument model itself, connections between the text arguments could be either explicit or implicit. In the case of X and Y, there was no explicit cross referencing, so any connection would be implicit. For example, *X disagrees with Y* would be one very general connection.

The global argument model can become quite expanded, however, beyond the simple case of two texts. Suppose Professor Y refers explicitly to a certain treaty, perhaps even describing its essential terms in detail. This treaty, say the 1846 Bidlack Treaty governing U.S.–Colombia relations in Panama, now can be part of the global argument representation: The U.S. intervention in the Panamanian revolution, according to Y, is a violation of the Bidlack Treaty, which stipulates such and such. Now the argument model contains three texts with an explicit relation between two of them. If X also refers to the treaty but interprets the treaty as allowing intervention, the representation is further enriched by explicit relationships among all three texts. The reader, in acquiring this global argument model, has an appreciation of the arguments made by texts and their relationship to each other. This model could be said to be built around rhetorical predicates such as *according to*, *interprets*, *claims*, *opposes*, *counters*, and so on. In the present

---

[33]Work using this model has been reported in Britt, Rouet, Georgi, and Perfetti (1994).

example, the representation would be something like this: Y *interprets* the Bidlack Treaty as *prohibiting* U.S. intervention in Panama and *criticizes* the intervention, thus *opposing* X's interpretation that the treaty allows U.S. intervention.

Figure 10.1 illustrates a representation of an idealized argument model that distinguishes texts and situations, indicating the rhetorical links among three texts and a single situation. The fully informed reader can take account of how the three texts relate to each other and to an interpreted situation.

This global level of argument representation actually depends on representations of the arguments of each of the texts, or *local representations*. The representations link the claims of a given text to its arguments, and thus constitute the reader's understanding of an author's arguments. So, in our example, a detailed representation of X's claim that the U.S. intervention was justified would include

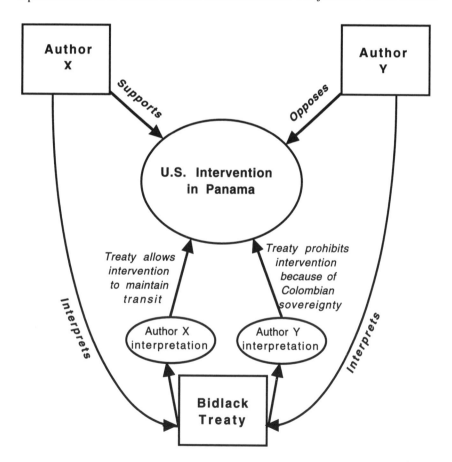

FIG. 10.1. Representation of an idealized global argument model for three texts. Text representations are rectangles and situation representations are ovals. Connectors are rhetorical predicates.

the arguments the author makes and the *evidence* he cites to support the arguments. Thus the local argument model represents claims, arguments, and evidence of a single text, whereas the global model represents the argument relations among a set of texts.

We claim that cognitive representations something like what we have just described are necessary to account for the ability to deal with related texts. More than a situation model and more than a model of a text, such an ability requires a model that interconnects texts and arguments with reference to a situation. But when is such an ability demonstrated? In the learning study we have described, there is certainly evidence that students used information from various texts in developing a model of the situation. And there is clear evidence that students were aware of the different stances taken by the authors on key issues concerning the Panama story. We would need to postulate that our students acquired some local argument models; for example, some subjects would have understood that Congressman X made certain arguments in support of his recommendation against the 1977 treaty revisions. For a global model, however, there is less strong evidence that anything more than a simple X-opposes-Y type of model is required.

To see a richer, more articulated global model, a more direct confrontation of texts around some problem seems to help. We have, in other research, arranged such conditions. The background for this research, which is discussed in Perfetti, Britt, Rouet, Georgi and Mason (1994) and reported more fully in Rouet, Britt, Mason, and Perfetti (1995) concerns document use.

Texts and Documents

Although the students in our minicourse showed good learning from multiple texts, they showed little inclination to go beyond the texts they were assigned. Various relevant treaties were made available to them as "optional" readings, but, except for one student, treaty documents were ignored. (Turning down optional assignments is a revered tradition among some undergraduate students, so we would not make too much of that.) Students also failed to show any spontaneous interest in cables, letters, and other documents that might have been useful, even when we asked them questions about what else they would like to know. Thus, we had found that multiple texts could be read to good effect, but not that students had developed a sense of document privilege. Students had learned only a story, certainly a story told by multiple authors, but only a story nonetheless.

The appreciation of document privilege is an important part of informed reasoning, for both expert scholars and student scholars. Many college students seem to have a weak sense of document privilege. They are more willing than their professors would like to cite textbooks and secondary sources when writing papers. Document privilege, however, is at the heart of rational argument-based reasoning. Such reasoning requires a sense that: (a) arguments require evidence, (b) evidence is documented, and (c) documents are not equal in their privilege as evidence. Of course, we do not intend to imply that a student should be expected to exhibit all three of these conditions in all circumstances.

Students vary widely in the extent to which they understand document privilege. Many students acquire most and even all of their education through textbooks. College classes generally move the student toward a sense of discipline-based document use, but this too can vary. We think that many, though certainly not all, underclass college students are similar to the kind of high school students studied by Wineburg (1991). These students, given a choice of various documents relevant for sorting out inconsistent interpretations about the Battle of Lexington, rated textbooks as the most trustworthy. Historians rated the text least trustworthy, because they could detect its inaccuracies and because they viewed historical documents as better evidence.

What we add to this picture, however, is a more favorable view of the student's potential to appreciate document privilege. Pursuing the Panama Canal story, but this time with documents of various types and with a different task—problem solving rather than learning—we found that college students did show an appropriate sense of document privilege. Students who were given primary documents (e.g., treaties and official cables), rated these documents highest in trustworthiness over both textbooks and secondary sources.[34] Students exposed to additional secondary sources, rather than primary sources, rated the textbook highest. Although all students rated the textbook as high in trustworthiness, students exposed to primary documents reduced their rating of the text's trustworthiness.

We think an important factor in encouraging students to value documents is the kind of task they are given. When students are asked to learn, textbooks are good functional sources. In the Rouet et al. (1995) study, the students were required to write brief essays addressing problems we posed to them about the Panama Canal story. One such problem required the students to write on *To what extent did the United States participate in the planning of the revolution?*. Under such circumstances, students correctly perceive the relevance of documents in trying to get the story right.

This study also provided evidence that students were able to take into account various features of documents in making their judgments. In justifying their evaluations of documents, students most often referred to the content of the document and characteristics of the author. In referring to an author, students cited

---

[34]The documents included two historians' essays, two accounts by participants in the 1903 events, two official documents including the 1846 Bidlack Treaty and a military cable, and one textbook excerpt. It is the official documents that we refer to as "primary." The participants' accounts, including a letter by President Roosevelt and an excerpt from a speech on the floor of the Senate by an opponent of American intervention, were classified as "intermediate" documents. Although these participant accounts are also a form of primary document, we placed them into the separate intermediate category because each had obvious persuasive goals.

his credentials (e.g., references to the author's position as professor or President), his motivations (e.g., "his reputation was at stake"), and his access to events (e.g., "he had first hand information"). In referring to the content of the document, students used a variety of justifications. They sometimes suggested merely that the document's conclusion on the question was the one they favored (e.g., that the document was "accurate"). Less frequent were justifications that referred to the type of document (e.g., commenting that a document was trustworthy because it was an "actual treaty"). And not all references to documents indicated a mature sense of document privilege (e.g., a "college text would not print false facts"). And only a few subjects, who were higher in history knowledge, made references to when documents were written.

The use of content-based justifications over document-based justifications may indicate that students are in the process of developing a sense of document privilege. Rather than a clear preference for citing document type, the author's credentials and access to evidence, we see that students use a mix of document features. Content-based justifications indicate that on some occasions at least some students are considering more about what is in a document than the status of the document as evidence. We can describe such students as comparing documents and other texts with their situation model rather than with an argument model. Texts that compare well with the student's model of what happened are considered trustworthy. We emphasize that many students, on some occasions, did appear to go beyond this level of comparison, evaluating the text as a document, either as the product of an author with certain credentials and motivations or as a class of documents that had important features that signalled bias, access to information, etc. We also emphasize that students differentiated the use they could make of a document in their assignment and the trust they placed in the document.[35]

This case of multiple text learning studied by Rouet et al. (1995) gives an opportunity to illustrate more directly the idea of an argument model. Because students had to write short essays addressing a problem, they were forced to consider more than one text at a time. And this meant representing the arguments and evidence of the text, at least to some extent. Certainly subjects could have chosen a simple one-text solution to the task we set for them, by ignoring most of what they had read. But they appear to have read a number of texts

---

[35]An interesting difference was observed between how subjects viewed the trustworthiness of documents compared with their "usefulness." Whereas subjects exposed to primary documents viewed them as more trustworthy than textbooks, they did not view them as more useful. Subjects were able to use information from all sources, and appeared to appreciate the use they could make of a textbook. In addition, in justifying usefulness, the content of the text was even more important than in the justifications of trustworthiness. Justifications for usefulness referred less to document type and author than did trustworthiness judgments. Thus students were quite able to appreciate information from wherever they could get it, and, at the same time to show a more selective appreciation of the documents' status.

and to have represented their relationships in an argument model, at least to some extent.

Argument Models in Essays.   Evidence that subjects established a multiple text argument model comes from their essays. Although they were not asked to cite documents when constructing their brief essays, the majority of essays referred to at least one document. Furthermore, although all students were exposed to the same number of documents, subjects exposed to primary documents referred to more documents than students whose document set excluded primary documents. Students referred to textbooks and other documents not defined as primary, but about half of the references were to primary documents. Thus, at least some students formed at least part of a global argument model. We cannot determine the extent to which their models were fully articulated (i.e., contained full connections among documents as well as a representation of each document). At least half of the students explicitly represented at least some text-argument relations.

Counting only students with explicit references underestimates the actual use of argument models. Britt, Rouet, Georgi, and Perfetti (1994) described a student who appears to have represented three arguments from three different texts, although he made only one explicit citation. Data from student essays suggest that students acquired local argument models as well. Of all students' citations, 91% turned out be accurate (i.e., the text actually stated what the essay claimed). Even the few errors were cases in which students referred to actual text information but attributed it to the wrong text. Students provided further evidence for their construction of local argument models by referring to the contents of the documents when they were asked to rank the trustworthiness and usefulness of documents. Although subjects were not asked to refer to the contents of documents, they sometimes did (14% of cases). When they did, their accuracy was impressive; 92% of these content-to-document links were accurate.

We draw modest but significant conclusions from these observations. Students, when faced with a problem solving task for which documents are useful, use the documents to reach an informed opinion and view document privilege appropriately. Their demonstrated ability to use the arguments of more than one text in a coherent way illustrates the sense of argument model we have proposed. Perhaps it is equally interesting that not all students showed clear evidence of representing multiple texts and their arguments, even in a task that encouraged them to do so. We suggest that we are observing college students who are in the midst of acquiring a certain approach to texts and arguments that they can use at least in academic settings that encourage their use. Some students are well on their way, others, perhaps more protected from document-based reasoning, are not.

DISCIPLINE PERSPECTIVE ON TEXT-BASED
REASONING

If students are moving toward an appreciation of document privilege and the role of evidence, it becomes of interest to consider students who are more sophisticated in their approach to texts and evidence. Graduate students in history represent such a group. They have developed, perhaps, not only general academic attitudes concerning texts, but a certain amount of domain knowledge and a discipline-centered approach to problems in this domain. We have, in some of our studies, given Panama Canal problems to one or more history graduate students. For example, in the document problem-solving study described earlier (Rouet et al., 1995), a history graduate student rated the same documents for trustworthiness and usefulness. As we would expect, he rated the primary documents as most trustworthy, and in that respect was similar to the undergraduates who were given primary documents. However, he showed a more differentiated judgment on the usefulness of documents, rating primary documents as most useful as well as most trustworthy. This contrasted with the pattern shown by the undergraduates (see footnote 35). This is sensible: For a discipline expert, only trustworthy documents are useful.

Rouet, Perfetti, Britt and Favart (1994) provided a fuller study of history students, this time through a comparison with graduate students in psychology. Notice that use of these groups removes a general education factor from the comparison. Furthermore, the comparison also reduces a domain expertise factor because the history graduate students involved were not experts on the topic. That is, they were neither Central American nor American specialists so the comparison instead involves *discipline expertise*. These students, enrolled at the University of Poitiers, read French translations of the materials used in the study of American college students (Britt et al., 1994; Rouet et al., 1995). Neither history nor psychology students scored well on our test of prior knowledge of the Panama Canal Story. They studied documents and wrote essays to address two controversies, including the justification for the U.S. military intervention in the 1903 Panamanian revolution.

The two groups produced some interesting comparisons. First, both history graduate students and psychology graduate students ranked the official (primary) documents as most trustworthy, followed by the textbook. Both groups, on the whole, trusted objective documents (treaties and military cables) and neutral documents (the textbook) more than texts expressing opinions (historian's essays, participants' letters, and speeches). However, there was an interesting difference: Psychology students considered the participants' accounts very untrustworthy, especially a letter by President Theodore Roosevelt denying U.S. intervention in the revolution. History graduate students rated both the Roosevelt letter and an opposing Congressional speech as more trustworthy than did the psychology graduate students.[36]

This implies a general heuristic that characterizes "novices" in a discipline. Texts that have a point of view are not trusted. History graduate students, on the other hand, have a more sophisticated approach. They clearly are suspicious of texts produced by participants who may be self-serving or opinionated, but they also consider the potential and partial veracity of a speech or letter by people participating in the events. It is interesting to suggest further that this reflects a true discipline difference between psychologists, who may place objectivity above all, and historians, who consider a wider range of contexts in evaluating texts. On the other hand, an expert in any field can use what Wineburg (1991) termed the *corroboration* heuristic in evaluating texts. Thus, a document that might have visible elements of bias would be considered trustworthy if other evidence converged on the same conclusion. In this case, however, we have no reason to believe that history students were using this heuristic more than psychology students, because they did not have significant knowledge of the Panama Canal. Furthermore, the two participants' texts were on opposite sides of the controversy, yet both were rated as more trustworthy by the experts.

To keep this difference in perspective, we must emphasize the high agreement between history students and psychology students in the privilege they accord to primary documents. Furthermore, the two groups provided the same pattern of justifications for their judgments. All students referred explicitly to source characteristics, especially when considering official documents and participants' accounts. Students in both groups noted the special status of a treaty, the self-serving nature of the letter by the President, and so on. Students, again students in both groups, used the content of the accounts less often when referring to these documents. When referring to the textbook and the historians' essays, students were much more inclined to refer to content in considering trustworthiness. In general, the more important the document is as a piece of historical evidence, the more important its characteristics as a document become in students' judgments of trustworthiness.

That discipline experts and discipline novices show similarities in their responses to documents points to the role played by factors beyond the discipline. Thus at least part of the appreciation of document privilege is a matter of education not specific to a discipline. Not any education, of course, because both groups were more advanced than our U.S. undergraduates. Graduate students in psychology and history are students who have not only acquired a more sophisticated view of the

---

[36]There was also a difference in how students viewed document usefulness. Psychology students, but not history students, viewed the historian essays as very useful, and psychology students viewed the textbook as more useful than did the history students. History students perceived the document's content as important for second-hand accounts, but for official documents they usually referred to the document's value in performing their task. Psychology students viewed usefulness consistently in terms of content.

role of documents and arguments in academic discourse, but have chosen to pursue advanced learning within some form of academic discourse. Thus, we see two factors here, neither a matter of domain knowledge. A general awareness of document status that comes with scholarship and cuts across disciplines, and a discipline-specific factor that places documents in the context of the discourse of the discipline—its cultivated style of problem analysis and argumentation.

To conclude our discussion of discipline factors, we consider the essays written by students. In the study of U.S. undergraduates, we have already noted that reading primary documents led to more citations of documents when students wrote essays addressing the problems we gave them. Essays in both this study and the Poitiers study were further analyzed by the claims and arguments framework (Rouet, Marron, Mason, & Perfetti, 1993). This framework analyzes students' written argument strategies by identifying argumentation units and classifying them according to categories of information and evaluation units, each category consisting of several subcategories.[37]

For our purposes, an especially interesting result concerns the framework's identification of claims, as opposed to arguments. The claim is the student's basic stance on the problem posed (e.g., *Was the U.S. intervention in Panama's revolution justified?*). Students sometimes provided explicit and *full claims* stating, for example, that "intervention was not justified because...." Or they could make *restricted claims* (e.g., "If one considers that a revolution would have threatened transit, then..."). Or they could have made *no claim*: "The U.S. intervention in Panama gave birth to two opposed interpretations." The interesting result was that history graduate students and psychology graduate students differed in the claims they made. Most of the psychology students' claims (73%) but only 31% of the history students' claims were in the full claims category. History students' claims were more often in the no claim (44%) and (25%) restricted claims categories.

Thus, we see an intriguing discipline-based difference. Discipline experts were more cautious about stating an opinion on the question at hand. This reluctance to express an unhedged opinion may seem completely warranted by the sparseness of the evidence presented. A history student may be more alert to the likelihood that there are many more documents that might be examined before reaching an opinion. A slightly different explanation suggested by Rouet et al. (1995) is one we think is more likely correct: To discipline experts, to "give an opinion" on a controversy is to develop the relevant arguments and evidence on the controversy. Solving the problem posed literally by "answering" the question it asks is not consistent with the discipline experts' framing of the problem.

---

[37]Information categories include facts, events, communications between characters, and characters' psychological states (motivations, goals, feelings). Evaluation units are the statements used by the subject in evaluating some aspect of the controversy or some information unit. The framework also identifies rhetorical adjuncts, including qualifications to opinions and citations of texts and documents.

Consistent with this interpretation is a second difference observed by Rouet et al. (1994). The essays of psychology students usually began with a claim (59%). By contrast, the essays of history students usually began with something else (69%). Some essays of history students began with a contextualizing statement (e.g., "On November 2, 1903, a revolution broke out in Panama"). Other essays began with a problem statement (e.g., "The controversy basically rests on an ambiguity of the 1846 treaty." Note this statement amounts to a claim about a solution of the problem. Rather than say whether intervention was justified, this student is going to explain why there is an argument about its justification.) Thus, discipline knowledge functions to define the space of the problem. For the history student, the problem is to analyze the controversy, develop the arguments and evidence, and, if possible, to explain why the controversy exists. This problem space does not include mere "justification" or other evidence-based opinions. Although the graduate student from a different discipline also uses evidence from documents, this use is in the service of responding literally to the question. The history student appears to use this evidence to understand the controversy at least as much as to resolve it.[38]

We caution against overgeneralization of these observations. Some psychology students followed the pattern we have attributed to the history students and vice-versa. Discipline influences are not deterministic. The discipline training cultivates a perspective toward analyzing texts and evidence, and individuals in the process of being trained in the discipline vary in the extent to which they reflect this training in a specific problem. And even a student from one discipline has the potential for demonstrating the pattern of another discipline. Some of the attitudes toward texts and evidence are more generally fostered across disciplines, as we have argued. Imagine a psychology student presented with a discipline problem such as *Is it justified to hold a distinction between short-term memory and long term memory?* The psychology student is very likely to show the same circumspect approach demonstrated by history students in their discipline: fewer unqualified claims, more attention to the reason for the "controversy," and less to the "right answer."[39] At least some of these students might be expected to apply this approach

---

[38]We observed a related difference, consistent with the suggestion that discipline experts make more use of contextualizing perspectives when dealing with a history problem (Wineburg, 1991). History students made more contextualizing statements (defined as referring to any information outside the text itself) than psychology students. Furthermore, their statements were both more elaborate and more "global" (i.e., placing events in broader historical contexts). Psychology students made contextual statements as well, but they were more often references to a local context regarding the Panama Canal story.

[39]This example illustrates how difficult it is to maintain a clear line between domain and discipline. The psychology example is analogous to the history example only for a student not an expert in cognitive psychology, the domain for memory concepts. It is unlikely, however, than any psychology student would not have some relevant domain knowledge to help this question. Similarly, our history students, although having no special knowledge about the Panama Canal have a large repertory of related knowledge dealing with treaties, international disputes, and so on.

to problems outside their discipline, provided they can acquire enough information from texts to do so.

These observations about discipline are relevant for questions of generalized and domain-specific knowledge. The similarities between psychology and history graduate students—their appreciation of objective official documents, their use of citations in their essays—point to a generalized attitude toward texts, arguments, and the use of evidence. This attitude does not spring from domains, although it might well have developed through learning in specific domains, the source of many generalized abilities (Glaser, 1984). The differences between these students—the history students' lessened distrust of participant documents, their reluctance to "answer the question," their use of historical contexts—all point to an additional kind of generalized ability. It is at least partly free of specific domain knowledge, although it too may be acquired as part of domain learning. But it is essentially discipline knowledge, an attitude toward the texts, evidence, and discourse that mark the discipline.

What we propose is a layered view of knowledge that gives a slightly different perspective on the question of domain-specific versus general knowledge. If we assume just three layers or levels—*domain* (e.g., Panama), *discipline* (e.g., history), and *supradiscipline* (e.g., academic disciplines), at least two of three are partly general. Furthermore, only lack of further analysis allows the fiction that domain knowledge itself is specific content knowledge exclusively. If we differentiate between knowledge about the Panama Canal story and the study of the story through discipline contexts, then domain knowledge has both story (specific content) and discipline components. And many more than three layers can be suggested. Perhaps, for example, there would have been even less difference between history and political science graduate students (or between history and classics students), suggesting a "discipline-family" level.[40] In this layers description, the acquisition of domain knowledge may or may not be the foundation for all generalized abilities. But it is clearly not all there is to reasoning about problems, either within or outside the domain.

HISTORY INSTRUCTION

We have discussed research projects on three kinds of history learning—learning from texts by undergraduates, reasoning from documents by undergraduates, and reasoning and writing from documents by graduate students. Let us reconsider the undergraduates who learned in our minicourse. What do documents and disciplines have to do with them? We know they learned from multiple texts, and they reasoned

---

[40]Although both may contrast with psychology, it is far from obvious that history and political science comprise a layer of discipline family. The social sciences and the humanities appear to differ substantially in their discipline discourses.

about what they had learned. But they were neither discipline experts nor psychology graduate students. Their learning of the story was good, their appreciation of authors' points of view was reasonably astute (but variable), but they were not forced to engage history problems at the same level as the graduate students did in our later studies. As we emphasized, these students were learning to reason as well as learning history. And the conclusions from that study were at least as much about learning from texts as learning history.

So too are the conclusions we draw from studies of history learning by younger students. In an unpublished study discussed in Britt et al. (1994), fourth through ninth grade students, along with college students, read a simple (fifth-grade level) text on the Panama Canal. Among many results from that study, we want to highlight just a few here. First, applying a causal–temporal model to the students' learning, including the content of summaries they wrote after reading the text, we examined the kinds of information children learned. Consistent with the adult learning study using multiple texts, we found that events were better learned than supporting facts by all grade levels, even the youngest students. Naturally, the amount learned increased with grade: College students learned virtually all the events and about 40% of the supporting facts, whereas all younger students showed only partial learning of the event structure and very few supporting facts. But more interesting is that older students, especially college students but also sixth graders, showed more learning of the causal connections between events than did fourth and fifth graders. The growth in learning of causal connections was quite substantial between fifth and sixth grades and even greater between sixth grade and college.[41]

Another result consistent with this growth in representing causal connections is the development of summarization skill. Fourth grade students tended to list facts rather than write coherent event-level narratives. College students wrote exclusively event-level summaries, just as they did in the learning study reported here. Over one half of the sixth graders also wrote these high-level event summaries of the main story, a large number were still at the fact-listing stage. Fifth graders showed a pattern in transition. About half of them wrote "substories," event-coherent narratives that were highly selective. All such summaries managed to omit the most central events of the story, selecting especially a substory about how tropical diseases ravaged workers on the French Canal project. The battle against malaria provided students with a vivid and engaging story, one off the central event chain. College students and most sixth graders placed this part of the story in an appropriately minor role, but fifth graders largely did not. It is an interesting transition: From listing facts, to representing noncentral but coherent substories, to a full representation of the central story events.

Thus, with schooling, the major developments in learning the stories of history appear to be an increased ability, at least in summaries, to pick out the central event

---

[41]Such growth may reflect development of sensitivity to causal relations of different kinds or the development of the ability to integrate information across texts (see van den Broek, 1989a).

chain of the story and to link its events together into a causal–temporal framework. Students move from an ability to recall events as discrete events to an ability to form coherent links among them. Some of this trend may be related to the linguistic expression of information rather than the representation of it, as children learn to mark connections more explicitly. But this is unlikely to be the whole story, because learning was assessed through oral interviews as well as written summaries. We suggest that part of this development reflects an increasing ability in representing more fully the causal event structure of a story. For these mundane texts, such a growth is more likely a matter of increased reading skill rather than something about history or causal reasoning. Indeed, reading skill was associated with summarization skill in this study (see Britt et al., 1994). Children already have the conceptual structure they need to handle the causal coherence of stories. The combination of texts that may fail to make the central causal connection easily visible and limitations in reading skill are what we think delays a fuller mastery of history stories.[42]

Nevertheless, our more general point is that story learning is the easy part of learning history. Even with the difficulties just noted, children's ability in learning stories makes history stories a good prospect for middle-grade learning, especially with texts that promote a clear view of the main story. So too with high-school students and college students. Taking advantage of young students' skills in narrative comprehension is an obvious component of history instruction.

If we turn from learning to reasoning, the simple story becomes a mixed blessing. A story is easy to learn, but it doesn't lend itself to critical analysis. Reasoning in the context of a single text has to be externally referenced—compared with the student's personal beliefs, experiences and expectations about the stories. Certainly students are challenged to respond to text stories in classroom instruction. But they are less often challenged to read multiple texts, to consider documents, and to engage in reasoning, except at a very personal and noncritical level. Asking students if they would like to be workers on a canal project or how they would feel if someone they knew had malaria may be useful for some goals, but it is unlikely to foster critical reasoning. At some appropriate grade level, it seems useful to deal explicitly with the complexities of the stories through evidence-based and document-based learning and discussion.

If multiple texts and documents can be a more routine part of instruction in history, there is a peripheral question about document and text management to consider. No one would recommend dumping a pile of papers, letters, maps, and treaties in the corner of a classroom and expect this to lead to document-based learning. The task of allowing effective access and promoting effective use of

---

[42]We mean to suggest that texts, as in the fifth grade text we studied, sometimes include substories that, while engaging, may attract attention away from the main story. This is what seemed to have happened to our fifth graders. Nearly every middle-grade text on the Panama Story includes the Malaria substory. We think this makes it a bit more difficult for the student to get the main story. (For other examples of how history texts can create problems for learners, see McKeown & Beck, 1994.)

documents is nontrivial. One helpful tool is *hypertext*. Our adult studies indicate that the use of hypertext can facilitate the management of multiple text learning.[43] We have presented documents for study in a hypertext format primarily as a management tool. In addition, we have carried out comparisons of linear and nonlinear presentation formats, in which students either control which documents they want to examine (nonlinear) or must access them in a fixed order (Britt, Rouet, & Perfetti, in press). We have found no particular advantage in the nonlinear format, although under the right circumstances, such an advantage might be expected (Dee Lucas & Larkin, 1992; Foltz, in press). We see the value of hypertext not so much as a superior format for learning, but as a way for a student or teacher to manage documents and facilitate document comparison. Document-based learning with hypertext management is an obvious classroom application for history instruction.

Our adult studies suggest that college students and even high-school students can deal with multiple texts effectively and can use documents in solving problems (Britt et al., in press). That middle-grade students could be expected to effectively learn in this manner is not out of the question. Clearly, high-school students can be expected to handle multiple texts and documents, and use them in solving problems. And this kind of document activity does occur in some classrooms. Our conclusion, based on what we can observe in our studies, is simply that there is value in multiple text learning. It allows students a richer representation of the situation to be learned. It forces an awareness of texts, as opposed to situations, and it can be structured so as to focus on thinking and problem solving. History seems to be an ideal subject around which to promote the use of multiple texts and documents—and from which to develop text-based reasoning skills.

---

[43]A high school classroom application of hypertext is reported in Spoehr and Shapiro (1991).

Motifs, Events, and States of the Acquisition of the Panama Canal[44]

Motifs	Events/States
1. Motives to Build	1. *United States interested in creating a shorter route*
	3. *Gold rush*
	7. Present routes (are long and dangerous)
	10. *Spanish–American War*
	11. United States expands trade
	13. United States gains new territories
2. Early Attempts	2. 1846 treaty (U.S.–Colombia treaty)
	5. *United States builds railroad*
3. British Involvement	4. Great Britain involved in region
	6. *Early U.S.–Britain treaty (for neutral ownership)*
	12. United States wants sole control
	14. United States–Great Britain renegotiate
	16. *Later U.S.–Britain treaty (for sole ownership)*
4. French Attempt	8. French–Colombia treaty (to let French build)
	9. *French attempt to build a canal*
	19. French company offers to sell rights and property to United States
	23. *French company lowers price for Canal property*
5. Find a Place to Build	15. *Committee set up to find a place to build the Canal*
	17. Committee recommends building in Nicaragua
	18. U.S. Congress debates about where to build Canal
	20. Lobbyists try to persuade United States to build in Panama
	21. Spooner Act (United States passes law to build in Panama)
	22. *Committee's final recommendation is to build in Panama*

(Continued)

---

[44]Core events are in italics; numbers correspond to node numbers in causal template (Fig. 2.2).

Motifs	**Events/States**
6. Need Permission	24. *Colombia owns Panama*
	26. United States negotiates with Colombia
	28. Colombia busy with internal problems
	27. *U.S.–Colombia treaty (to build a canal)*
	29. *Colombian congress rejects treaty*
7. Panamanian Revolution	25. Panama not happy being ruled by Colombia
	32. Colombian military force present in Panama
	30. *Panama revolts*
	31. *United States supports Panama in revolution*
	33. *Panama gains independence*
	34. *United States recognizes Panamanian independence*
8. U.S.–Panama Treaty	35. United States negotiates with Panama
	36. *U.S.–Panama treaty (right to build in Panama)*
	37. Panamanians unhappy with treaty
	38. Panamanian Congress ratifies treaty
	39. *United States builds Canal*

The Neutral Texts Used in Part 1

TEXT 1: THE PANAMA CANAL[45]

There are two parts to the Panama Canal Story. The first is how the United States came to acquire the Canal Zone and build the Canal. The second is how it happened that the United States agreed to return the Canal Zone to Panama in the year 2000 under the agreements signed in 1977.

Part 1: Acquisition of the Canal

American interest in having a canal to connect the Atlantic and Pacific Oceans goes back to the Gold Rush of 1848. The discovery of gold increased the need for transportation between the East and West coasts. There was as yet no transcontinental railroad, so the trip was a long and difficult one. There were sea alternatives to a long journey across the continent, but they involved sailing to the Isthmus of Panama, or some other stretch of land in Central America, and then crossing by land to the Pacific.

This state of affairs led, in 1849, to plans to build a railroad across the Isthmus of Panama. The railroad, which took five years to complete, cost $8 million dollars and its construction took the lives of more than 800 men who worked on it.

There were also political problems concerning the Isthmus. Great Britain did not like the idea of a U.S. controlled railroad across the Isthmus. Nor did they like the idea, popular in the U.S., that there would be a U.S.-built canal across the Isthmus in the future. The British, demonstrating their intention to be the dominant power in the area, made a show of force in the area in 1848. Differences between the United States and Britain over the area were resolved by a treaty compromise reached in 1850. In the Clayton–Bulwer treaty, the two nations agreed to guarantee the neutrality of any canal built across the Isthmus. The treaty also provided that

---

[45]This text was written by the experimenters.

neither country would "exercise any dominion" over Nicaragua, Costa Rica, the Mosquito Coast, or any part of Central America.

Although U.S. interest in a canal across the isthmus was renewed following the completion of the railroad, it was actually the French who began a canal project. In 1879, Ferdinand de Lesseps, the builder of the Suez Canal, decided to build a canal across the Isthmus of Panama. At that time, Panama was a part of Colombia, so a canal project required Colombian agreement. The French bought a concession from Colombia to build a canal, but the effort collapsed in 1889. Malaria, yellow fever, floods, landslides, and other problems, including financial ones, led to the failure of the project.

American interest in a canal had not disappeared during the period of the French attempt. Indeed, in 1880, as the French effort was about to get underway, President Rutherford B. Hayes made clear the U.S. interests in the control of any canal: "The policy of the U.S. is a canal under American control. The United States cannot consent to the surrender of this control to any European power..." In this statement, Hayes was repeating a theme that had been pronounced by Henry Clay in 1826, and repeated in various forms since then by U.S. Presidents and other government officials.

The next impetus for an American canal effort came in 1898 as a result of the Spanish–American War. The war was fought on two fronts, one in the Caribbean and one in the Pacific. The need to move ships rapidly between the two oceans refocused U.S. interest in a canal. This need was especially dramatized when the battleship Oregon sailed 12,000 miles from the Pacific Coast around Cape Horn to join battle off the coast of Cuba. The trip took 67 days. President William McKinley, in December of 1898, declared that an American controlled isthmanian canal was "indispensable."

The conclusion of the war brought the U.S. additional territories: The Philippines, Guam, Hawaii, and Puerto Rico, as well as a protectorate in Cuba. Having these new territories increased the need for military security, and their locations reinforced the need for a canal to connect the two oceans. During the same time, trade interests in the Far East added to U.S. enthusiasm for the canal. The main impetus, however, was military security.

One obstacle to the U.S. canal objective was the Clayton–Bulwer treaty. Over the years, however, British interests had changed. The British were busy with war in South Africa and had become less interested in Central America and more interested in American friendship. Thus, American diplomatic efforts to abrogate the treaty were successful, resulting in two Hay–Pauncefote treaties. The second, signed in November of 1901, specifically superseded the Clayton–Bulwer treaty. The Hay–Pauncefote treaty established that a canal, when completed, would be neutral and open to use by all nations. It avoided issues of military fortification, but the treaty gave the United States police powers. The main effect of the treaty was to remove British interests from the region, thus allowing the United States to pursue its interests.

There remained a question about where a U.S. Canal would be built. A canal route across Nicaragua had always been an alternative to one across Panama, and such a route in fact had many supporters in the U.S. Congress. In 1899, the Isthmanian Canal Commission, headed by Admiral J. G. Walker, was established to study canal options and their costs. Walker, in an opinion based largely on cost, informed President Roosevelt that Nicaragua was the preferable route. The main problem with the Panama option was the price—$109 million—requested by the French Canal Company for its Panama holdings. Roosevelt authorized negotiations to begin with both Colombia and Nicaragua. The Nicaraguan President, Jose Zelaya, was receptive to the American overtures. When the French learned about the increasing chances of the Nicaraguan option, they dropped their price to $40 million, making the Panama option once again attractive.

Thus, in January of 1902, the Commission made a report that recommended the Panama route for a canal. The report stipulated that the grant for a Canal Zone must not be for a specified period, but "in perpetuity" and that it include "a strip of territory from ocean to ocean...under the control of the United States."

During the same year as the Walker report, Congress passed the Spooner Act, authorizing the President to acquire the rights to build a canal across Panama. The Spooner Act further provided that if the attempt to acquire rights for a project in Panama "within a reasonable time" failed, the President was to take steps to build a canal in Nicaragua. Congress' decision in favor of the Panama route was the result of considerable debate and maneuvering to overcome the support in Congress for the Nicaraguan option. A key event in the Congressional decision concerned the eruption of a volcano in Nicaragua in the previous year and the issuance of a stamp picturing the volcano. Philippe Bunau-Varilla, the chief French engineer for the de Lesseps canal project, bought up a large supply of the stamps in Washington and placed one on each Senator's desk with a note referring to "Official testimony regarding volcanic activity in Nicaragua."

To pursue the Panama route, Secretary Hay negotiated with Colombia for the rights to the Canal Zone. Negotiations were frustrating and time consuming, but finally resulted in the Hay–Herran treaty, signed in January of 1903. The treaty gave the U.S. the rights to acquire the holdings of the French company and provided that Colombia would lease to the United States a zone 10 kilometers wide. The lease was for 100 years, renewable at the option of the U.S. In return, Colombia would be paid $10 million and $250 thousand annually, beginning 9 years after ratification of the treaty.

The Unites States Senate approved the treaty in March of the same year, but the Colombian Congress did not. Colombian concerns included financial considerations and also concerns about guarantees for their sovereignty.

Colombia's refusal to sign the Hay–Herran treaty came at a time when revolutionary groups were becoming active in Panama. In the first week of November, 1903, a successful revolution in fact occurred. On November 3, 1903, Panamanian nationalists proclaimed independence and the Colombian forces were unable to offer effective resistance. Three days later the U.S. recognized the sovereign nation of Panama.

On November 18th, 1903, about two weeks after the Panamanian revolution, a canal treaty was signed between Panama and the United States. Panama was represented by the Frenchman Bunau-Varilla. The Hay–Bunau-Varilla treaty was similar to the Hay–Herran treaty but with some differences:

The treaty with Colombia did not require Colombia to give up sovereignty over the zone. By contrast, the treaty with Panama gave the U.S. "all the rights, power and authority within the zone...which the Unites States would possess if it were the sovereign of the territory...to the entire exclusion of the exercise by the Republic of Panama of any such sovereign rights, power, or authority."

The length of the lease was also different: The Colombian treaty would have granted the U.S. a renewable 100 year lease, whereas the treaty with Panama provided for U.S. rights in perpetuity.

The width of the canal zone also differed. From Colombia, the width would have been 10 kilometers. From Panama the width was 10 miles.

Finally there was a difference in courts. With Colombia, the treaty called for three sets of courts, U.S., Colombian, and mixed. The treaty with Panama gave exclusive rights to U.S. courts.

The treaty conditions were written by Bunau-Varilla, with Hay making only one change about the wording of the term of the lease. Nevertheless, the treaty conditions produced a negative reaction in Panama. Panamanian officials objected that their representative had exceeded his authority and had even defied his written instructions. Bunau-Varilla persuaded his government to sign the treaty by suggesting that, if they did not, the U.S. would reopen negotiations with Colombia. On December 2, 1903, one month after the revolution, Panama formally approved the treaty without modification.

President Roosevelt signed the treaty and the United States Senate ratified the treaty on January 4, 1904 by a vote of 66–14. On May 4th, 1904 a young lieutenant raised the American flag over the old French headquarters in the new U.S. canal zone. Canal construction was started in that same year and the first ship passed through the Panama Canal ten years later, on January 7, 1914.

TEXT 2: THE HISTORICAL PERSPECTIVE[46]

Before the Canal

The idea of an Isthmian canal has a history stretching back more than 400 years, but this history did not become deeply involved with that of the United States until

---

[46]This text is from *Panama: Canal Issues and Treaty Talks.* Reprinted on a one time only basis by permission of the Center for Strategic & International Studies, Washington, DC.

1848, when the acquisition of California and the discovery of gold there started a mass rush from the Atlantic to the Pacific coasts of North America. There were only five ways to reach the new gold fields from the eastern seaboard: by the long ocean voyage around Cape Horn at the Southern tip of South America; by the arduous overland route across the continental United States; or by three ship and portage routes across, via the Isthmus of Tehuantepec, Nicaragua-Costa Rica, or the Isthmus of Panama.

The portage across the Isthmus of Panama was a cruel one. The burro or foot trip over the Panamanian mountains and the hazards from insects, disease, bad food, and impure water took their toll of travelers. The solution was a transisthmian railroad, and there were men in the United States who undertook the building of it.

The Panama Railroad Company was incorporated on April 7, 1849 with a stock capitalization of $1 million, a full 20 years before the final golden spike was driven into the U.S. transcontinental railroad at Promontory, Utah in 1869, connecting the eastern United States with its western frontier by rail. The job of connecting the two oceans by rail through Panama took five years and cost $8 million. More than 800 of the 6,000 who worked on the project died of disease and accident. The road was completed on January 27, 1855.

But construction of the railroad encountered serious political as well as practical problems. Great Britain did not like the idea of a U.S.-controlled railroad across the Isthmus and refused to accept the growing national sentiment in the United States that a future canal would be built by the United States alone. Early in 1848, the British made a show of force in Central America, seizing control of strategically important San Juan del Norte (Greytown) at the mouth of the San Juan River in Nicaragua on the Caribbean side of the Isthmus, in an attempt to monopolize the area. It took two years for Great Britain and the United States to compromise their differences in the Clayton–Bulwer Treaty of 1850, by which the two countries guaranteed the neutrality of any transisthmian canal and provided that neither would "fortify or colonize or assume or exercise any dominion over Nicaragua, Costa Rica, the Mosquito Coast, or any part of Central America." The British also agreed not to interfere with building of the U.S.-controlled railroad across Panama and the work proceeded.

In 1853 the policy of the United States towards Isthmian crossings took further form with the signing of the Gadsden Treaty with Mexico by which the United States acquired the right for free transit across the Isthmus of Tehuantepec by any form of crossing that might be constructed there.

Already in hand was a treaty between the United States and Colombia (then called New Granada) offered by the Colombians and signed on his own initiative by the farsighted minister of the United States in Bogota, Benjamin Bidlack, in 1846. The treaty guaranteed the neutrality of the Isthmus of Panama, which was then a Province of New Granada, and "the rights of sovereignty and property which New Granada has and possesses" in it. In Washington the treaty had been accepted by President James K. Polk, approved by the Senate, and ratified with the understanding that it was applicable only to the "single Province of the Isthmus of Panama" and only "for a purely commercial interest." It embraced all modes of transisthmian crossing including natural roads as well as any future railroads or canals. The railroad completed, United States interest in a canal grew. Subsequently, further canal-centered negotiations were conducted with Colombia in 1866–68 and again in 1870 but they came to nothing. The United States consequently shifted its attention to the potential canal route through Nicaragua. In 1880, President Rutherford B. Hayes, without expressing any preference as to canal routes, committed the United States to the policy of an Isthmian canal "under American control." Such a canal when constructed, he declared, must be "virtually a part of the coastline of the United States."

While the United States, New Granada, Great Britain and others were formulating policies and plans for an Isthmian canal, the people of the Province of Panama, stimulated by the California gold seekers' need for the Isthmian passage, were laying the foundation of their autonomy and eventual independence. A particularly important step in that direction was taken in 1855, when the congress of New Granada granted department status and autonomy to Panama and other provinces. Through the grant of autonomy, the Panamanians gained a substantial amount of power over their own internal affairs, and though this authority was retracted when the Colombian constitution of 1863 was abolished in 1885, it had been held long enough to give the Panamanians a sense of independence and of the commercial value of the Isthmus.

The French Attempt

The French also had their eyes open to the possibility of a transisthmian canal, especially after the Suez Canal triumph of Ferdinand De Lesseps. While Washington kept up a running battle of words with the British and studied canal crossing routes from Mexico to Panama, French entrepreneurs acted.

The Geographical Society of Paris, with de Lesseps as its president, convened an international congress at Paris in May 1879 to examine the subject of an interoceanic canal across Central America. And though other routes were considered, the congress overwhelmingly favored the one across Panama.

Several months after the conference de Lesseps organized the Compagnie Universelle du Canal Interocéanique, which proceeded to purchase Colombian concessions that had been obtained by the French engineer, Lucien Napoléon Bonaparte Wyse, a year earlier. In 1881, the company also purchased a controlling interest in the Panama Railroad Company from its New York owners for the inflated sum of $25 million. The owners were happy to sell because their profits were being drastically cut by the competition of the new transcontinental railroad across the United States.

The French canal project was an ill-starred venture that created scandals and brought financial disaster to hundreds of thousands of French investors. De Lesseps was 73 years old, and he rushed through the concept of a sea-level canal, though at least one farsighted engineer, Aldophe Godin de Lepinay, insisted that the canal could be constructed only by damming the Chagres River and Rio Grande to create lakes that would reduce the depth of the cut necessary, joining the lakes with a channel across the continental divide, and connecting the lakes with the oceans by locks. But de Lesseps rejected this plan; and the French engineers, beset by landslides, floods, yellow fever, malaria, and countless other problems, had a horrible time. Their financial plight was aggravated by the necessity of paying for the worn-out American railroad.

By 1887 de Lesseps conceded that the Isthmus could be conquered only with a lake and lock type canal, but all the money was gone and no more could be raised. On May 15, 1889 all work ceased and the French left their earth-moving equipment to rust and disappear in the jungle. They had completed two-fifths of their planned excavations, but even this effort proved of little assistance to those who later picked up the canal project.

Building the Canal

Less than a decade later, the United States, by its war with Spain, suddenly acquired possessions in the Caribbean and the Pacific. With two coasts to defend and an overseas empire, the United States became acutely aware of the need for a transisthmian canal, especially when one of its warships, the *Oregon*, required two months to go from California to the Caribbean by way of Cape Horn.

The first order of business was to secure the abrogation of the Clayton–Bulwer Treaty. When Secretary of State John Hay began negotiations with the British, he found them surprisingly agreeable; at that time they were fighting the Boers in South Africa and, being isolated in international diplomacy, they sought the friendship of the United States. The results were two Hay–Pauncefote treaties. The second, signed November 18, 1901, specifically superseded the Clayton–Bulwer treaty. This treaty removed British obstacles to U.S. construction of a transisthmian canal. The troublesome questions of the right to defend the canal were eliminated by leaving out any reference to fortifications. Police powers were turned over to the United States. The treaty stipulated further that the canal when completed should remain neutral and should be free and open to the vessels of commerce and of war of all nations on terms of entire equality, with the United States as the sole guarantor of these provisions.

As the political pressure for a transisthmian canal built up, the United States recognizing that the popular Nicaraguan canal route was only a part of the overall problem, by act of March 3, 1899, established the Isthmian Canal Commission, of which Admiral J. G. Walker was president. This Commission in its report estimated the value of the French holdings in Panama at $40 million. For these same holdings, the French were asking $109,141,500, but faced with the threat of losing their entire investment the French company accepted the U.S. offer and was eventually paid.

The Isthmian Canal commission submitted a supplementary report on January 18, 1902 recommending the Panama route. It stipulated that the grant of a Canal Zone "must not be for a term of years, but in perpetuity, and a strip of territory from ocean to ocean of sufficient width must be placed under the control of the United States. In this strip the United States must have the right to enforce police regulations, preserve order, protect property rights, and exercise such other powers as are appropriate and necessary." In the same year Congress in the Spooner Act, authorizing the president to acquire a canal zone, stipulated that he must ensure "perpetual control" over it by the United States and must obtain "the right..to excavate, construct, and to perpetually maintain, operate, and protect" a canal.

But Panama was a department of Colombia, and any arrangements for the construction of a canal through the department would have to be made with the parent nation. Moreover, the French contract had given Colombia the right to approve or disapprove arrangements with a third party as to the canal situation. President Theodore Roosevelt's Secretary of State John Hay called upon Bogotá to confer. The result was the Hay–Herrán Treaty of 1903, which gave the U.S. government the right to acquire the holdings of the French canal company and proceed with construction of a canal neutral and open to all the world. It granted the United States a strip of land 10 kilometers (6 miles) wide and the rights to police and administer it under a system of dual sovereignty with mixed courts. Colombia was to receive in gold coin $10,000,000 in payment, and nine years after exchange of ratifications, an annual payment of $250,000, to Colombia. The U.S. Senate approved the treaty on March 17, 1903, but the Colombian congress denounced Herrán and the terms he had signed. They demanded $15,000,000 and rejected establishment of U.S. courts in the zone.

Some Colombian leaders believed that they might collect the entire $40,000,000, which the United States would otherwise have to pay the French. But they misjudged Roosevelt as well as the loyalty of the government of the Department of Panama. The Panamanians had attempted to secede in 1840 and 1850, and, while the Colombian legislature debated, revolutionary groups were again forming in the area. Secret agents were dispatched to New York City and Washington to raise money for the cause. A Frenchman, Philippe Bunau-Varilla, a former engineer on the canal, was especially active in this revolutionary effort.

Historians still dispute what role the United States played in the revolution, but the arrival of the *U.S.S. Nashville* in Colón harbor on the evening of November 2, 1903, and the refusal of U.S. officials of the Panama Railroad Company to transport Colombian troops across the isthmus, leaves little doubt that the United States favored the independence of Panama. On November 3, 1903 the revolution took place and Panamanian independence from Colombia was declared. Three days later, on November 6, the United States recognized the sovereign nation of Panama.

And, on November 18, 1903, the United States signed a treaty in Washington with the Frenchman, Bunau-Varilla, who diplomatically represented the new nation.

Other diplomatic representatives of Panama's new government, who were en route to Washington to discuss treaty terms, arrived in Washington several days after the signing and were unhappy to learn that they had journeyed in vain. The provisions of the treaty were not what they had hoped for or contemplated. The Hay–Bunau-Varilla Treaty followed the outline of the Hay–Herrán Treaty—but with four major differences:

1. In the treaty with Colombia, Colombia was not asked to give up sovereignty over the zone; Panama granted the United States "all the rights, power and authority within the zone...which the United States would possess if it were the sovereign of the territory...to the entire exclusion of the exercise by the Republic of Panama of any such sovereign rights, power or authority."

2. Colombia was asked to grant the United States rights over the zone for a term of 100 years with the right of renewal; from Panama the United States received a term in perpetuity.

3. Colombia was asked to make available a width of 10 kilometers for the Canal Zone; from Panama the United States obtained a zone 10 miles wide.

4. And finally, the treaty offered Colombia provided for three sets of courts—U.S., Colombian, and mixed; from Panama, the United States obtained full rights for U.S. courts exclusively.

These major differences were written into the new treaty by Bunau-Varilla on his own initiative. His reason for the changes appeared to have been at least twofold. He feared the terms of the Hay–Herrán Treaty were stigmatized, in the eyes of the Panamanians, as a result of the long struggle they had waged against Colombia. Probably more significantly, Bunau-Varilla feared the U.S. Senate would not favor treaty terms it had already approved once, but which had been rejected by another government. Bunau-Varilla's motives may have been even deeper and darker, especially judging by his actions before and after composing the treaty, but at the time of authorship he had the authority to compose the document as he saw fit, and the U.S. Secretary of State John Hay's only suggestion before accepting the draft as final was a change in the clause governing the transfer of the Zone to the United States, which Bunau-Varilla accepted. Hay's phrase which "grants to the United States in perpetuity the use, occupation, and control" was substituted for Bunau-Varilla's original phrase which simply stated "leases in perpetuity."

Almost from the beginning the Hay–Bunau-Varilla treaty was criticized on the grounds that it resulted from a conspiratorial action, which was responsible for establishing Panama as an independent nation, and that it gave excessively generous concessions to the United States. The grievances of Colombia were satisfied when the United States paid her $25 million and gave her certain preferential use of the canal under the Thomson–Urrutia treaty, signed in April 1914 and ratified in 1922. In return Colombia acknowledged that the title to the

Panama Canal and the Panama Railroad were "now vested entirely and absolutely in the United States, without any incumbrances or indemnities whatever."

A lake-lock canal constructed according to the later plan of de Lesseps with a dam at Bohío was contemplated; U.S. engineers started construction in 1904. Still the old and discredited project of a sea-level canal was revived by the first Chief Engineer, John F. Wallace, who, however, soon resigned. Though Wallace had reopened the "battle of the levels," the issue was settled by President Roosevelt in February 1906 in favor of a high-level, lock-lake plan. For the rejection of the sea-level plan at that time the new Chief Engineer, John F. Stevens, was partly responsible, because he found no advocate of a sea-level canal among the engineering force on the Isthmus, so mammoth was the remaining task of excavation and the danger of slides, particularly in the Culebra Cut. Roosevelt's decision in favor of a lock-lake canal enabled Stevens to predict that the canal could be opened by January 1, 1915.

The Panama Canal was brought to completion under the direction of the Isthmian Canal Commission, which was a civilian agency supervised by the Secretary of War. When Stevens resigned after finishing his task of planning, the remaining problem was one of coordination and administration. This monumental work was carried through by Colonel George W. Goethals as Chairman and Chief Engineer of the Isthmian Canal Commission. Colonel William C. Gorgas, the sanitary officer, also played a key role in the project by controlling the insects that spread yellow fever and malaria.

A force of men, who eventually totalled 30,000, was assembled. The old railroad was rebuilt. Huge steam-shovels, locomotives, and flatcars were sent to Panama. The engineers harnessed the Chagres River by building a huge dam to create Gatún Lake, 85 feet high. They constructed the Gatún Locks, two sets of three each. By 1909, they were at work on the locks on the Pacific side: the lock at Pedro Miguel, where ships descend from Gatún Lake to Miraflores Lake, and the two lock-steps down to the Pacific Ocean. They attacked the job of cutting a valley through the ridge of Culebra with forty steamshovels. They were obliged to construct huge dams to hold back flash floods and landslides.

In May 1913, the gangs working from opposite ends met at the bottom of the cut through Culebra. By the end of that year, in the administration of President Woodrow Wilson, the waters of Gatún Lake, the lake that serves as the central reservoir for the Canal, were flowing through the Canal and were discharging into both the Atlantic and Pacific Oceans. The first ship to pass through the Canal from end to end made the transit on January 7, 1914, but the formal opening was not held until August 15, 1914, when the *Ancon*, laden with dignitaries, came in from the Atlantic side in the morning and reached the Pacific that afternoon.

The United States had built a canal that is 40.27 statute miles in length and 50.72 miles from deep water points on either side. It runs from northwest to southeast so that the Pacific terminus at Panama City is actually 20 miles east of Colon, the Atlantic terminal.

The Canal is at sea level for about seven miles on the Atlantic side and eight on the Pacific. Gatun Lake is about 24 miles long and the Culebra, or gaillard, Cut is eight miles long. The dimensions of the locks are 110 feet wide by 1,000 feet long, with a navigable depth of 41 feet.

The estimated cost of the canal to the United States, not including the payments to France and Panama and the cost of military installations, ranges from $354 million to $380 million at a time when wages of canal workers totaled only twenty or thirty cents an hour. The question of whether the investment has been amortized is arguable. Amortization of the cost of the Canal through toll revenues was not given serious consideration at the time the Canal was built. Then the main argument favoring the building of the Canal centered on national defense. The Canal as a self-supporting commercial enterprise is a new conception that became current at the end of World War II and resulted in the Panama Canal Company–Canal Zone Government reorganization.

Appendix C

Opinion Statements

The students were asked *To what extent do you agree or disagree with the following statements?* They placed their answers on a 5-point scale where 1 was "strongly disagree" and 5 was "strongly agree." The questions were in a random order when the students answered them but are presented in categories here.

General U.S. Policy in Central America

- The United States has treated Central American countries poorly.
- The United States has the right to keep order in Central America even if it means invading a country.

Specific U.S. Policy in Panama

- After lengthy debates in the 1970s, the United States made the right decision to turn the rights to the Canal over to Panama.
- The United States was wrong in its December invasion of Panama.
- In 10 years, Panama will have complete control over operations and ownership rights over the Canal. The United States should relinquish control of the Canal, regardless of changes in the Panamanian government.

U.S. Domestic Policy

- The United States should provide day care opportunities for all families.
- The United States should only sponsor artists whose work is deemed "tasteful."
- The United States should provide drug addicts with needles to prevent the spread of AIDS.
- The United States should not pay for drug rehabilitation programs for drug addicts who don't have insurance.

- The United States needs stricter gun control laws.
- The United States needs more restrictions on abortion.
- Capital punishment should be stopped.
- Americans today have taken their Bill of Rights freedoms too far (i.e., flag burning).
- The U.S. government should provide health services for all citizens.
- The ACLU (American Civil Liberties Union) is an important institution.

U.S. Foreign Policy

- The United States should help countries in which free and democratic elections are in jeopardy.
- The United States has the obligation to protect the world from communism.
- Political and economic sanctions should be placed on countries which harbor terrorists.
- The United States should cut off all aide to countries with governments that do not support U.S. policies.
- One nation has the right to invade another if it is to protect its citizens residing in that country.
- Ethnic minorities should be allowed to govern themselves even if it means civil war.
- Violence is an acceptable method in fights against minority governments (i.e., IRA vs. British rule in Ireland).

Personal Beliefs

- It is my obligation to be well informed about local and global events and concerns.
- My political views in comparison to my peers are:[47]

---

[47]This question was slightly different from the others because it used the same 5 point scale but 1 was "liberal" and 5 was "conservative."

Short Summaries Following
Congressman X's Text (Part 1)

Eileen: U.S. interest in a transisthmian canal stems from the desire to get from one coast of the U.S. to the other the easiest way possible. A transisthmian railroad was built and the Bidlack treaty of 1846 gave U.S. right to protect that railway. Britain was concerned with U.S.'s growth and Clayton–Bulwer treaty of 1850 signed to ensure neutrality of any future zone. This treaty eventually was superseded by the Hay–Pauncefote treaty in 1902. U.S. purchased rights to build from the old French Panama Canal company for 40 million. Hay Herran treaty with Colombia was superseded after Panamanian revolution by the Hay–Bunau-Varilla Treaty in 1901.

Dave: The U.S. canal in Panama was created by a treaty between the U.S. and the newly independent Panama. The Panamanians accepted the treaty, although it provided for extensive U.S. intervention and control in their land, for political, military and economic reasons. The canal would provide a boost to an otherwise flat economy; U.S. alliance would prevent Colombian reacquisition of Panama; and the canal treaty demonstrated the Panamanian's ability to conduct their own affairs. The U.S. gained a vital trade and military link between the Atlantic and Pacific.

Jen: After the gold rush in 1849 the U.S. began to seriously discuss the need for a canal. A treaty was signed with Great Britain stating that neither country could claim rights to a canal. After much debate the U.S. decided to build a canal in Colombia. They bought out the failed French attempt. Yet the Colombian congress decided against the treaty. When Panama gained its independence the U.S. negotiated a treaty with them.

Mitch: After the Spanish–American war the U.S. was ready and willing to build a canal. They were aided by a few treaties signed by Great Britain, a revolution in Panama, an unsigned treaty in Colombia, and by the lowering of the price for the canal spot by the French. At this time there is nothing and no one standing in the way of the U.S. to build a canal.

Robbie: U.S. was always interested in canal across isthmus. We first signed treaty with Great Britain which shared control. Then signed treaty that gave U.S. control. France tried to build a canal but failed. They eventually sold rights to U.S. for 40 million. We almost signed with Colombia but Panama revolted and we ended up signing with them. Varilla spoke for them and we (U.S.) ended up with a better deal anyway.

George: California's gold rush of 1849 spurred on need for U.S. canal in Panama. British did not want U.S. run canal and conflicts occurred for two years. The Clayton–Bulwer Act of 1850 assured neutrality of canal on behalf of both nations. The French attempted in 1879 and failed in 1889. The Spanish–American war brought the U.S. possessions in both Pacific and Atlantic oceans, so need for canal became great. The Hay–Pauncefote treaty of 1901 nullified Clayton–Bulwer act in 1850. The Hay–Herran treaty of 1903 with Colombia did not pass the congress and Panama became independent the same year. The Hay–Bunau-Varilla act, 1903, began construction of canal.

Robbie's Long Summaries Showing Learning of Treaty Information (Part 1)

Reading 1: United States was interested in building a canal across Panama for many years. Great Britain had control first but when they started fighting with Africa they wanted U.S. as friends. We had some control but could not build a canal. France also had control of the property and they wanted U.S. to pay 109 million for it but the U.S. had then gotten offers to build a canal in Nicaragua. Many Congressmen supported the Nicaragua offer so France lowered their money price to 40 million. U.S. took it but we still needed permission from Panama to start work. They could not give this to U.S. right away because a revolution had started in their country. U.S. started negotiations with Colombia so Panama then gave us the right. Several treaties were passed along the way to come to this point. Some treaties crossed out others. So 10 years after we had it we could finally start building it.

Reading 2: U.S. was interested in building a canal across Panama since 1848. We really wanted one when the Gold Rush came into effect. People were traveling many unnecessary miles when if we had a canal it would be easier. Great Britain and U.S. shared the canal and when U.S. became in a war with Spain or it was the Spanish American war we wanted it badly. Great Britain gave it up easily though because they were in a war also and wanted Americans as friends. The French had a part in this also. They were building but they spent great deals of money and lost out a lot. They would sell the right to build to the U.S. for 109 million. We said "let's look other places." With this they said 40 million. We took it. But we needed to have the right by Colombia. We made a deal but Panama revolutionized and we again had to wait. When Panama finally beat Colombia in their revolution we made another deal. We talked to Buena Villa [*sic*] who represented Panama and we got more land and other options. The canal finally opened August 14th 1914.

Reading 3: U.S. had strong intentions to build a passageway across the isthmus for years. The isthmus was known for terrible human beings to go there. U.S. needed it for a short cut more than anything. We first signed a treaty with Britain that was called the Clayton Bulwar treaty which gave U.S. and Great Britain control of the land. We got rid of Britain after an amount of time but De Lesopps [*sic*] of France (who built the Suez canal) tried to build a canal there first. He had very bad luck. After 10 years he quit. The only way the U.S. could build one there though was if they wanted to pay 109 million for it. So U.S. senators took votes and decided to look at Nicaragua for a route. Then France dropped price to 40 million. We took it and almost agreed a treaty with Colombia but they didn't like it. Panama rebelled and we backed them up in a way that we looked good and Panama won and they dealt with U.S. Varilla talked for Panama and we ended up getting full control of the canal and 10 miles of property. We also had police powers and could exercise them. This canal is used by U.S.

Reading 4: U.S. was interested in a "pathway" across the isthmus for years. This all started with a treaty with Great Britain called the Clayton Bulwar treaty. This treaty shared equal rights for U.S. and Great Britain. U.S. then wanted total control so we talked with Great Britain and finally signed the Hay–Paunceforte [*sic*] treaty. This gave U.S. rights. Great Britain did this not willingly but wanted U.S. as friends. Meanwhile Colombia gave rights to France to start building. They tried with Delesseps but failed to make it work. U.S. was looking at a Nicaraguan route also because France was selling theirs for too much money. Then they dropped price to 40 million and we took it. We then signed treaty with Colombia. This was Hay Herran treaty but never worked because Panama revolted. We let Panama know that we would deal with them if they won. We did not fight but backed them up. Panama won revolution and then we signed Hay–BV treaty. Varilla was a leader for Panama and this treaty gave U.S. more land than we would of in the Hay Herran treaty. Varilla was supposed to wait to sign the treaty but wanted to collect his money in it. Turned out good for U.S.

Students' Long Summaries in Part 2

LONG SUMMARIES FOLLOWING CONGRESSMAN X

Eileen (272 Words)

Despite the signed Panama Treaty (in 1977), some Americans feel that giving up U.S. control of the Panama Canal Zone was not a good idea. Advocates of the 1977 treaty believe the canal is not as important as those opposed. They argue, for one, that not all ships can fit through this canal and that use is the important thing, not control and the Neutrality Treaty of 1977 ensures U.S. will have use. A very strong argument is made in favor of those opposed to the 1977 treaty. Ships are now being designed to be small enough to fit through the canal yet carry more due to technology. Also, the 1977 treaties are carefully analyzed to show that U.S. could easily lose use of the canal under the terms of the treaties. One Panamanian official is quoted from a speech as having claimed that after 1999 the U.S. will have no authority in the Panama Canal Zone and that the U.S. warships will not be given preferential treatment in case of war. The canal will be placed entirely under Panamanian control after 1999. The workers of the canal will be given the freedom to form international labor unions enabling them to possibly strike. Also, all ships passing through the canal must meet health and sanitary regulations—thus the U.S. ships could be postponed indefinitely. The Panamanians also think that they need not follow the Neutrality Treaty in a time of crisis. Another concern with losing the Panama Canal Zone is appearing weak towards a nation that, according to the author, respects strength and decisiveness.

Dave (235 Words)

The last reading documented reasons why the United States should not relinquish control of the canal. Primary reasons given include the following: (1) it is still a vital economic factor in the trade of the U.S. and many other countries; (2) it is still an important strategic resource for the U.S.; (3) releasing the canal to Panama will be seen as an act of weakness by the U.S., both at home and abroad.

To support his stand, [Congressman X] uses many sources, including the turbulent political history of Panama, statements by the U.S. military officials attesting to the strategic importance of the canal, economic statistics and trends showing the continual role in trans-ocean trade that the canal has, and evidence of rising communist influence in Central America. [Congressman X] states that U.S. control of the canal is vital to U.S. military, economic and psychological needs, and declares that U.S. operation of the canal has been a model of fairness and efficiency. He worries that the 1977 treaties give the Panamanians too many opportunities to close the canal or restrict its use, and maintains that it would be better to continue control of the area than to have to re-take control by force, should the canal be threatened. He also believes the Panamanian government to be consistently repressive, unreliable and leftist, with allegations of torture, terrorism and drug trafficking.

Jen (177 Words)

In this article [Congressman X] gives a summary of what occurred between the time of the signing of the Hay–Bunau-Varilla Treaty and the signing of two more treaties in 1977 which surrendered the canal to Panama. [X] explains first how the canal was built. He then goes on to describe how vitally important the canal is to many of the Latin American and other countries. [X] discusses the political history of Panama since the building of the canal. He describes how the President is almost always a member of the group of elite families (Los Dorados) of Panama. [X] discusses the uprising of the dictatorial leader Torrijos and what his part was in the surrendering of the canal. The background treaties were discussed (those occurring between 1903–1977). Opposition to these treaties were many. Many naval officers testified against the surrendering of the treaty. The treaties consisted of two main points. The first one turned the canal over to Panama until Dec. 31, 1999 and the second one made the canal neutral after the year 2000.

Mitch (134 Words)

The article that I read was an argument against the treaties of 1977. [Congressman X], who believed that the U.S. was sovereign over the land of Panama, wrote this in order to sway the public into taking an anti-treaty stance. [X] believed that the canal was an important asset to the American people. It was extremely necessary in respect to the navy and he believed that no one else could run the canal like the U.S. Many people were afraid of the Domino effect, while others believed the U.S. would be excluded from using the canal. The one thing that the U.S. was afraid of was losing face or showing a weakness. This is why the U.S. can not and should not give in to the demands of Panama.

Robbie (199 Words)

The article that [Congressman X] wrote actually seemed like several articles put together. It went from talking of the times way back when to talking of future events to come. It spoke a lot of General Torrijos of Panama. It spoke down on him as if he was not a political figure but a tyrant. It gave great explanations of this and examples were also given. It spoke of his family and how they were in fact definitely trafficking heroin to U.S. This era of 60's and 70's heroin was often used. It spoke of the 1936 treaty and that did really nothing except give Panama 430,000. It spoke of 1955 treaty which gave Panama 1.5 million instead of 430,000. Then it spoke about U.S. thinking of giving up the canal. We in fact signed Panama Canal Treaty and Neutrality Treaty which Panama Canal Treaty gave millions to Panama and said by 1999 at 12:00 Panama would fully rule the Canal— Fully! This was going to slowly take effect. The Neutrality act said that all nations would be able to go across the canal. It also said that U.S. was not able to intervene in any opposition.

George (254 Words)

In 1903 the United States made a treaty with the Republic of Panama for the provisions of a canal in the latter country. The treaty, named Hay–Bunau-Varilla, provided the following: (1) 10 miles of "canal zone"; (2) American sovereignty in the Zone; (3) a lease of "in perpetuity", meaning the lease would expire when the U.S. saw fit; (4) the Zone would be managed under U.S. jurisdiction only; and (5) 10 million dollars would be awarded to Panama, with an annual payment of $250,000 each year. Panama was not pleased with the treaty but signed anyway. Colombia complained about U.S. intervention in their affairs in making Panama independent and President W. Wilson awarded them 25 million dollars, which was accepted in 1921. In 1936 President F. Roosevelt, as part of his Good Neighbor Policy, raised the annual payment from $250,000 to $430,000. In 1955 President D. Eisenhower increased the annual payment from $430,000 to 1.93 million. He also granted Panama titular sovereignty of the Zone. The Panamanians, however, were not satisfied and wanted to see their flag raised over the Zone. In 1964, the "flag riots" boiled to a head and 23 people were killed, along with millions of dollars of damage to the canal. The Panama flag was raised next to the American flag from then on. By 1967, the abrogation of the 1903 treaty was getting some serious consideration and in 1977 President W. [sic] Carter did just that. By 2000, all canal operations will fall under Panamanian hands.

LONG SUMMARIES FOLLOWING PROFESSOR Y

Eileen (304 Words)

[Professor Y's] text discussed the problems preceding the signing of the 1977 Panama Canal Treaty in light of a third cold war. This cold war is caused by the economic development of third world nations in the face of the declining ability of the United States to dictate to them. A major debate proceeded [*sic*] the signing of the treaty between those who favored the new treaties and those who felt that the U.S. should keep the original treaty of 1903. A major question raised was whether or not the U.S. owned the Panama Canal Zone as it owned Alaska. The initial treaty negotiations of the early seventies found Ronald Reagan appealing to the hearts rather than the heads of voters by claiming the U.S. did own it and thus trying to gain the republican nomination for presidential candidate over Gerald Ford who failed to take what could be viewed as a firm public stand one way or the other over the treaty issue. Carter won with Gerald Ford's stand rephrased to state he hoped the U.S. would have the capacity to control the canal if need be. The treaty was signed after gaining support in the Senate due to Senators Byrd and Baker, American public opinion changing little during the debates. After the treaty was signed the question of whether it had the support of all Panamanians was raised as well as the question of whether it would be better for the U.S. to leave sooner than 2000. The presence of the U.S. until 2000 may serve to promote ill will between Panamanians and the U.S. while serving no other important cause. The Senators wished to forget the Panama treaty while Carter wished to call attention to it as a big step forward in U.S. foreign policy.

Dave (315 Words)

[Professor Y's] second article describes events concerning the Panama Canal from the 1903 treaty up to modern times. He places particular emphasis on developing anti-American sentiments in Panama as well as describing the political and diplomatic manipulations that occurred in the U.S. while attempting to revise the 1903 treaty. American sentiment was sharply divided on the issue of whether or not to return the canal to Panama. Conservatives generally felt that the canal was still an important trade and military link and that the unstable political climate in Central America required that the canal be kept under U.S. control. Liberals tended to believe that the U.S. would best serve its own interests by divesting itself of its Central American colonies and protectorates, and to instead establish economic and trade ties to assist those colonies in gaining their independence; as the Panama Canal was Panama's chief resource, it should be given to Panamanian control as a first step in establishing a strong independent Panamanian economy. Considerable diplomatic dealing over the period of several U.S. presidential administrations was necessary before a new treaty was reached; however, in 1977 the U.S. and Panama agreed to and signed a new treaty that would give control of the canal to Panama by the year 2000.

Jen (184 Words)

[Professor Y] creates a feeling of fright in his text. He does not go in any particular historical order but jumps around a lot. He gives the background on how the U.S. finally arrived to write two treaties in 1977. One particular argument he uses is the way that the Presidential campaigns of the late 60's and 70's revolved around the question of what was going to happen to the canal. One particular anti-treaty sentiment was stated by Ronald Reagan, who at the time wanted the party nomination for President. He felt that the U.S. owned the canal and the Canal Zone just as the U.S. owns Alaska and Texas. We bought Alaska and Texas and we also bought the Canal Zone. This text also brings up the people living in the Zone. One argument stated that because the U.S. owned all the businesses in the Zone area that the economic level of the Canal Zone is controlled by the U.S. Yet the treaties were signed in 1977 despite opposition from all sides on why and what they said.

Mitch (119 Words)

The third cold war was an important obstacle for the U.S. to overcome. They (the U.S.) were becoming very unpopular thanks to General Torrijos. After the many outbursts of violence it became apparent that the U.S. would have to re-negotiate. The presidential race and the election of Jimmy Carter were also very important. The two treaties signed and Carter's hard work led to the peace in Panama. The Senate played a big part but strangely public opinion mattered little. The Snyder Act made things difficult for a while but never brought things to a standstill. Ron Reagan played an important part in the pre-election year. But as usual no one took him seriously.

Robbie (180 Words)

The article I read is not about the events leading up to the building of a canal across Panama, but rather it is about the negotiations and the fights that occurred after everything was supposedly figured out. The Panamanians wanted more control then [sic] they had. This was shown through student movements which eventually lead to riots etc. This whole deal also made politicians which were running for office very alert of [sic] what U.S. citizens wanted. The politicians wanted to figure out negotiations so they could be elected. Reagan was doing this well. I remember Kissinger wanted to almost tell Panama tough luck, that the canal is ours. A lot of people disagreed. Carter wanted negotiations but with U.S. control indefinitely. Reagan looked at the Panama Canal as Alaska or Texas, that we owned it. Well finally we made negotiations in 1984 [*sic*] that said we would move Panamanians into positions working the canal. U.S. also gave millions and millions of money to Panama. There was a staff of 5 U.S. and 4 Panamanians to further discuss issues.

George (236 Words)

Panamanian unrest about the treaty of 1903 had been occurring since that year, despite many attempts by the United States Government to appease them. By 1974, however, the text described what can be called the "third cold war" between the U.S. and its southern Latin American neighbors. At this point the U.S. needed economic support and Latin America was needed for this, especially when the Arab oil embargo of 1973 went into effect. President R. M. Nixon authorized negotiations for a new treaty for the canal, and Secretary of State H. Kissinger and Panamanian Ambassador Tack came up with an eight point plan. The United States Senate, however, did not want to see sovereignty of the canal handed over to Panama and thus negotiations came to a dead end. Torrijos, President of Panama, bided his time and in the 1976 U.S. Presidential election, the topic of the treaty became a major issue for debate; the victory going to Jimmy Carter. Carter first tried to persuade the people of America, with little result, on the virtues of a new treaty. Next came the Senate, and advocates for a treaty finally persuaded a Senatorial majority. Last were the Latin Americans themselves. The Panamanians wanted full control, without U.S. interference in any way. What the 1978 treaty provided was full control by Jan 1, 2000, with the right to American intervention to keep the canal open.

References

Abelson, R. P. (1988). Conviction. *American Psychologist, 43*, 267–275.

Baron, J. B., & Sternberg, R. J. (Eds.).(1987). *Teaching thinking skills: Theory and practice.* NY: Freeman.

Black, J. B. (1985). An exposition on understanding expository text. In B. K. Britton & J. B. Black (Eds.), *Understanding expository text: A theoretical and practical handbook for analyzing explanatory text* (pp. 249–267). Hillsdale, NJ: Lawrence Erlbaum Associates.

Bovair, S., & Kieras, D. E. (1984). A guide to propositional analysis for research on technical prose. In B. K. Britton & J. B. Black (Eds.), *Understanding expository text* (pp. 315–362). Hillsdale, NJ: Lawrence Erlbaum Associates.

Britt, M. A., Bell, L., & Perfetti, C. A. (1990). *Learning from middle grades science and history texts: General comprehension skills and domain specific knowledge.* Unpublished report.

Britt, M. A., Marron, M. A., Foltz, P. W., Perfetti, C. A., & Rouet, J.-F. (1994, July). *Memory for arguments in history texts.* Paper presented at the fourth annual meeting of the Society for Text and Discourse, Washington, DC.

Britt, M. A., Rouet, J.-F., Georgi, M. C., & Perfetti, C. A. (1994). Learning from history texts: From causal analysis to argument models. In G. Leinhardt, I. L. Beck, & C. Stainton (Eds.), *Teaching and learning in history* (pp. 47–84). Hillsdale, NJ: Lawrence Erlbaum Associates.

Britt, M. A., Rouet, J.-F., & Perfetti, C. A. (in press). Using hypertext to study and reason about historical evidence. In J.-F. Rouet, J. J. Levonen, A. P. Dillon, & R. J. Spiro (Eds.), *Hypertext and cognition.* Hillsdale, NJ: Lawrence Erlbaum Associates.

Carretero, M., Asensio, M., & Pozo, J. I. (1991). Cognitive development, historical time representation and causal explanations in adolescence. In M. Carretero, M. Pope, R. J. Simons, & J. I. Pozo (Eds.), *Learning and instruction: European research in an international perspective* (Vol. 3, pp. 27–48). Oxford: Pergamon Press.

Center for Strategic & International Studies (1967). *Panama: Canal issues and treaty talks.* Washington, DC.

Cheng, P. W., & Holyoak, K. J. (1985). Pragmatic reasoning schemas. *Cognitive Psychology, 17*, 391–416.

Crismore, A. (1984). The rhetoric of textbooks: Metadiscourse. *Journal of Curriculum Studies, 16*, 279–293.

Dee Lucas, D., & Larkin, J. H. (1992). Text representation with traditional text and hypertext (Tech. Rep. H.P. #21). Pittsburgh: Carnegie Mellon University, Department of Psychology.

Eagly, A. H., & Chaiken, S. (1993). *The psychology of attitudes.* Fort Worth, TX: Hartcourt Brace Jovanovich.

Fletcher, C. R. (1989). A process model of causal reasoning in comprehension. *Reading Psychology*, *10*, 45–66.

Foltz, P. W. (in press). Comprehension, coherence and strategies in hypertext and linear text. In J.-F. Rouet, J. J. Levonen, A. P. Dillon, & R. J. Shapiro (Eds.), *Hypertext and cognition*. Hillsdale, NJ: Lawrence Erlbaum Associates.

Glaser, R. (1984). Education and thinking: The role of knowledge. *American Psychologist*, *39*, 93–104.

Graesser, A. C. (1981). *Prose comprehension beyond the word*. New York: Springer-Verlag.

Graesser, A. C., & Goodman, S. M. (1985). Implicit knowledge, question answering, and the representation of expository text. In B. K. Britton & J. B. Black (Eds.), *Understanding expository text: A theoretical and practical handbook for analyzing explanatory text* (pp. 109–171). Hillsdale, NJ: Lawrence Erlbaum Associates.

Hample, D. (1977). Testing a model of value argument and evidence. *Communication Monographs*, *44*, 106–120.

Holland, J. H., Holyoak, K. J., Nisbett, R. E., & Thagard, P. R. (1986). *Induction: Processes of inference, learning, and discovery*. Cambridge, MA: MIT Press.

Johnson-Laird, P. N., Lagrenzi, P., & Sonino Lagrenzi, M. (1972). Reasoning and a sense of reality. *British Journal of Psychology*, *63*, 395–400.

Just, M. A., & Carpenter, P. A. (1992). A capacity theory of comprehension: Individual differences in working memory. *Psychological Review*, *99*, 122–149.

Kieras, D. E. (1985). Thematic processes in the comprehension of technical prose. In B. K. Britton & J. B. Black (Eds.), *Understanding expository text: A theoretical and practical handbook for analyzing explanatory text* (pp. 89–107). Hillsdale, NJ: Lawrence Erlbaum Associates.

Kintsch, W. (1988). The role of knowledge in discourse processing: A construction-integration model. *Psychological Review*, *95*, 163–182.

Kintsch, W. (1992). How readers construct situation models for stories: The role of syntactic cues and causal inferences. In A.F. Healy, S. M. Kosslyn, & R. M. Shiffrin (Eds.), *From learning processes to cognitive processes: Essays in honor of William K. Estes* (Vol. 2, pp. 261–278). Hillsdale, NJ: Lawrence Erlbaum Associates.

Kintsch, W., & van Dijk, T. A. (1978). Towards a model of text comprehension and production. *Psychological Review*, *85*, 363–394.

Kuhn, D. (1991). *The skills of argument*. New York: Cambridge University Press.

Leinhardt, G. (1993). Weaving instructional explanations in history. *British Journal of Educational Psychology*, *63*, 46–74.

Leinhardt, G. (1994). History: A time to be mindful. In G. Leinhardt, I. L. Beck, & C. Stainton (Eds.), *Teaching and learning in history* (pp. 209–255). Hillsdale, NJ: Lawrence Erlbaum Associates.

Leinhardt, G., Stainton, C., Virji, S. M., & Odoroff, E. (1994). Learning to reason in history: Mindlessness to mindfulness. In M. Carretero & J. F. Voss (Eds.), *Cognitive and instructional processes in history and the social sciences* (pp. 131–158). Hillsdale, NJ: Lawrence Erlbaum Associates.

Mackie, J. L. (1980). *The cement of the universe: A study of causation*. Oxford: Clarendon.

Mandler, J. M., & Johnson, N. S. (1977). Remembrance of things parsed: Story structure and recall. *Cognitive Psychology*, *9*, 111–151.

Mayer, R. E. (1985). Structural analysis of science prose: Can we increase problem-solving performance? In B. K. Britton & J. B. Black (Eds.), *Understanding expository text: A theoretical and practical handbook for analyzing explanatory text* (pp. 65–87). Hillsdale, NJ: Lawrence Erlbaum Associates.

McCloskey, M., Caramazza, A., & Green, B. (1980). Curvilinear motion in the absence of external forces: Naive beliefs about the motion of objects. *Science*, *210*, 1139–1141.

McKeown, M. G., & Beck, I. L. (1990). The assessment and characterization of young learners' knowledge of a topic in history. *American Educational Research Journal*, *27*, 688–726.

McKeown, M. G., & Beck, I. L. (1994). Making sense of accounts of history: Why young students don't and how they might. In G. Leinhardt, I. L. Beck, & C. Stainton (Eds.), *Teaching and learning in history* (pp. 1–26). Hillsdale, NJ: Lawrence Erlbaum Associates.

McKoon, G., & Ratcliff, R. (1986). Inferences about predictable events. *Journal of Experimental Psychology: Learning, Memory, and Cognition, 12*, 82–91.

McKoon, G. & Ratcliff, R. (1992). Inference during reading. *Psychological Review, 99*, 440–466.

Meyer, B. J. F. (1985). Prose analysis: Purposes, procedures, and problems. In B. K. Britton & J. B. Black (Eds.), *Understanding expository text: A theoretical and practical handbook for analyzing explanatory text* (pp. 11–64). Hillsdale, NJ: Lawrence Erlbaum Associates.

Miller, J. R. (1985). A knowledge-based model of prose comprehension: Applications to expository texts. In B. K. Britton & J. B. Black (Eds.), *Understanding expository text: A theoretical and practical handbook for analyzing explanatory text* (pp. 199–226). Hillsdale, NJ: Lawrence Erlbaum Associates.

Omanson, R. C. (1982). The relation between centrality and story category variation. *Journal of Verbal Learning and Verbal Behavior, 21*, 326–337.

Perfetti, C. A. (1985). *Reading ability.* New York: Oxford University Press.

Perfetti, C. A. (1989). There are generalized abilities and one of them is reading. In L. B. Resnick (Ed.), *Knowing, learning and instruction: Essays in honor of Robert Glaser* (pp. 307–335). Hillsdale, NJ: Lawrence Erlbaum Associates.

Perfetti, C. A. (1990). The cooperative language processors: Semantic influences in an autonomous syntax. In D. A. Balota, G. B. Flores d'Arcais, & K. Rayner (Eds.), *Comprehension processes in reading* (pp. 205–230). Hillsdale, NJ: Lawrence Erlbaum Associates.

Perfetti, C. A., Britt, M. A., Rouet, J.-F., Georgi, M. C., & Mason, R. A. (1994). How students use texts to learn and reason about historical uncertainty. In M. Carretero & J. F. Voss (Eds.), *Cognitive and instructional processes in history and the social sciences* (pp. 257–283). Hillsdale, NJ: Lawrence Erlbaum Associates.

Perkins, D. N. (1985). Postprimary education has little impact on informal reasoning. *Journal of Educational Psychology, 77*, 562–571.

Ravitch, D. R., & Finn, C. E. (1987). *What do our 17-year-olds know? A report on the first national assessment of history and literature.* New York: Harper & Row.

Rhine, R. J., & Severance, L. J. (1970). Ego-involvement, discrepancy, source credibility, and attitude change. *Journal of Personality and Social Psychology, 16*, 175–190.

Rouet, J.-F., Britt, M. A., Mason, R. A., & Perfetti, C. A. (1995). *Using multiple sources of evidence to reason about history.* Manuscript submitted for publication.

Rouet, J.-F., Marron, M. A., Mason, R. A., & Perfetti, C. A. (1993). *Claims and arguments: A framework for analyzing historical arguments.* Unpublished manuscript, University of Pittsburgh, Learning Research and Development Center.

Rouet, J.-F., Perfetti, C. A., Britt, M. A., & Favart, M. (1994, July). *Situation models and argument models in students' representation of historical controversies.* Paper presented at "Learning and Instruction in History" Conference, Autonoma University, Madrid, Spain.

Rumelhart, D. E. (1975). Notes on a schema for stories. In D. G. Bobrow & A. Colling (Eds.), *Representation and understanding: Studies in cognitive science* (pp. 211–236). New York: Academic Press.

Schank, R. C., & Abelson, R. P. (1977). *Scripts, plans, goals and understanding: An inquiry into human knowledge structures.* Hillsdale, NJ: Lawrence Erlbaum Associates.

Spoehr, K. T., & Shapiro, A. (April, 1991). *Learning from hypermedia: Making sense of a multiply-linked database.* Paper presented at the annual meeting of the American Educational Research Association, Chicago, IL.

Stein, N. L., & Glenn, C. G. (1979). An analysis of story comprehension in elementary school children. In R. O. Freedle (Ed.), *New directions in discourse processing* (pp. 53–120). Hillsdale, NJ: Lawrence Erlbaum Associates.

Stein, N. L., & Miller, C. A. (1991). I win—you lose: The development of argumentative thinking. In J. F. Voss, D. N. Perkins & J. W. Segal (Eds.), *Informal reasoning and education* (pp. 265–290). Hillsdale, NJ: Lawrence Erlbaum Associates.

Thibadeau, R., Just, M. A., & Carpenter, P. A. (1982). A model of the time course and content of reasoning. *Cognitive Science, 6,* 157–203.

Thorndyke, P. W. (1977). Cognitive structures in comprehension and memory of narrative discourse. *Cognitive Psychology, 9,* 77–110.

Toulmin, S. E. (1958). *The uses of argument.* New York: Cambridge University Press.

Trabasso, T. (1989). Causal representation of narratives. *Reading Psychology, 10,* 67–83.

Trabasso, T., Secco, T., & van den Broek, P. (1984). Causal cohesion and story coherence. In H. Mandl, N. L. Stein, & T. Trabasso (Eds.), *Learning and comprehension of text* (pp. 83–111). Hillsdale, NJ: Lawrence Erlbaum Associates.

Trabasso, T., & Sperry, L. L. (1985). Causal relatedness and importance of story events. *Journal of Memory and Language, 24,* 595–611.

Trabasso, T., & van den Broek, P. (1985). Causal thinking and the representation of narrative events. *Journal of Memory and Language, 24,* 612–630.

van den Broek, P. (1988). The effects of causal relations and hierarchical position on the importance of story statements. *Journal of Memory and Language, 27,* 1–22.

van den Broek, P. (1989a). Causal reasoning and inference making in judging the importance of story statements. *Child Development, 60,* 286–297.

van den Broek, P. W. (1989b). The effects of causal structure on the comprehension of narratives: Implications for education. *Reading Psychology, 10,* 19–44.

van den Broek, P. (1990). The causal inference maker: Towards a process model of inference generation in text comprehension. In D. A. Balota, G. B. Flores D'Arcais, & K. Rayner (Eds.), *Comprehension processes in reading* (pp. 423–445). Hillsdale, NJ: Lawrence Erlbaum Associates.

van den Broek, P., & Trabasso, T. (1986). Causal network versus goal hierarchies in summarizing text. *Discourse Processes, 9,* 1–15.

van Dijk, T. A., & Kintsch, W. (1983). *Strategies of discourse comprehension.* New York: Academic Press.

Varnhagen, C. K. (1991). Text relations and recall for expository prose. *Discourse Processes, 14,* 399–422.

Voss, J. F., Fincher-Kiefer, R., Wiley, J., & Silfies, L. N. (1993). On the processing of arguments. *Argumentation, 7,* 165–181.

Voss, J. F., Perkins, D. N., Segal, J. W. (1991). *Informal reasoning and instruction.* Hillsdale, NJ: Lawrence Erlbaum Associates.

Voss, J. F., Schooler, T. E., Kennet, J., Wolfe, C., & Silfies, L. (1990, November). *Argument structure and argument generation.* Paper presented at the annual meeting of the Psychonomic Society, New Orleans, LA.

Warren, W. H., Nicholas, D. W., & Trabasso, T. (1979). Event chains and inferences in understanding narratives. In R. O. Freedle (Ed.), *Advances in discourse processes: Vol. 2. New directions in discourse processing* (pp. 23–52). Norwood, NJ: Ablex.

Wineburg, S. S. (1991). Historical problem solving: A study of the cognitive processes used in the evaluation of documentary and pictorial evidence. *Journal of Educational Psychology, 83,* 73–87.

Author Index

Subject Index